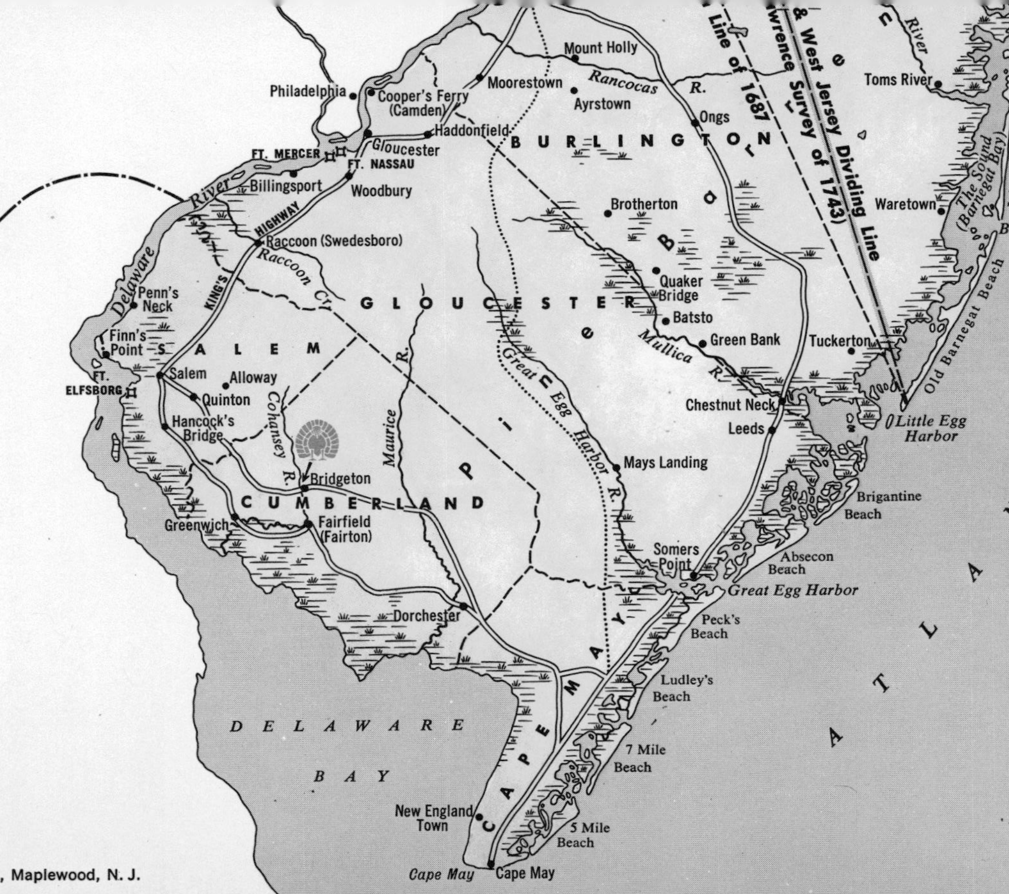
ATLANTIC
Toms River
River
Island Beach
The Sound (Barnegat Bay)
Waretown
Barnegat Inlet
Old Barnegat Beach
& West Jersey Dividing Line
wrence Survey of 1743)
Line of 1687
Tuckerton
Little Egg Harbor
Brigantine Beach
Absecon Beach
Great Egg Harbor
Peck's Beach
Ludley's Beach
7 Mile Beach
5 Mile Beach
Cape May
Cape May
New England Town
Mount Holly
Moorestown
Rancocas R.
Ayrstown
Ongs
BURLINGTON
Brotherton
Quaker Bridge
Batsto
Green Bank
Mullica R.
Chestnut Neck
Leeds
Mays Landing
Great Egg Harbor R.
Somers Point
GLOUCESTER
CAPE MAY
Philadelphia
Cooper's Ferry (Camden)
Haddonfield
Gloucester
FT. MERCER
FT. NASSAU
Billingsport
Woodbury
Delaware River
KING'S HIGHWAY
Raccoon (Swedesboro)
Raccoon Cr.
Penn's Neck
Finn's Point
SALEM
FT. ELFSBORG
Salem
Alloway
Quinton
Hancock's Bridge
Cohansey R.
Maurice R.
Bridgeton
CUMBERLAND
Greenwich
Fairfield (Fairton)
Dorchester
DELAWARE BAY
© C. S. HAMMOND & Co., Maplewood, N. J.

Painting and Sculpture in New Jersey

THE NEW JERSEY HISTORICAL SERIES

Edited by

RICHARD M. HUBER WHEATON J. LANE

New Jersey from Colony to State—1609-1789	Richard P. McCormick
New Jersey and the Civil War	Earl Schenck Miers
New Jersey and the English Colonization of North America	Wesley Frank Craven
The Story of the Jersey Shore	Harold F. Wilson
Princeton and Rutgers: The Two Colonial Colleges of New Jersey	George P. Schmidt
Architecture in New Jersey	Alan Gowans
Elementary Education in New Jersey: A History	Roscoe L. West
The New Jersey High School: A History	Robert D. Bole and Laurence B. Johnson
The New Jersey Proprietors and Their Lands	John E. Pomfret
The Early Dutch and Swedish Settlers of New Jersey	Adrian C. Leiby
New Jersey and the Revolutionary War	Alfred Hoyt Bill
Fundamental Laws and Constitutions of New Jersey	Julian P. Boyd
Medicine and Health in New Jersey: A History	David L. Cowen
New Jersey in the Automobile Age: A History of Transportation	H. Jerome Cranmer
Religion in New Jersey: A Brief History	Wallace N. Jamison
The New Jersey Governor: A Study in Political Power	Duane Lockard
The Research State: A History of Science in New Jersey	John R. Pierce and Arthur G. Tressler
Radicals and Visionaries: A History of Dissent in New Jersey	Morris Schonbach
Historic New Jersey Through Visitors' Eyes	Miriam V. Studley
The Decorative Arts of Early New Jersey	Margaret E. White
Where Cities Meet: The Urbanization of New Jersey	John E. Bebout and Ronald J. Grele
A Narrative and Descriptive Bibliography of New Jersey	Nelson R. Burr
The Literary Heritage of New Jersey	Laurence B. Holland, Nathaniel Burt and Arthur W. Litz
Painting and Sculpture in New Jersey	William H. Gerdts, Jr.
Life in Early New Jersey	Harry B. Weiss
The Geology and Geography of New Jersey	Kemble Widmer

SUPPLEMENTS

Woodrow Wilson, Reform Governor	David W. Hirst
Banking and Insurance in New Jersey: A History	Bruce H. French
Tours of Historic New Jersey	Adeline Pepper

Volume 24

The New Jersey Historical Series

Painting and Sculpture in New Jersey

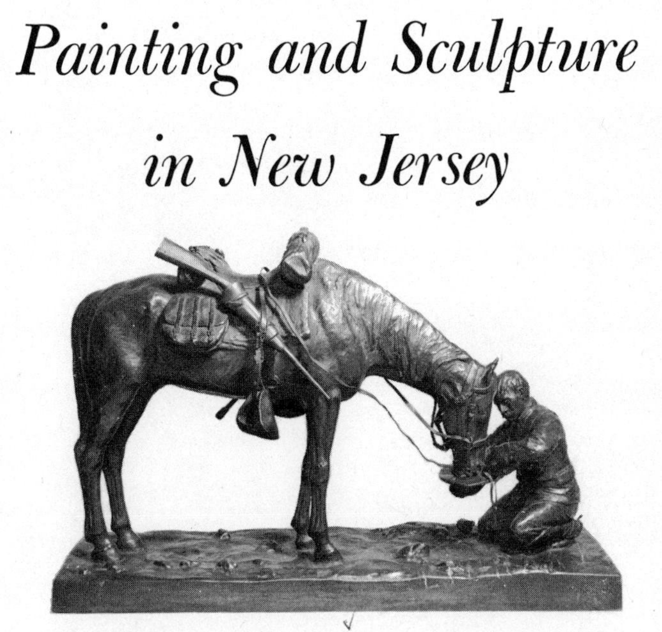

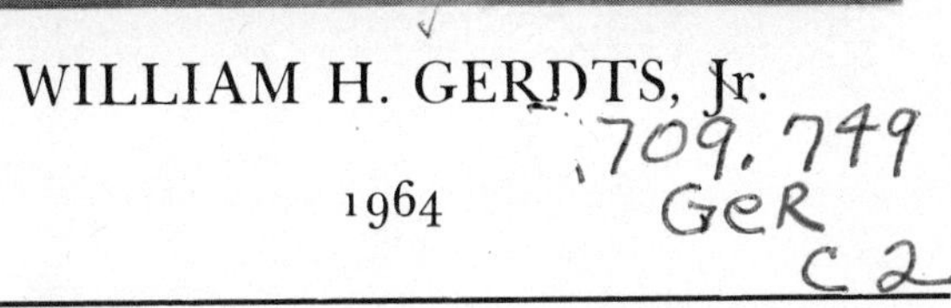

WILLIAM H. GERDTS, Jr.

1964

D. VAN NOSTRAND COMPANY, INC.

Princeton, New Jersey

New York, N. Y. • Toronto, Canada • London, England

D. VAN NOSTRAND COMPANY, INC.
120 Alexander St., Princeton, New Jersey (*Principal office*)
24 West 40 Street, New York 18, New York

D. VAN NOSTRAND COMPANY, LTD.
358, Kensington High Street, London, W.14, England

D. VAN NOSTRAND COMPANY (*Canada*), LTD.
25 Hollinger Road, Toronto 16, Canada

Published simultaneously in Canada by
D. VAN NOSTRAND COMPANY (Canada), LTD.

PRINTED IN THE UNITED STATES OF AMERICA

FOREWORD

Many tracks will be left by the New Jersey Tercentenary celebration, but few will be larger than those made by the New Jersey Historical Series. The Series is a monumental publishing project—the product of a remarkable collaborative effort between public and private enterprise.

New Jersey has needed a series of books about itself. The 300th anniversary of the State is a fitting time to publish such a series. It is to the credit of the State's Tercentenary Commission that this series has been created.

In an enterprise of such scope, there must be many contributors. Each of these must give considerably of himself if the enterprise is to succeed. The New Jersey Historical Series, the most ambitious publishing venture ever undertaken about a state, was conceived by a committee of Jerseymen—Julian P. Boyd, Wesley Frank Craven, John T. Cunningham, David S. Davies, and Richard P. McCormick. Not only did these men outline the need for such an historic venture; they also aided in the selection of the editors of the series.

Both jobs were well done. The volumes speak for themselves. The devoted and scholarly services of Richard M. Huber and Wheaton J. Lane, the editors, are a part of every book in the series. The editors have been aided in their work by two fine assistants, Elizabeth Jackson Holland and Bertha DeGraw Miller.

To D. Van Nostrand Company, Inc. my special thanks for recognizing New Jersey's need and for bringing their skills and publishing wisdom to bear upon the printing and distributing of the New Jersey Historical Series.

My final and most heartfelt thanks must go to William H. Gerdts, Jr., who accepted my invitation to write *Painting and Sculpture in New Jersey,* doing so at great personal sacrifice and without thought of material gain. We are richer by his scholarship. We welcome this important contribution to an understanding of our State.

RICHARD J. HUGHES
Governor of the
State of New Jersey

January, 1964

PREFACE

This book is the first ever to deal with the overall subject of painting and sculpture in New Jersey. A list of more specialized published discussions appears in the Bibliographical Note. While it might have been advantageous to include all aspects of the fine arts in this volume, space limitations have made it necessary to eliminate a consideration of the graphic arts and of the fields of illustrative art and cartoons, in the development of all of which New Jersey artists have played a significant part. Perhaps, someday, their history will be recorded.

The more information that is gleaned in regional studies, such as this, concerning both recognized and neglected artists and the more that is known about regional interests, developments and styles, the better we can assess the total nature of the pictorial arts of the nation. State boundaries provide a basic geographic framework within which scholars can work. Uncertainty arises however as to the precise meaning of the claim to an artist in such chronicles. Must an artist be a resident of a state to qualify for consideration, and if so, how long must his residency be? Must he have worked as well as lived in the state? What consideration should be given artists who produced a significant body of work dealing with some aspect of the region, although no proof of residence can be found? Should notice be paid to artists who were born or who died in the state although their creative years were spent elsewhere?

The present volume is concerned with the art and artists of the State of New Jersey, and the problems suggested above are of concern here. That New Jersey has some claim to the lives and activities of many artists was shown in the exhibition, "Early New Jersey Artists," held in 1957 at the Newark Museum. This show dealt only with painters and sculptors, and only with those who were active in the eighteenth and nineteenth centuries. One hundred and nine original works by 99 artists, professional, primitive, and amateur were shown, but the catalogue listed almost twelve hundred artists who had some connection with the State of New Jersey. Since that date, another fifty or so names have been added to the original group, and work by about one hundred and fifty of the total number of painters and sculptors has been located or is known. Undoubtedly more artists have yet to be discovered—at the moment of writing the author has just seen a highly skillful drawing by a mid-nineteenth-century German named Frederick Ochs, heretofore unknown, who later came to Newark.

On the face of it, then, New Jersey might lay claim to a large, varied and important place in the development of American art. Unfortunately, this is not quite the case. True, many of America's leading artists did paint in New Jersey, including such portraitists as Charles Willson Peale and Gilbert Stuart. Significantly located as it is, New Jersey was the birthplace of important artists from Colonial times to such well-known contemporaries as Grace Hartigan. Yet, accidents of birthplace and occasional work created here does not make an artist a Jerseyman, any more than the deaths of both George Catlin, the Indian painter, and John Quidor, the Washington Irving illustrator, in Jersey City entitles that city to claim them as native sons.

Culturally, New Jersey presents a complex problem in the analysis of her place in American developments. Situated as it is between the two most important artistic centers of the nineteenth century, the State was traversed by many of the country's most illustrious artists, but few of these stopped for long and when they did, it was not for the purpose of professional practice. That, after all, could be found far more profitably at the two termini—across the Hudson and the Delaware in New York and Philadelphia.

On the other hand, the conception of New Jersey as an artistic desert, either in the past or the present, is quite false. If claims too great to be sustained have been made for artistic representation in New Jersey, it is equally true that not enough attention has been paid to those painters and sculptors who lived and worked here and who are part of the State's heritage. This is partly due to the fact that the activity of some of America's leading painters and sculptors in New Jersey is little known, and also that a number of artists of perhaps less significance but undeniable talent and ability have not been given their due.

This is naturally a generalization and like all generalizations has its exceptions. The early portraitist John Watson is certainly known for his New Jersey connections and his historic place in American art is recognized. The landscapists Asher B. Durand and George Inness are acknowledged as among the leading New Jersey painters, and, indeed, New Jersey's role in the development of American landscape painting, although less significant than that of the Hudson River Valley and the White Mountains, has not been ignored. In the twentieth century, the activity of Jerseymen such as John Marin have gained great respect, although even here their connections with the State have often been overlooked.

That New Jersey had artists of capability and significance will be shown in this book, but the question may still be asked as to whether or not New Jersey art has a distinctive, recognizable character. In a large, overall sense, the answer is probably "no," but then, few regions do. Perhaps a Quaker tradition does exist in the art of Pennsylvania; a bayou school of landscape painting did develop in and around New Orleans in the late nineteenth century; and regional schools in the twentieth century can be analyzed not only in New York and California, but also in the Pacific Northwest, in Maine, in the Southwest, in Chicago, and perhaps elsewhere. Nevertheless, a continuous artistic tradition of distinct style is seldom found in any state or region. In New Jersey, rather, one can trace the general history and development of American art on a more local scale. The Colonial portraitists, the early landscape school, the development of the sentimental genre and *trompe-l'oeil* still life, the precisionist movement, abstraction and beyond—all have had their local practitioners. Some of these artists were, indeed, the leading painters in the country, but more often they were followers, imitators, or even quite independent creative spirits reacting to the *Zeitgeist*. The analysis of the work of many of these artists may throw new light on the richness and abundance of fine, competent painting not only in New Jersey but in the country as a whole.

But New Jersey offers more than this concentrated view of American art. Situated as it is between Philadelphia and New York, it was, in the eighteenth and nineteenth centuries particularly, truly a garden spot where artists as well as others might flee from the hectic life (and the occasional epidemic diseases, too!) of the great urban centers. At the same time, this characteristic was conducive to the flowering of landscape painting, for the State offered visiting artists many verdant scenes from which to choose subjects in the growing art of landscape painting. Some of these artists are known to have remained in New Jersey for a time or to have had seasonal studios here, but others crossed the rivers and visited the coasts for short but repeated visits. It is not surprising, therefore, that many of the leading early artists in the state were landscapists.

Many of the artists of New Jersey are associated with the tradition of landscape painting and drew their inspiration from the meadows, the hills and valleys, the rivers and the coast. But for the most part, the resident artists lived in the larger cities—Jersey City, Elizabeth, and above all, Newark. Yet, other communities had a place in the history of New Jersey art, larger than their population and size might suggest. Perth Amboy, for instance, was very important in the early history of the arts, although few artists lived there after the early nineteenth century. At that time, due to the temporary importance of the area, Bordentown was something of an artistic center. During the whole of the nineteenth century, however, no community of its size figured as importantly as Hoboken, where a number of leading New Jersey artists lived in mid-century. At the end of the century, both Montclair and Nutley were communities of considerable importance in the arts.

There are thus distinct qualities in the artistic development of the state of New Jersey which merit attention, not only by local historians but by those striving for a better understanding of America's cultural heritage. The present volume does not intend to be a catalogue of all those who painted and sculpted in New Jersey but rather to present a general history of that development in terms of those artists who seem to represent the highest standard of achievement set in this state. But a volume such as this must be thought of rather as an interim report than a definitive study, for the future will not only extend our knowledge of the past, but will bring its own rewards.

As already stated, the research herein contained is based principally upon the results of the project that culminated in the exhibition, "Early New Jersey Artists," held in the Newark Museum in 1957. The sources acknowledged in the catalogue of that show can also be credited with assistance here. However, much further research has gone into this publication, particularly in the field of twentieth-century New Jersey painting and sculpture, which was not included in the show nor in the research project which preceded it.

Assistance in the preparation of this volume is acknowledged from the librarians of many public libraries throughout the State and particularly to Miss Julia Sabine and Mr. William Dane of the Art Department of the Free Public Library in Newark, and to Miss Miriam V. Studley of the New Jersey Room of that library. The staffs of the Montclair Art Museum, the State Museum at Trenton, The New Jersey Historical Society, the Rutgers University Library, and Mr. Lindabury, editor of the *Proceedings of The New Jersey Historical Society,* have all been most helpful. With their permission, articles by the author on Henry Inman, Edward Kranich, Rembrandt Lockwood, and Ralph Blakelock which have appeared in the *Proceedings* are reproduced in this volume either in whole or in part. Among private collectors of American art, special assistance should be noted from James Ricau and Henry Fuller. Many dealers, particularly in New York City and Boston, such as Victor Spark, Charles Childs, Mrs. Edith Gregor Halpert of the Downtown Gallery, George Schriever of Kennedy Galleries, Robert Vose, Jr., George P. Guerry, Ira Spanierman, and Robert Kashy of the Thompson Gallery, have provided valuable and significant information.

Many art historians, scholars, and laymen in the Americana field have been most helpful. These include Dr. Richard Carrott, Chairman of the University of California in Riverside; Alfred Frankenstein of the *San Francisco Chronicle;* Mr. William Steinschneider of Hastings-on-Hudson; New York; Miss Brenda Kuhn of New York City; Mr. John C. Long of Princeton; Mr. Jay B. Tomlinson and Orson H. Brown of Bordentown; Mrs. David B. Gross of Mount Holly; Mr. and Mrs. Robert Price of Lake Openaka; Miss Gertrude Tubby of Montclair; Mr. Lyman G. Douglas of Westfield; Miss Mary Bartlett Cowdrey of Passaic; Mr. Julian Foss of Verona; Mr. Robert Martin of Ridgefield; Mr. Edwin A. Gauntt of Jobstown; Mr. and Mrs. Laurence Babbage and Miss Joan Babbage of Montclair; Mr. Woodruff English of Summit; Mrs. Donald Liddell of Englewood; and Mrs. Earl LeRoy Wood of Newark. Particular gratitude is due to Mr. Bernard Rabin and the late Mr. Nathan Krueger, of Rabin & Krueger Gallery in Newark, for their unfailing help and for their constant interest in twentieth-century New Jersey art.

Deepest appreciation should be accorded, too, to those at the Newark Museum who provided opportunity, inspiration, and assistance. To Miss Katherine Coffey, Director, for her understanding of the problems involved in this project and the ultimate purposes such a study might serve; to Mrs. Mildred Baker, Associate Director, for all her advice, particularly in the later sections of the book where her assistance proved invaluable; to Robert Riggs Kerr, Librarian, for his willingness to aid in countless problems of research, for advice in matters of overall planning and for editing the text so conscientiously and thoroughly; and finally to my secretary, Miss Lorna Clohosey, for her great assistance in the typing of the manuscript and for her patience and sympathy with the problems of organization and revisions.

WILLIAM H. GERDTS, JR.

New York City
June, 1964

TABLE OF CONTENTS

	Foreword	v
	Preface	vii
	List of Illustrations	xvii
I	Colonial Artists	1
II	Portraiture: Three Generations	13
III	Landscape Painting Before the Civil War	50
IV	Newark at Mid-Century	80
V	Other Themes in Nineteenth Century New Jersey Painting	104
VI	Landscape and Seascape Painters of the Late Nineteenth Century	142
VII	Nineteenth Century Sculpture	180
VIII	Art in the Early Twentieth Century	196
IX	New Jersey Painting and Sculpture Today	235
	Bibliographical Note	253
	Index	263

LIST OF ILLUSTRATIONS

Lilly Martin Spencer, "The Children of Marcus L. Ward," c. 1858 — *Frontispiece*
John Watson, "Governor William Burnet" — 5
John Watson, "Portrait of Lewis Morris," 1726 — 6
Patience Wright, "Portrait of Admiral Richard Howe" — 11
Gilbert Stuart, "Portrait of Miss Anne Penington," 1805 — 18
William Dunlap, "The Dunlap Family," 1788 — 21
Henry Inman, "The Children of Bishop Doane," 1835 — 28
Thomas J. Natt, "Portrait of a Newark Gentleman," 1831 — 30
Rembrandt Peale, "Portrait of William Rankin," 1834 — 32
Oliver Tarbell Eddy, "Children of William and Abigail Rankin," 1838 — 34
Benjamin Trott, "Mrs. Alexander N. Macomb," 1823 — 37
Jefferson Gauntt, "Portrait of Uz Gauntt," 1833 — 39
Micah Williams, "Portrait of Sarah Hasbrouck," c. 1830 — 41
Charles Loring Elliott, "Portrait of Mrs. Thomas Goulding," 1858 — 43
George Gates Ross, "Portrait of James Ward," 1845 — 45
John Alexander McDougall, "Portrait of a Lady" — 47
Thomas W. Whitley, "Passaic Falls in Spring" — 54
Joshua Shaw, "English Landscape with Two Figures" — 58

Asher B. Durand, "Portrait of Mrs. Durand and Her Sister," 1831 — 62
Asher B. Durand, "Landscape," 1849 — 64
John Jesse Barker, "East Entrance to Rahway," 1843 — 68
Edward Kranich, "The Old Homestead" — 70
Jasper Francis Cropsey, "Greenwood Lake," 1862 — 74
William R. Miller, "Weehawken Bluff on the Hudson," 1871 — 76
Martin Johnson Heade, "Jersey Meadows," 1877 — 78
Rembrandt Lockwood, "Last Judgment," c. 1850 — 96
Paul Lacroix, "Still Life with Grapes and Watermelon," 1866 — 107
Mrs. E. B. Duffey, "Lillies," 1866 — 110
Susan Waters, "Still Life with Squirrels" — 112
John Frederick Peto, Still Life — 116
William Tylee Ranney, "The Pipe of Friendship" (Completed by William Sidney Mount), 1857 and 1859 — 124
Lilly Martin Spencer, "The War Spirit at Home," 1866 — 127
Edward Lamson Henry, "Station on Morris and Essex Railroad," 1864 — 130
William Page, "Venus Guiding Aeneas," 1862 — 135
Julian Scott, "Scene of the Civil War," 1872 — 140
George Inness, "On the Delaware River," c. 1861 — 148
George Inness, "Winter Morning, Montclair," 1882 — 152
Andrew Melrose, "Valley of the Hackensack" — 158
Thomas Moran, "Lower Manhattan from Communipaw," 1880 — 160
T. Worthington Whittredge, "Millburn, New Jersey" — 164
Ralph A. Blakelock, "Grace E. Washburn in Her Garden" — 169
William Trost Richards, "Twilight on the New Jersey Coast," 1884 — 174
Winslow Homer, "Long Branch, New Jersey," 1869 — 176
James E. Buttersworth, "New York Harbor Scene" — 178
John Frazee, "Bust of Judge Story," 1834 — 183

William John Coffee, "Bust of a Man," 1824 186
Jonathan Scott Hartley, "Portrait of George Inness," 1894 189
Charles Schreyvogel, "The Last Drop," 1903 192
Everett Shinn, Murals, Trenton City Hall, 1911 202-203
Stuart Davis, "Hoboken," 1915 207
Reginald Marsh, "Hudson Burlesk Chorus," 1950 210
George O. "Pop" Hart, "Cock Fight, Mexico," 1926 212
Walt Kuhn, "Harlequin," 1918 214
Man Ray, "Woman Asleep," 1913 217
John Marin, "Eastern Boulevard, Weehawken, New Jersey," 1925 220
Charles "Gus" Mager, "Country Road," 1932 226
Louis Lozowick, "Relic," 1949 229
José Ruíz de Rivera, "Flight," 1938 232
Ben Shahn, "Bartolomeo Vanzetti and Nicola Sacco," 1931-1932 238
Adolf Konrad, "End of Day," 1952 240
Leo Dee, "Reflections in White," 1959 241
Lee Gatch, "High Tension Tower," 1945 242
Burgoyne Diller, "Construction #16," 1938 244
Seymour Shapiro, "W. C. W.," 1960 246
Dorothea Greenbaum, "Bathsheba" 248
James Kearns, "Seated Model" 249
George Segal, "Model in the Studio," 1963 251

Lilly Martin Spencer,
"Portrait of the Children of Marcus L. Ward," c. 1858
Collection of The Newark Museum

I

COLONIAL ARTISTS

SEVENTEENTH-CENTURY "American" paintings are all portraits. There were many reasons for this thematic preoccupation which lasted, really, into the early nineteenth century. The portrait had, in a sense, a utilitarian function: to remind the beholder of a relative or loved one, one who might have departed, either for a long voyage or from life itself. The portrait too could be inspirational, calculated to inspire in the onlooker the spiritual endowments of the subject depicted. Also to be remembered is the importance of the portrait tradition in the British Isles. Beginning with Hans Holbein the Younger, there was in England a sequence of brilliant portraiture in the hands of continental artists such as Holbein from Germany, Anthony van Dyck from Flanders, Peter Lely from Holland, and others. This tradition of formal portraiture must have been known to the Colonists and, in their desire to transplant to American shores the civilization from which they came, it was only natural that they encouraged that art form which they knew best and which dominated the visual arts of their homeland.

The artists who painted the portraits of seventeenth-century American Colonists are, for the most part, unknown. It is probably true that they were not professional portraitists and that they made their livelihood in other fields, as merchants, sea captains, builders, or perhaps as house and sign painters, which might have prompted them to try their hands at portraiture. For that matter, there were probably not enough commissions available among the Colonists to provide constant employment for full-time portrait painters. Nevertheless, these early artists show a familiarity with the successive styles of European art. Some of the earliest portraits are painted in a flat, sharply outlined, and decorative style akin to the art of Elizabethan England; others are more solid and monumental, modeled boldly with vigorous contrasts of light and dark, typical of the seventeenth century baroque era.

These early artists may or may not have had any artistic training before they came to the Colonies. Some appear a good deal more gifted than others, but none of them can be called a professional painter. It was only in the early years of the eighteenth century that professional artists first began to come to America, settling in the larger towns where they might find employment. Their work, at least that which has survived, is nearly all portraiture, though a few classical and religious works by at least one of these painters, Gustavus Hesselius, are known to survive. Hesselius was a Swede who emigrated to America in 1711, settling in Philadelphia. Justus Englehardt Kühn, a German, came even earlier, settling in Annapolis before the end of 1708. Henrietta Johnston was working in Charleston, South Carolina, still earlier, and bears the distinction of being certainly the earliest woman artist in America and also one of the earliest painters who might be called professional. Her work consists almost entirely of pastel portraits.

John Watson (1685-1768), who settled in Perth Amboy, New Jersey, as early as 1714, is not, then, the earliest professional American painter, but he was certainly one of the first. William Dunlap, the first historian of American art, wrote in his *History of the Rise and Progress of the Arts of Design in the United States* of 1834 that the earliest artist about whom he could find information was Watson; but then, Dunlap, himself an artist, was also from Perth Amboy, and information about his predecessor was more readily available to him than that about even earlier artists who had worked in distant communities. Indeed, Dunlap was able to interview collateral descendants of the artist and ascertain some essential information about Watson's life and career, to which various other writers have since added.

Watson, like his more illustrious contemporary, John Smibert, the leading New England portraitist of that generation, was a native of Scotland. He was born on July 28, 1685. Little is known of his life in Europe except that he may have been born near Dumfries, Scotland, and that he was a house painter before turning to portraiture there. Jilted, after a long courtship, by a wealthy young woman, and having squandered his money, he sought refuge in the Colonies. Dunlap records him as coming to America immediately after the Jacobite rebellion in England at the end of 1715. However, Watson brought a suit against Thomas Turnbull of Perth Amboy, for the payment of wine valued at £24, in June of 1714. He was described in the dispute as a limner of Perth Amboy and therefore must have been in that town earlier than the date Dunlap gives.

Watson was known in Perth Amboy as a miser and a usurer. He seems to have been financially successful, although his activities were not limited to painting. Watson engaged in real estate transactions and in the selling of merchandise, as well as money-lending. In 1744, a young Scots physician, Dr. Alexander Hamilton, visited Perth Amboy and saw Watson, whom he described as a very rich man who kept no servants and took care of his cow and poultry himself. He seems to have presented a very distinctive appearance, suggesting poverty and eccentricity, but Hamilton reported him as owning most of the houses in Perth Amboy. Watson had begun purchasing property there in 1726 and extended this activity to the purchase of property in New York City in John Street.

In 1730, Watson returned to Scotland for a visit. When he came back to Perth Amboy, he brought his orphaned niece and nephew with him, and also a collection of pictures which enabled him to form an art gallery, certainly one of the first in the New World. The painter built a studio and gallery to house this collection, adjacent to his home. Watson never married, and his nephew Alexander supervised his uncle's business transactions and took care of him along with his sister Sophia, who acted as housekeeper. Watson's will, made on September 28, 1756, named his nephew as executor, and left him the bulk of his estate. Watson died on August 22, 1768, at the age of eighty-three, and was buried in the cemetery of St. Peter's Episcopal Church, just south of his home.

In his own time, Watson appears to have been a painter of some reputation, and among his sitters were men and women of distinction, such as Governor William Burnet of New York and New Jersey, and Lady Burnet, Sir William Keith and his wife of Pennsylvania, and subjects from Rhode Island, Virginia, and even from the islands of Antigua and Madeira. The distant subjects, however, were probably depicted on visits to New York, and there is no evidence that Watson ever journeyed beyond New York and New Jersey. Although Watson was naturally known for his portraiture, he was also remembered locally for the window shutters of his painting house, which were adorned with painted heads of heroes, kings, and other figures, crowned or helmeted in antique costume. One of these, representing a priestess of Bacchus, was described in detail as the result of nineteenth-century investigations into the life of this earliest New Jersey artist.

Although this relatively full general account can thus be given of Watson's life, very little can be said about his art, or at least about his paintings in oil, which must have been a major portion of his work. Few portraits can be assigned to him with any certainty, although the attributions of several, such as that of Governor Burnet, owned by the State of Massachusetts, and that of Governor Lewis Morris, in the collection of the Brooklyn

John Watson, "Governor William Burnet"
Collection of The New Jersey Historical Society, Newark

Museum, seem well founded. In addition, probably the most interesting work by Watson is the painting of Gaius Caesar Caligula, one of the studio shutter paintings. Undoubtedly, other works by Watson still exist and some of these may yet come to light and be attributed to him.

We are more fortunate, however, in our knowledge of

John Watson, "Portrait of Lewis Morris," 1726
Collection of The Brooklyn Museum

Watson's drawings. Thirty-three of these are extant and located today, and more are known to have existed. The medium varies among these; some are pencil, some make use of wash; some are on paper, and others are on vellum. They are mostly portrait drawings, but some represent historic and classical figures. A pencil sketch of a nude athlete is known to have existed in the nineteenth century.

John Watson's works, both drawings and oils, are of considerable interest as a visual record of the early eighteenth century. They are typical of the kind of portraiture practiced in the Colonies in these early years, and a number of the portraits present the physical appearances of personages of the time, including the several governors heretofore mentioned and also Watson himself. Since one of the oil paintings and a number of the drawings are taken from characters of the historic past, and one drawing, that of Hercules, from classical mythology, there is a greater range within Watson's *oeuvres* than that known of most of the other Colonial portraitists.

It must be admitted that, esthetically, Watson's work shows the artist to have been one of very limited talent. His oil portraits, such as those of William Burnet and Lewis Morris, are typical baroque works with a solidity and monumentality reflecting distantly the art of Sir Godfrey Kneller and other British portraitists of the era. They are painted, however, according to a rather lifeless formula, with perfunctory treatment given to the costumes and large wigs, and somewhat insensitive treatment of the features themselves. It is surprising, perhaps, that they retain the sense of life that they do. The Caligula is a more dramatic piece, and gives credence to the suggestion once made that his copies were his best executed works. Even the portrait drawings, although more lively and with a distinctive lightness and airiness, are somewhat weak and insensitive.

Still, it could hardly be otherwise. Had Watson been an artist of exceptional or even reasonable skill, he would probably not have emigrated from Great Britain to a small New Jersey town; he would certainly have remained to rival his contemporaries in London or at least practice his art in his native Scotland, rather than seek the role of a "large fish" in a very small pond. His work is not, after all, unlike that of the other early professionals in America—Gustavus Hesselius and Henrietta Johnston—and only a little less interesting than that of Justus Englehardt Kühn. If Watson is much inferior to John Smibert who came to these culturally inhospitable shores in 1729, it is all the more astounding that the Colonies could attract an artist of Smibert's caliber. Meanwhile, Watson, along with others, had carried over from Great Britain and begun in the Colonies a tradition of professional portraiture which was to remain esthetically vital well into the nineteenth century.

In the field of American sculpture even more than in painting, New Jersey can claim a famous "first." Sculpture in America began, on a professional level, a good deal later than painting. As with all the arts, sculptural forms in the New World were created when they were functional and practical. Three basic categories of these exist, in three different materials: stone grave markers, mental weathervanes, and wooden figureheads. The creation of these began early—obviously so with the first-named form. This sculpture was often very decorative and extremely ingenious, and is highly prized today, but the artists who created it are mostly anonymous and their work falls under the heading of "folk art," though in their own time they were thought of as artisans or craftsmen.

Certain connections and relationships can be made between folk sculpture and the professional counterparts which began to be developed on a monumental scale in the early nineteenth century. Professional sculpture, however, finds its tentative beginnings in America in the late eighteenth century and the only Colonial products that have been documented are the works of Patience Lovell Wright (1725-1786) of Bordentown. She was a Quaker, born in a low frame house on the east side of Main Street, and legend has it that she was a niece of John Wesley. Nothing is known of her parents, but her sister, Rachel Lovell Wells, was likewise a sculptor. On March 20, 1748, Patience Lovell married a farmer, Joseph Wright, who died in 1769 after fathering four children: Joseph, Phoebe, Elizabeth, and Sarah, the first three of whom had their place in the history of the arts. During this period in Bordentown, Patience Wright began to model likenesses, first in bread dough to amuse her children and later in wax. It was in the latter medium that Mrs. Wright found distinction, as did her sister, remembered for her likeness of the Reverend George Whitefield, and her daughter Elizabeth, who worked in New York and London after her marriage to Ebenezer Platt.

After the death of her husband, Mrs. Wright moved from Bordentown to New York City, where she is noted because of a fire in her waxworks in June, 1771; she sustained damage and loss to the value of several hundred pounds, although some of her better statues were saved. Her sister assisted her in the repair of the waxworks but in the following year Patience Wright left with her family for London and opened a celebrated waxworks there. Horace Walpole made mention of her in 1773, and the list of notables whom she depicted is quite long: Lord Chatham, Lord Lyttleton, Thomas Penn, and others. The fidelity of the work of this "Promethean Modeller," as she was called, was greatly praised, and stories exist of the deceptively real quality of her statues. Her life in London was exciting in another way, for she served Benjamin Franklin as a spy during the Revolution, and removed from London to Paris in 1781. There she modeled a bust of Franklin, but she soon returned to London where her daughter Phoebe married the well-known English portraitist, John Hoppner. In 1785, she wrote to Thomas Jefferson concerning a bust of Washington which she was contemplating; this project was never completed but she did make a wax profile of Washington, probably from the clay bust created by her son Joseph. In the following year, Mrs. Wright died as the result of a fall in returning from a visit to the American Ambassador, John Adams. Her countryman, Joel Barlow, wrote a final tribute to her in *The Columbian Muse* of 1794:

> Two kindred arts the swelling statue heave,
> Wake the dead wax, and teach the stone to live.
> While the bold chisel claims the rugged strife,
> To rouse the sceptered marble into life;
> While Latian shrines their figure's patriots boast
> And gods and heroes crowd each orient coast;
> See Wright's fair hands the lives her fire control;
> In waxen forms she breathes the impassioned soul;
> The pencill'd tint o'er moulded substance glows,
> And diff'rent pow'rs th'unrivall'd art compose.

Although Mrs. Wright must have produced many works in wax—miniature profile portraits, complete busts, and even a full-length effigy of William Pitt the Elder (Lord Chatham), in Westminster Abbey—few are known today. Profile busts of Franklin and Washington also survive as well as busts of James Johnson, Bishop of Worcester, Admiral Richard Howe, and of Charles Fox. None of these relates, of course, to her early career in New Jersey, or for that matter to the work that she did in New York City before going abroad. For the most part, her profile portraits seem more like extensions of the popular field of minature painting and bear little relationship to a tradition of monumenal carving. Nevertheless, Mrs. Wright inaugurated the sculptural medium in America and gained even international fame in an art which boasted a number of other practitioners in this country, including not only Mrs. Wright's sister, son, and daughter, but also John Christian Rauschner and Robert Ball Hughes a little later.

The careers of the two earliest New Jersey artists, Watson and Mrs. Wright, are curiously dissimilar. They lived in two of the most important Colonial New Jersey

Patience Lovell Wright, "Portrait of Admiral Richard Howe"
Collection of Jay B. Tomlinson

communities, one in the northeast, the other on the Delaware. They were among the first to introduce the two basic forms of the fine arts. Watson, the first, was born in Europe but came to America and made New Jersey, where he gained a modicum of local fame, his home. Mrs. Wright was born here and began her art in New Jersey, but achieved fame on a far broader plane in the capitals of Europe. It is intriguing to speculate whether or not either had ever heard of the other.

Despite the beginnings of artistic expression in New Jersey, there was little immediate succession. Mrs. Wright, of course, had left the state and moved to New York before leaving the country, and it may be surmised that much of Watson's work was also done in New York. Even Mrs. Wells moved to Philadelphia after her marriage. Cosmo Alexander (c. 1724-1772), a portraitist from Scotland who was later to become the teacher of Gilbert Stuart, was active in Burlington for a number of weeks in the winter of 1768-1769, where he stayed with Governor William Franklin, painting for the Governor and several of his friends. The only other important figure of the Colonial era to express artistic talent was an amateur rather than a professional artist: Francis Hopkinson (1737-1791), signer of the Declaration of Independence. Hopkinson was born and educated in Philadelphia, where he studied law. In 1763 he was Collector of Customs at Salem, and then he went to England for a year in 1766. On his return he settled in New Castle, Delaware, but soon removed to Bordentown. He undoubtedly must have known Mrs. Wright before she left for New York; later he was friendly with her son Joseph and acted as intermediary between him and Jefferson. Although he is most noted, of course, as a lawyer, politician, and writer, he was both an artist of ability and a musician of note. It is believed that he probably received some training in England from the Anglo-American artist, Benjamin West. A number of his crayon portraits survive, and he also employed his talents in making heraldic devices such as seals for the American Philosophical Society, the Great Seal of New Jersey, and one for the University of the State of Pennsylvania. His pastel portrait of his son, James Hopkinson, probably drawn in 1773, is owned by the Maryland Historical Society in Baltimore and is a more naïve version of pastel portraiture made popular at the time by such Colonial artists as John Singleton Copley and Benjamin Blythe.

II

PORTRAITURE: THREE GENERATIONS

COLONIAL PAINTING in America reached its culmination in the portraiture of the Boston artist, John Singleton Copley. Until his appearance on the painting scene in the late 1750's, portrait painting in America was basically very much what one might expect: a distant reflection of the current styles in vogue in Europe, particularly in England. John Watson's art is very much a part of that development. By the third quarter of the eighteenth century, native-born artists had appeared, and the best of these, such as Robert Feke, showed a real individuality in portrait interpretations, but all of them based their art firmly upon the examples of European models known either in originals or through engravings, or upon the art of European-trained painters who continued to come to America.

Nor, in terms of basic compositions and props, do Copley's portraits differ from the accepted mode. But both technically and interpretively, Copley introduced a style of portraiture into America which, although bearing some similarity to the work of such English artists as Joseph Wright of Derby and the early George Romney, had been totally unheralded on this side of the Atlantic. There is a mastery of precise form created by dramatic studio lighting in his paintings, in which a heightened sense of reality is brought about by an emphasis upon three-dimensional, plastic qualities. And, instead of the graceful and mannered interpretations of predecessors who cast their subjects into set formulae, Copley's style, although monumental, is hard-bitten and strong, revealing tremendous character and individuality in his Colonial sitters.

The Federal Period

Copley visited New York and Philadelphia but does not appear ever to have painted in New Jersey, although he probably passed through the Colony. Furthermore, he left these shores at the time of the Revolution, never to return. The art of the succeeding period, however—the Federal Period, from the Revolution to about 1810—was dominated by his style. The leading practitioners of portraiture—for portraiture still remained almost the only art form practiced—were Charles Willson Peale of Philadelphia and Ralph Earl of Connecticut. Both of these artists studied in England but they returned to America and to the unflattering, unsparing realism which was Copley's legacy.

The late eighteenth century, however, was a peculiarly barren period in New Jersey art. There were no resident artists of high professional caliber in the State. Those artists who may have painted there worked in New Jersey only briefly and sometimes only in transit. Charles Willson Peale himself, for instance, was in New Jersey during the Revolution as a captain of volunteers in the Battle of Trenton; and, while serving there, he did likenesses of some of his officers, for example, a miniature of Captain Boyd. Peale's own son, the artist Rembrandt Peale, asserted that his father was employed in painting a miniature of George Washington at a farmhouse in New Jersey.

In this period, the towns of Bordentown and Burlington stand out strongly as the major centers for painting in New Jersey for those few artists who had any connection with the State. The painter who was probably most closely associated with New Jersey in this period was Joseph Wright (1756-1793), a son of Patience Wright, who was, after all, born in Bordentown and grew up there in something of an artistic environment. His mother had moved the family to New York and later to London, however, before Wright began to study painting and to practice this art; he exhibited several canvases in London including one, in 1780, at the Royal Academy of "Mrs. Wright Modelling a Head in Wax." In 1782 he went to France for further study. In the following year he embarked for America and by August of 1783 he was back in Bordentown after being shipwrecked off the coast of Spain and arriving in Boston destitute. In October of that year, Wright was at Rocky Hill with a letter from Benjamin Franklin to George Washington. Since Congress was sitting in Princeton at that time, Wright was able to paint a portrait of Washington. He was also employed to take a mold in plaster of Paris from which a cast could be made to be sent to a European sculptor as a guide for a marble bust or statue of Washington. However, when the artist removed the mold it fell and broke to pieces, and the General was reluctant to undergo a second attempt.

Wright painted a number of portraits of George Washington; the best-known version is his profile portrait, one example of which is owned by the Cleveland Museum of Art. The Rocky Hill portrait, which was not a profile, was acknowledged as the finest likeness taken of the General. Wright's career relates no further to New Jersey. He was in Philadelphia until 1786; from 1786 to 1790 in New York; and from 1790 until his death three years later in a yellow fever epidemic, an Philadelphia. In his last year he had been appointed die sinker to the Mint. His portraiture is marked by a sober realism which, if uninspired, is straightforward and typical of the art of the period.

Yellow fever accounts for the brief residence of one other artist in New Jersey. Edward Savage (1761-1817) is known primarily for his large group composition of

"The Washington Family." He was born in Massachusetts, but his residences were numerous, since he worked in Boston, New York, London, and Philadelphia, before returning to Princeton, Massachusetts, where he died. In 1798, however, he left Philadelphia during the yellow fever epidemic for a brief stay in Burlington, but no work by him is known from that visit. Savage was back again in New Jersey in 1806, this time at the Passaic Falls; he did a drawing of the falls on July 29 of that year which is now in the Rush Rhees Library at the University of Rochester. The portrait of James Ewing, Mayor of Trenton, attributed to Savage and now in the Newark Museum, may also have been done about that time, though not necessarily in New Jersey. Savage was moreover the teacher of John Crawley (1784-1842), the first Newark-born artist of any note, but the instruction took place in New York City and Crawley's connection with New Jersey occurred only in his youth.

At exactly the same time as Savage's stay in Burlington, another artist of note took residence there. Charles Balthazar Julien Févret de Saint-Mémin (1770-1852) had been born in Dijon, France, and his family, being sympathetic to the Old Regime during the French Revolution, emigrated to Switzerland and then to America about 1793. They had hoped to reach Haiti where they had large estates, but the insurrection there of Toussaint L'Ouverture made the situation too chaotic for them to continue their journey. Saint-Mémin had had some training in drawing and painting before reaching this country and, being in need of a means of livelihood, turned to drawing and engraving. Although he began by doing topographical landscape subjects, he gained his fame in portraiture. Saint-Mémin made use of a machine called the "physionotrace," which enabled the artist to produce with speed a profile outline of the sitter in a continuous line and with mathematical exactness, the artist then shading and working out the interior detail. Saint-Mémin's profiles were usually produced on a pink paper, and the image was then reduced upon a copper plate which could be engraved.

In 1798 Saint-Mémin's mother and sister came to New York, and the family shortly after went to Burlington where they established a girls' school, while the artist's father journeyed to the West Indies in an attempt to recover his property. Saint-Mémin drew some portraits in Burlington itself, but for the most part he wandered up and down the Eastern seaboard, to Baltimore, Annapolis, Washington, Richmond, and Charleston, wherever customers could be found. In 1810 he returned to France; he came back once more to this country in 1812, and then returned, finally, in 1814 to Dijon, where he became director of the museum.

Among the works by Saint-Mémin of pertinence to New Jersey is his portrait of Captain James Lawrence, an engraving of which is in the Lawrence House in Burlington. A 1798 advertisement listed his prices for an original drawing, an etched copper plate of the drawing, and 12 impressions as $35.00 for ladies, and $25.00 for gentlemen. The precise, accurate approach of Saint-Mémin's art and the realism implicit in his use of mechanical devices was perfectly in keeping with the forthright stylistic approach of the time, and Saint-Mémin takes his place among our important Federal portraitists, with Peale, Savage, and Wright.

The most significant American portraitist of all who may have lived in New Jersey for a brief time was Gilbert Stuart (1755-1828). Born in Rhode Island, Stuart had gone to England to study and later became a successful portraitist in London and then in Dublin. In 1792 he returned to this country, to New York and later to Philadelphia; after Washington became the nation's capital, he moved there, in 1803. He did not take his family with him, however, but settled them in Bordentown, New Jersey, where it is believed that he painted the portraits of Mr. and Mrs. Edward Stow. He himself must have been in Bordentown in 1805, for his lovely portrait of

Gilbert Stuart, "Portrait of Miss Anne Penington," 1805
Collection of the Powel House, Philadelphia

Miss Anne Penington, the daughter of Isaac and Sarah Penington of Bordentown, is signed "G. Stuart, Bordentown, 1805," one of the few portraits by the artist signed with his name. After this short stay in Bordentown, Stuart removed to Boston, with which city he is most closely associated, and he remained there until his death.

Stuart's art is far different from that of Copley, Peale, and the other Federal portraitists. In England, his style was completely consistent with the best of English painting of the period, and he was able to compete with such artists as Thomas Gainsborough and Sir Joshua Reynolds with his emphasis upon idealized refinement—a facet of aristocratic portraiture which dominated English painting from the period of Sir Anthony van Dyck. Stuart brought this form of portraiture back to America, and it was immediately accepted. The elegance and beauty of his style are very evident in his portraits of Mrs. Stow and Miss Penington, with their elongated forms, smooth, unmodeled limbs and features, and broad, fluid brushwork. Costumes and furnishings are up-to-date, and a bright, cheerful, and confident atmosphere fills the canvases.

The Empire Period

The style which defines American portraiture, and American art in general, during the Empire Period, from about 1810 to 1845, is quite distinct from that which preceded it. This was the most romantic period in American art, and romanticism characterized not only the fine arts but literature as well, as in the novels and short stories of Washington Irving and James Fenimore Cooper. The sources of this romanticism can be found in English and Continental art, and its hallmark is an emphasis upon emotional appeal rather than strict veracity to nature. Thus, Gilbert Stuart's portraiture was a prototype for this development and, living as he did well into the Empire Period, it is not surprising that he was acknowledged as America's foremost portraitist and that his art stood as a model for the artists of this generation.

In the past each American city had its particularly noted portraitist, but now the number of portraitists greatly increased as well as the number of cities that had their local, resident painters and the number of painters that could be found in each of the larger centers. Thus, Thomas Sully was the leading portrait painter in Philadelphia throughout his long lifetime. In Boston, Stuart held sway until his death, when his place was taken by Chester Harding. New York had a series of leading portrait painters: John Wesley Jarvis early in the century, and in the second quarter Jarvis' pupil, Henry Inman. But in addition, there were many other talented painters particularly in Philadelphia and New York—John Neagle and Jacob Eichholtz in the former, John Trumbull, Samuel F. B. Morse, and Samuel Waldo in the latter. Some of the lesser masters, in smaller towns, such as Ezra Ames of Albany, also achieved a style of distinction.

Compared to the small number of artists who worked in New Jersey during the preceding era, there was a tremendous amount of activity in the State during the Empire Period. Some of this is well documented but more needs to be done to define precisely the activities of the painters of this time in New Jersey. Bordentown and Burlington, however, lost their position as the most active area in the state for the arts, and many communities could now count one or two portrait painters of ability among their temporary or permanent residents. The greater number of portraitists naturally lived in the more populous area of the state: George Conarroe 1803-1882 or 1884), however, lived in Salem, in 1829 when he began exhibiting his work in Philadelphia. Conarroe's art, however, is closely allied to that of Sully, and he lived most of his life in Philadelphia. The Salem County Historical Society owns his portrait of Anne L. Hubbell.

One of the most noted figures in the history of American art, connected with New Jersey, was William Dunlap (1766-1839). Perhaps his greatest contribution to the arts was not the portraits, miniatures, and occasional landscapes which he created, but his two-volume *History of the Rise and Progress of the Arts of Design in the United States* of 1834, which is the first and most important chronicle of the early history of the fine arts in this country; for this work, Dunlap drew upon his own knowledge and reminiscences and wrote to all his colleagues for information about their lives and their recollections. Much of what is known about such artists as John Watson and Patience Wright, for instance, comes from Dunlap's history. Dunlap was in a particularly fortunate position for research into Watson's life because he was born in Perth Amboy and grew up there. He was in England from 1784 to 1787, studying painting; shortly after his return to this country he turned his attention to the theatre as both writer and manager, and later, in 1832, as an historian of the American theatre.

Nevertheless, Dunlap never lost his interest either in the field of painting or his native home. Throughout his lifetime he spent his summers in Perth Amboy and

William Dunlap, "The Dunlap Family," 1788
Collection of The New-York Historical Society

it served as a sort of base of operations from which he took many trips in search of commissions. Around 1805, while in Perth Amboy, and again about 1811 he turned his interest to miniature painting. It is at this time perhaps that his miniature self-portrait, in the Yale University Art Gallery, and other miniatures of his family were painted. Dunlap was quite peripatetic, wandering up and down the East Coast of the United States and into Canada, first as an itinerant miniaturist and then seeking commissions for large oil portraits, while also exhibiting vast religious paintings the whereabouts of which are not known today. He remembered very vividly, throughout his whole life, the opportunity he had as a young man of seventeen, in 1783, of painting George Washington at Rocky Hill, at the same time that Joseph Wright made his first portrait of the General.

As an artist, Dunlap was only a secondary figure, exaggerating the limitations of the Empire style with an emphasis upon soft, weak forms, never achieving the loveliness and sweet emotional appeal that the finest portraitists of the era did. His miniatures are more fortunate, but it is really as an historian of the arts that Dunlap is, rightly, best remembered.

The most important portrait painter of this period to have lived in New Jersey was Henry Inman (1801-1846). A pupil of John Wesley Jarvis, he succeeded his teacher as the most successful New York portraitist of his day, holding the same position in that community that Thomas Sully, his contemporary, held in Philadelphia. He was also considered the first successful genre painter in America, a landscapist of note and, early in his career, a fine miniaturist. He was one of the first artists concerned with the new graphic technique of lithography. He had been born in Utica, New York, but came to New York City in his early youth. As early as 1826 he had assumed a position of importance among prominent American artists as a founder and the first vice-president of the National Academy of Design. Later in the same decade he increased his growing fame by his connection with *The Talisman,* the leading gift-book annual published in New York, which brought together some of the principal literary and artistic talents in the United States.

Although visiting other communities, Inman's associations during the 1820's were almost completely with New York City. However, a drawing in the collection of the Pennsylvania Historical Society bears witness to his first known visit to New Jersey. This is a pencil sketch inscribed "Paterson, July 25th, 1828," depicting an artist—undoubtedly Inman himself—seated on a rock and sketching, his back to the spectator. The drawing is done rapidly in a sketchy yet sure technique, typical of Inman, and has a sense of air and atmosphere. Although no other evidence has so far come to light concerning Inman's visit to Paterson, it is reasonable to assume that he came there for the same reason so many other early nineteenth-century American artists did: to see and to paint the Falls of the Passaic, New Jersey's greatest natural wonder.

Undoubtedly Inman passed through New Jersey during this period and earlier, on trips to Philadelphia and to southern communities. At such times he must have been impressed by the charm of the New Jersey countryside, for in 1832 he moved to Mount Holly, the only early artist to be associated with that attractive community. A number of reasons led him to move from the busy New York environment to the peaceful quiet of a rural New Jersey town. One of these was the change he had made the previous year in centering his artistic activity upon Philadelphia rather than New York. In 1831 he moved to Philadelphia in order to enter into a partnership with Colonel Cephas Childs in the establishment of a lithographic firm. Inman and Childs had had contact in previous years when Childs was practicing the art of engraving, and to add prestige to his project, Childs invited Inman to join him in the firm of Childs and Inman, Lithographers. Inman himself did very few lithographs, but many of his oil portraits were lithographed by Albert Newsam and others in the firm. The real inducement for Inman was the promise of numerous commissions in oil, in Philadelphia, which he knew that Childs could procure for him.

Nevertheless, Inman was not content to make the city itself his home, and on February 11, 1832, he purchased 105 acres of land at Mount Holly for $5000. The land was between the Mount Holly–Rancocas and the Mount Holly–Burlington roads, almost within town limits. Henry T. Tuckerman, in his *Book of the Artists,* summarizes Inman's reasons for the move as his love of the outdoors:

> . . . circumstances and traits combined to make him a lover of the country where, in the height of his metropolitan success, he determined to make his home; and took up his abode at a beautiful rural estate at Mount Holly, New Jersey. . . . Inman's studio had long been the rendezvous for the eminent and gifted in the land; he enjoyed his trout fishing, his sketching from nature, the birds, flowers and domestic pleasures of his rural home. . . .

Anther reason for Inman's wish to live in the country was undoubtedly the severe epidemics of cholera which were prevalent at this time in the United States, particularly in the major cities; these, as the artist's letters indicate, were a very real worry to him.

Among the portraits painted by Inman at Mount Holly was that of his friend, the Philadelphian James McMurtrie. A letter by the artist to McMurtrie, now in the possession of the Pennsylvania Academy of the Fine Arts, bears witness not only to the painting, but also to the mode of travel—doubtless used many times by Inman—between Philadelphia and Mount Holly. Inman wrote to McMurtrie on August 15, 1832:

> I recd. yours of last evening and hasten to tell you that I shall be proud of an opportunity to oblige you in the matter of the 'leetle Piktur.' As to the 'con-sid-e-ra-tion' I will thus ordain; that the execution of the 'Piktur' shall extinguish

a certain debt of $10, I owe you, and in addition you may give me, in any matters of Art, you are disposed to part with, a like sum of $10.

We shall be right happy to see you at our 'Jersey' shantee, and I will suggest the following mode of getting here. You will get this tomorrow afternoon 16th. Yr. best plan will be to take the next morning steam boat, (17th) for Burlington, which leaves I believe at 6 A.M. In two hours you will reach Burlington, where you will find yr. humble servant with a vehicle which will convey you, to my house in ½ an hour. At ½ past 1, the same day the Stage passes my door, for Burlington to take the return Boat.

If however I should not be able to get through with one sitting, we will be most happy to keep you with us until the next morning when you can take the early stage.

So come with 'yr. lady,' in your hand.

Sterling Farms was, to Inman, a rural retreat and actually very little of his painting was done there. Perhaps the most famous picture that he created at his home was the "Self-Portrait in a Top Hat." John Sartain, in his *Reminiscences of a Very Old Man,* speaks of the work as follows:

It was here that he painted the small portrait of himself, half his face shaded by the brim of a straw hat, which is now the property of the Pennsylvania Academy. It was done at one brief sitting to show three young artists how he worked. Two of them, Debeaugh (Deveaux?) and another whose name I fail to recall, had received an invitation to visit the artist. On their way to the Camden ferry, whom should they meet but Matthew Parker, who hailed them with 'Whither away, boys?' They told him, when he promptly said he would go too. He was not of the kind to inquire if his company was agreeable, and neither of the two had the courage to try and shake him off.

When the lesson was over Inman gave them the picture, and it was decided by lot which of the three should possess it. To the vexation and mortification of the others, it was the interloper, Matthew Parker, who drew the prize.

The prize was sold, when Parker fell ill, to John

Towne; Cephas Childs, Inman's former partner, owned it after Towne; on Childs' death, in 1871, it was bequeathed to the Pennsylvania Academy of the Fine Arts. On the back of the painting is inscribed: "Sketch of H. Inman by himself at 33, June, 1834." The painting is probably the best known of all Inman's self-portraits, and it is a very beautiful piece of work, strongly painted, yet quite informal, with a general romantic personal mood enhanced by the strong shadow across the face.

Though little is known of Inman's personal life and his friendships in New Jersey, we do know that one of his important patrons was a near neighbor. Inman had a high reputation as a portraitist for the clergy, particularly in the Episcopal Church, of which he was a member. It is not surprising, then, that he was commissioned to paint the portrait of George Washington Doane, Protestant Bishop of New Jersey, who became rector of St. Mary's Church in Burlington on October 1, 1833. The portrait of Doane was painted in 1834 and exhibited in New York at the National Academy in 1835. The painting was commented upon in the *New York Mirror* on June 20, 1835, in reviewing the exhibition, as "Mr. Inman's best male portrait in the present exhibition. It would be difficult to say more in its praise." It was given in 1858 to Union College, in Schenectady. It is a handsome work, very spirited and colorful. A second version, without hands and darker, is owned by a descendant of the subject, in New Lebanon, New York. Judging by the date of the painting and the exhibition, it is probable that the Doane portrait was begun in Mount Holly and finished on Inman's return to New York City.

That the relationship between Inman and Doane was more than merely that of artist and patron is indicated by a letter from Doane to Inman which is preserved by the Historical Society of Pennsylvania. Although the letter is undated, it must have been written between October, 1833 and October, 1834, since it is addressed to Inman at Mount Holly from St. Mary's Parsonage, and that one year is the only period when both lived in New

Jersey. Doane wrote solicitiously of Inman's health and discussed a meeting between them, perhaps in reference to his portrait. The letter is signed, "Truly your friend."

One of Inman's most charming pictures is the double portrait of the children of Bishop Doane. The picture depicts George Hobart Doane and William Croswell Doane and is a disarming depiction of childhood, broadly and freely painted, with a fine contrast between the characters of the two children. Although the landscape is undoubtedly a reference to Bishop Doane's ecclesiastic position and the church's geographic location on the banks of the Delaware, St. Mary's Church was not a Gothic structure; so the church in the picture must bear only a general reference to the Bishop.

The "Portrait of the Children of Bishop Doane" is signed and dated "Inman 1835." It was therefore completed in New York City, although it is probable that it was begun in 1834; Inman also received a commission from Bishop Doane to paint a full-length portrait of Bishop White of Pennsylvania, and he wrote to Asher B. Durand, inquiring if Durand would do the engraving of the subject, for which subscriptions would be raised at $10 each. Inman quotes Doane as expressing himself thus: "It will be very hard if a production combining the three names of White, Durand, and Inman should not succeed."

Nevertheless, Durand did not do the engraving, and it appears that the project was actually carried out by Inman several years later in conjunction with the English engraver Wagstaff and the Philadelphia art patron James McMurtrie.

Toward the end of 1834 Inman returned to New York City, having severed his connection with the lithographic firm (Childs took a new partner and renamed the firm Childs and Lehman, though he and Inman remained lifelong friends). Inman sold his Mount Holly property to George Haywood on September 18; one of the witnesses to the transaction was Charles Wesley Jarvis (1812-1868), Inman's pupil and the son of his former teacher,

Henry Inman, "The Children of Bishop Doane," 1835
Collection of The Newark Museum

John Wesley Jarvis. Undoubtedly Inman's reason for returning to New York was to reclaim his former position as the leading portraitist of the metropolis, and his association with New Jersey ceased at that time. Nevertheless, New Jersey played a significant role in the career of this most important portrait painter. Interestingly enough, Charles Jarvis himself was a portrait painter in Newark during the last ten years of his life, practicing the more dramatic and realistic art of the mid-century, but with overtones still of the idealizing style he had learned from Inman. His portrait of Henry Clay in New York City Hall is flanked by many likenesses by his illustrious teacher. Another pupil of Inman's, Ferdinand Thomas Lee Boyle (1820-1906), taught art as a young man at the academy run by Eloise Chagaray between 1837 and 1842, where the College of St. Elizabeth is now, at Convent Station. This institution appealed to the French immigrants from the West Indies who had settled in the region. At that time Boyle painted portraits such as those of the Ford family; he was later to work in St. Louis and New York City, and for many years in later life he served in the art departments of Brooklyn Institute and Adelphi College.

Among other portraitists in Newark were the father and son team of James Pine (fl. 1834-1859) and Theodore Pine (1828-1905), who were in that city in the 1840's and 1850's. They were both talented painters who also worked in New York City and Ossining, New York. In addition, Theodore Pine, whose works are more numerous than those of his father, was active in several Western communities and died in Ogdensburg, New York. An earlier father and son who worked in New Jersey, and about whom even less is known, are John Paradise (1783-1833) and John Wesley Paradise (1809-1862). John Paradise was born in Hunterdon County, but was trained in Philadelphia and worked most of his life in New York City, although he died at the home of his sister in Springfield, New Jersey. A number of his portraits appear to have been painted in Pennington, New Jersey, in 1807, such as those of the minister Joseph Rue and his wife. John Paradise painted distinctively in the sharp, realistic style of the early years of the nineteenth century, while his son's work—little known today—is characterized by a more flattering, sweeter approach. He too was born in New Jersey, but seems to have spent his life in New York City, as an engraver and portraitist.

Thomas J. Natt, "Portrait of a Newark Gentleman," 1831
Collection of The Newark Museum

In the early 1830's, Newark does not appear to have had a resident portraitist, but was rather dependent upon artists who visited the city for short periods of time. Thomas J. Natt (fl. 1824-1859) was a Philadelphia portraitist who advertised from a studio on Bank Street, Newark, in the *Sentinel of Freedom* on July 5, 1831. A strong, if slightly primitive portrait painted in that city is known to be by him; he may also be the painter of an attractive landscape of Belleville created at this time. In November of the following year, Horace Rockwell (1811-1877) inserted an advertisement in a local Newark newspaper: "Portrait Painting—The Subscriber, lately from the city of New York, would respectfully inform the public that his Painting Rooms, three doors above Broad-street House, are now open, where the ladies and gentlemen of Newark are invited to call and examine specimens of his work. His portraits and miniatures are warranted likenesses, and will be taken on the most reasonable terms." Like Natt, Rockwell's work would be classed as "semi-primitive" or "semi-professional," but he was to develop into a more sensitive painter. His later work, painted in Fort Wayne and Roanoke, Indiana, beginning about 1836, is better known and includes several extremely large and complicated family groups. In July and August of 1833, an otherwise unknown artist named P. B. Marshall also advertised in Newark in a fashion almost identical to Rockwell's.

A far better-known portraitist who may have visited Newark during this period was Rembrandt Peale (1778-1860), the best known of the painter sons of Charles Willson Peale. In addition to numerous trips to Europe, studying in London and Paris, Rembrandt Peale spent most of his life variously in Baltimore, Philadelphia, and New York. There is no record of an actual residence in New Jersey. However, a fair number of portraits by him of prominent Newark and other New Jersey residents are known, which might have been painted either in New York or in New Jersey.

Among the finest of Rembrandt Peale's New Jersey

Rembrandt Peale, "Portrait of William Rankin," 1834
Collection of The Newark Museum

portraits is his likeness of William Rankin, painted in 1834. Peale also painted other members of the Rankin family, including Mrs. Rankin, but the artist who created the largest number of portraits of the Rankin family was Oliver Tarbell Eddy (1799-1868). Indeed, Eddy may be thought of as Elizebeth's and Newark's local portrait painter of distinction, in much the same way that Inman is primarily associated with New York, Sully with Philadelphia, etc. Eddy was the son of a pioneer engraver and printer in the little hamlet of Greenbush, Vermont, where the artist was born. He received what was probably his only training from his father whom he assisted in his printing establishment, and it is possible that the father also taught his son the art of portraiture. Several copper-plate engravings are known, youthful works of Oliver Tarbell Eddy. He married Jane Maria Burger in Newburgh, New York, in 1822, but his whereabouts are not known after that date until 1826, when he is listed in the New York City directories. He exhibited in the National Academy of Design in 1827, but in 1831 the Eddy family was in Elizabeth. They remained in Elizabeth at least through January, 1835, when he advertised in the *New Jersey Journal.* During this period a son, Henry Clay, and a daughter, Mary Louisa, were born. No paintings from his Elizabeth years have yet come to light.

In 1835 Eddy was in Newark, and was listed as a portrait and miniature painter on Broad Street. He remained in that city through 1840. It was in 1838 and 1839 that Eddy painted his numerous portraits of members of the Rankin family, including one of William Rankin. Rankin had been born in Nova Scotia and came to Elizabeth as a young man, later moving to Newark and founding a successful hat factory. He was very prominent in Newark affairs as President of the Board of the Newark Academy and was one of the founders of the Newark Library Association. Probably Eddy's masterwork of his New Jersey years is his large group portrait of the four youngest children of William Rankin, which epitomizes the artist's very individual style.

Eddy's work is not so broadly and fluidly painted as the portraits of his better-known contemporaries, yet his style is characterized by great sweetness and charm, pale, smooth surfaces, and a quiet seriousness which are uniquely his. In addition, he had a great fondness for details of costumes, furnishings, and furniture, so that his portraits often not only present a likeness but give a suggestion of the environment of his subjects. One detail found in numerous Eddy portraits is an emphasis upon fringe, either as part of actual coverings or hangings, or as a prominent detail of the stock motif of a hanging curtain.

Rankin's daughter, Phebe Ann, writing to her brother William about the family portraits, stated:

Oliver Tarbell Eddy, "The Four Youngest Children of William Rankin and Abigail Ogden Rankin," 1838
Collection of The Newark Museum

The large picture which was home was much admired and your portrait was pronounced admirable. . . . I am sitting for mine at Pa's request. It is to be quite a large picture and is to hang over the dining room mantlepiece. I am taken in a sitting posture—my whole form nearly to my feet. Shall be taken in my wedding dress sitting on a sofa with my eyes turned toward the window. . . .

The large portrait of Phebe Rankin was much admired; Edward E. Rankin wrote that it was "worthy of a more celebrated limner than Mr. Eddy."

Other portraits known to have been painted by Eddy in Newark include those of Matthias Day and his wife; David Hayes, a prominent Newark attorney; and several members of the Alling family. Eddy also painted a portrait of the Reverend Ansel Doane Eddy, a distant relative. The Reverend Mr. Eddy became pastor of the First Presbyterian Church in Newark in 1835, and it is possible that this event was the reason for the artist's moving to Newark. By 1841, however, he may have run out of commissions, for in the following year he moved to Baltimore where he remained for a decade, and numerous portraits by him are known from his Baltimore years. At this time Eddy was also involved in the invention of a writing machine, but this early typewriter proved to have been too elaborate despite efforts on his part to perfect his invention. By 1850 he had moved to Philadelphia, where he lived the remainder of his life, continuing to paint portraits but also working on other inventions, including cork linoleum, a barrel-making machine, and a cartridge belt. His later portraits are more sophisticated and show a relationship to photography. In both his Newark and his Baltimore paintings, Eddy created works which are fascinating records of the period as well as charming and thoughtful likenesses.

There were still other prominent portraitists who maintained connections in New Jersey during the period. Outstanding among those was William Jewett (1789/1790-1874), a partner in the New York firm of Waldo & Jewett, with Samuel Lovett Waldo. Jewett had studied under Waldo and by 1818 had been taken into the firm as a partner, collaborating on portraits until 1854. The exact contribution each made to their collective efforts has never been fully determined, and it is difficult to ascertain the individual styles of the two men, although a few works, signed by each alone, are known. Jewett moved to Bergen Hill, living in the Jewett homestead at Jewett and Bergen avenues, until his death. He painted in New York City, but particularly related to New Jersey are the Waldo & Jewett portraits of Mr. and Mrs. George Dummer of 1840. Dummer was a mayor of Jersey City and founder of the Jersey Glass Company. He was an intimate friend of Jewett's and it is possible that the portraits may have been painted in New Jersey.

Another painter who worked in Jersey City was George Linen or Linnen (1802-1888). Linen was the leading portraitist in America during this period of "cabinet" pictures, portraits larger than miniatures but smaller than the life-size oil paintings. He emigrated from Scotland to America in 1834 and worked mainly in New Jersey and New York, although he traveled as far as Richmond, Virginia, and Terre Haute, Indiana. In 1859 he was listed in the Newark City Directory; he may have died on a farm near Bloomsdale. Cabinet portraits were particularly popular during this period; Samuel F. B. Morse, among others, began his artistic career painting them, but they seem to have suffered the same fate as miniature paintings, and they dissappear after the arrival of photography.

Although some of the portraitists already mentioned, such as Oliver Tarbell Eddy, are known to have painted miniatures, specialists in this branch of portraiture do not seem to have chosen New Jersey for their abode during this period. William Russell Birch (1755-1834) was a painter of enamel miniatures who came to Philadelphia from England in 1794; he became the most noted American artist in this specialized branch of minature painting, and he is supposed to have lived in Burlington in 1797. The one important American miniature painter who is known definitely to have lived in New Jersey in the early nineteenth century was Benjamin Trott (c. 1770-1843). He traveled extensively throughout his whole lifetime, seldom staying more than a few years in any locality. He had gained encouragement from Gilbert Stuart on that artist's return from Europe, and in the first decade of the nineteenth century he was

Benjamin Trott, "Mrs. Alexander N. Macomb," 1823
Collection of The New-York Historical Society

one of the leading minaturists in this country. Around 1823 he moved to Newark where he lived for a number of years. Although the move was made more for personal than for professional reasons—he had made what Dunlap referred to as a "mysterious marriage and moved to Newark to be able to obtain a divorce there"—he nevertheless does seem to have had some employment in Newark. It is about this time that his work began to decline in quality, but his miniature of Mrs. Alexander Macomb, painted in Newark, is lively and sparkling and typical of Trott's style.

It could not be expected that truly professional artists would take up their residence in the more rural areas of New Jersey unless, as with Inman, they were seeking a pastoral retreat. Jefferson Gauntt (1805/1806-1864) was born into a leading Quaker family of Jobstown near Mount Holly, and brought up on the family farm, Haninicon. His talents so impressed his father, Uz Gauntt, that he was sent to the Pennsylvania Academy of the Fine Arts for study; his subsequent career is connected with Philadelphia and later with Brooklyn, but a number of family portraits are preserved in the Jobstown area, particularly that of his father, one of the strongest paintings to come out of New Jersey. It depicts the rugged, devout Quaker with a surprisingly early, and deceptively real, still life of books on shelves behind.

A number of the most interesting, more primitive portraitists of the period worked in Middlesex and Monmouth counties. George Henry Durrie (1820-1863) is one of these. He is usually associated completely with New Haven, where he was born and grew up, and where he later gained great reputation as America's foremost painter of winter scenes, but earlier—after having studied portraiture in New Haven with Nathaniel Jocelyn, the best-known local portraitist there, equivalent in New Haven to Oliver Tarbell Eddy in Newark—Durrie went to Freehold, in 1840. He returned to Connecticut sometime in 1841, but was back in Monmouth County in 1842. In these few years he painted quite a number of

Jefferson Gauntt, "Portrait of Uz Gauntt," 1833
Collection of Edwin A. Gauntt

portraits under the patronage of Judge James S. Lawrence at prices ranging from five to fifteen dollars. The artist supplemented his income by such odd jobs as altering portraits, varnishing, and even painting window shades. His portraits of Tunis V. Conover and his family, now in the Monmouth County Historical Association, are hard, clear, and formal, simplified and patterned with great skill.

Another, more completely primitive artist, was Ira Goodell (c. 1810–after 1860), also born in Connecticut, who worked in New Brunswick in 1859. He produced sharp-featured, bold portraits in which stock costume models were used and only the sitter's individual features differed. Earlier than Goodell was Micah Williams (1782/1783-1837), perhaps the most distinctive of all of New Jersey's primitive painters and the one who has been studied most fully. Williams also worked in and about Freehold and New Brunswick, and died in the latter town where his descendents live today. Williams' work, with only one or two exceptions, is all pastel portraits, highly stylized and utilizing a minimum of different colors. Again, as with Goodell, costumes and poses are sometimes almost identical. The artist was formerly identified as "Henry Conover," but research has revealed that this was the name of one of the artist's sitters. There is in Williams' work simplicity and a decorative sense which characterizes the best of American folk painting.

Mid-Nineteenth Century and Later

American art in the mid-nineteenth century, not only portraiture but painting and sculpture in all their branches, changed quite decisively during the 1840's. In portrait painting the graceful forms and the artistocratic interpretations of Inman and Sully were abandoned in favor of what was considered greater naturalism and truth to nature. In place of the emphasis upon beauty and occasionally upon sentiment, the portrait painter stressed character and individuality. Forms became very

Micah Williams, "Portrait of Sarah Hasbrouck," c. 1830
Collection of The Newark Museum

solid and much more dramatic, and, although from very different motivation, there was a return to Copley-like realism.

By far the finest portraitist of this period in America was Charles Loring Elliott (1812-1868), who succeeded Henry Inman as the leading portrait painter in New York, about 1845. He was born in upstate New York and studied painting in New York City. During the 1830's he was an itinerant portrait painter throughout his native state, working in the style of the period and also painting an occasional landscape. After 1840, however, he painted chiefly in New York City. Nevertheless, by 1850 and perhaps earlier, Elliott had a home in Hoboken, which was becoming something of an artistic haven at mid-century. Thomas W. Whitley, a landscape painter who was also living there and who will be noted in future chapters, showed in the annual exhibition of the National Academy of Design in 1850 a painting of the "Country Seat of Charles L. Elliott in Hudson County, N. J." From 1854, Elliott was listed in the Hoboken City Directories and gave his home as Hoboken in the 1860's also.

The reason for the popularity of Hoboken at the time is not difficult to fathom. New York City was growing and many artists sought the quiet and relaxation of the countryside. Hoboken was extremely convenient to New York; it was a prosperous community; and, strangely contrasting with its present appearance, it was at the time an attractive suburban community with beautiful houses. It was easily possible for artists to live there and yet maintain studios in New York City. There seems to have been patronage for the arts in Hoboken, too. George William Curtis, writing to the painter and author, Christopher Pearse Cranch, in Italy, stated: "Undoubtedly, there is a greater general respect for art and artists here. It is quite 'the thing' to know them and to have them. Then Belmont and Aspinwall and Wright, at Hoboken, open their galleries as marquises do in London to ticketed people."

Charles Loring Elliott, "Portrait of Mrs. Thomas Goulding," 1858

Collection of the National Academy of Design, New York
Photograph Courtesy of the Frick Art Reference Library

Such was the role that communities such as Hoboken, and to a degree the State in general, played in American art life at mid-century. Most of Elliott's painting, therefore, must have been done in New York City itself, although when he was depicting a resident of New Jersey, it is very possible that the subject may have sat at Elliott's home instead of at his New York studio. Such, for instance, may have been the case with Mrs. Thomas Goulding, of Jersey City, whose portrait, now in the National Academy of Design, has always been considered Elliott's masterpiece. It is a powerful, solid portrait, totally unflattering, but a brilliant analysis of a strong, independent-minded woman. About 1860, much of Elliott's work became rather dry and photograph-like, but during the 1850's he was America's finest portraitist.

Elliott, like Inman before him, had chosen a New Jersey residence as a rural retreat. The successor to Oliver Tarbell Eddy as Newark's "resident" portraitist was George Gates Ross (1814-1856). He was born in Springfield, New Jersey, but was working in Newark by 1835 and remained active in that city until his death. He was well recognized locally, and the *Newark Daily Advertiser* reported on his activities a number of times. On June 5, 1850, Ross' painting was recalled to the attention of its readers, and the paper noted: "Few, if any, among the numerous competitors for distinction in the department of portrait painting in our country, at the present day, can justly claim precedence." On June 11, 1852, Ross arranged for an exhibition of the work of his landscape-painting colleague, William Mason Brown, also a resident of Newark, in Ross' painting rooms in Library Hall. In December of that year, however, Ross moved his studio to 250 Broad Street. The paper commented on December 3:

> The remarkable facility with which he reproduces the features, and almost the animation indeed, of the "human face divine," upon his canvas, has rendered him well and widely appreciated as one of the most successful artists in the country, and his pictures are sought as well for the accuracy of their likenesses,

George Gates Ross, "Portrait of James Ward," 1845
Collection of The Newark Museum

as for their real artistic finish. His pencil will be the means of transmitting to posterity the looks of many of our citizens in a manner so attractive that they will be cherished as pictures, when the originals would otherwise be forgotten.

Many of Ross' paintings of local residents have been preserved, and while they do not have the power and monumentality of Elliott's work, they do mark Ross as a strong, competent portraitist in the realist tradition. In December of 1854, the paper reported that he had recovered from a long illness, but in August of 1856 it sorrowfully announced his death.

In 1838, George Ross had advertised in Newark the partnership of McDougall and Ross, portraitist and miniaturist, on Broad Street near City Hall. He made this liaison with John Alexander McDougall (1810/1811-1894), a native of Livingston who spent most of his career in Newark. McDougall seems to have traveled a good deal more than Ross, visiting Saratoga Springs, Charleston, and New Orleans, but Newark remained his home where several of his children also engaged in the arts. McDougall also had a studio in New York City. The partnership would seem to have been an ideal one, since Ross specialized in large oil portraits and McDougall in miniature painting. In addition to miniatures, McDougall painted numerous landscapes and seems to have practiced lithography, too.

McDougall's miniatures, like Ross' large oils, are in the tight, realistic style of the middle of the century. They are rather hard and uninspired work, but McDougall's gradual abandonment of this art was in all probability due more to the decline in miniature painting that set in at the time than to his own deficiencies. Photography became extremely popular in science-minded America immediately upon its emergence in the 1840's. It is probably unfair to claim too great an influence for photography upon the arts; it might be more accurate to suggest that the scientific experimentation which resulted in photography was reflected in the arts

John Alexander McDougall, "Portrait of a Lady"
Collection of The Newark Museum

in the new emphasis upon truth, realism, and individuality. Nevertheless, because the photograph could match the miniature, even in size, and surpass it in realistic detail, the photograph successfully rivaled miniature painting which was abandoned by many of its leading practitioners. In fact, like many another former miniaturist, McDougall ended his days as a photograper, and his painting talents were reduced to touching up and coloring photographs he had taken.

Lilly Martin Spencer, whom we will discuss later, did fine portraiture in Newark in mid-century, and Thomas Buchanan Read painted in Bordentown, but he too is better known for other art forms. Samuel Bell Waugh (1814-1885) was a superior portraitist who also painted in Bordentown in 1853, although he is primarily associated with Philadelphia.

Perhaps a word should be said also about portraiture at the turn of the century. Portraits continued to be painted and artists to find patronage, but at this time very few really creative or distinguished painters specialized in this theme, and the hard, photographic likenesses of the period deserve little attention. Perhaps the best portraitist to work in New Jersey in the third quarter of the nineteenth century was John Hagny (1833-1876), who had a studio in Newark as early as 1855, and whose photographic likenesses can be found today in most of the public institutions in New Jersey, such as the State Capitol, Rutgers and Princeton Universities, The New Jersey Historical Society, and the Newark Museum.

Joseph G. Beitl (1841-1929) worked into the twentieth century. He began his career in Newark in 1868 or 1869, in partnership with Charles Leyers, a photographer. He had a studio and drawing school in Newark, and was active there, principally as a portraitist; he also worked in Elizabeth, Old Bridge, Livingston, and Orange. Douglas Volk (1856-1935) was one of the best known American portraitists. Son of the famous sculptor of Abraham Lincoln, Leonard Volk, he lived in Montclair from about 1890 to 1895, at a time when that town was the leading art center in the state. Another art-conscious town of the period was Nutley, where the portraitist Frank Fowler (1852-1910) built a famous residence and studio in the "Enclosure," which has remained the home of prominent artists through succeeding generations. Fowler had worked with Carolus-Duran on the frescoes in the Luxembourg Palace in Paris; during his years in Nutley he was engaged in creating the frescoes for the smaller ballroom of the Waldorf-Astoria. He painted portraits of such well-known figures as William Dean Howells and Madame Helena Modjeska and died in New Canaan, Connecticut.

Louis Charles Moeller (1855-1930), a portrait and figure painter, was born in New York City and studied there and with Frank Duveneck in Munich; his last years were spent in Weehawken. He developed a very detailed, blocky figure style, and often incorporated his portrait subjects into their settings and environments, so that his paintings appear to be genre pictures or "informal conversation pieces." This made for a distinct and rather engaging style, and he was probably the most interesting artist to paint portraits in New Jersey at the time. However, the revival of interest in portraiture, represented internationally by the American expatriate artist, John Singer Sargent, does not find reflection in New Jersey, and important creativity in portrait painting in New Jersey had long since disappeared.

III

LANDSCAPE PAINTING BEFORE THE CIVIL WAR

DESPITE THE NUMBER of portraitists who were active in New Jersey during the nineteenth century, the State's legacy in the fine arts is greater in landscape. The "Garden State" was truly that for many an artist, even into our own time. On the other hand, New Jersey landscape painting begins later than portraiture. This is, after all, not surprising, for this branch of the arts began much later in America in general than portraiture. Indeed, it was only in the early nineteenth century that, with the emergence of a wealthy leisure class who supported the artists of their own newly-founded nation, professional landscape painting began to emerge.

This does not mean, of course, that no landscapes were painted in America during the eighteenth century, but surprisingly few were—or have survived. Most of the known eighteenth-century scenes are more topographical than inventive: almost "portraits" of a harbor, a town, or a natural formation. Only in the very late eighteenth century can one find a professional artist such as Ralph Earl painting pure landscapes, still in a very naturalistic style, and even here there was little enough demand for such scenes. But, in the second and third decades of the nineteenth century, some artists, such as Thomas Birch and Thomas Doughty in Philadelphia, Thomas Cole in New York, and Alvan Fisher in Boston, began to explore and record the American landscape in a rather romantic, sometimes inventive style, and to find patrons who purchased or even commissioned such works.

The earliest New Jersey landscapes of which we have knowledge are depictions of scenic wonders or are related to the routes which travelers took to journey from one Colonial center to another. Because of this, many of the earliest landscapists to work in New Jersey were not residents but travelers themselves, and some were amateurs who were struck by the attractiveness of a scene. Indeed, the most important subject in New Jersey during the whole of the eighteenth and nineteenth centuries, was the Passaic Falls in Paterson. As early as 1680, Jasper Danckaerts, a leader of the Dutch Labadists, who was also an amateur artist, sketched the Passaic Falls. In the late 1750's, Lieutenant Governor Thomas Pownall (1722-1805) sketched the Falls; a number of scenes by Pownall, who was a topographical artist, including the Falls, were engraved and published. Perhaps best known of the artists who sketched in New Jersey and drew the Falls during that century was Archibald Robertson (1765-1835), a Scottish miniature and portrait painter who came to New York City in 1791. A number of his sketches are preserved in The New Jersey Historical Society.

The Passaic Falls remained a popular spot, particularly during the romantic period. Indeed, newspapers, periodicals, and gift books contain many accounts of visits to the Falls, sentimental poems written about them or about a loved one visiting the Falls, or even, occasionally, in memory of one who perished in the waters of the Falls—usually intentionally. Waterfalls, with their suggestion of the power of Nature and their movement and turbulence, were popular among travelers in the period, and the Passaic Falls were only surpassed by Niagara Falls and the Trenton Falls near Utica in popularity. Furthermore, they were the most accessible to visitors, so that many journeyed over from New York to see them, artists included. It is not surprising, therefore, that a number of New Jersey's resident landscapists also took advantage of the proximity of this scenic wonder, and succeeding styles of landscape painting can be studied in the various depictions of the Falls.

The most romantic view among those in the collection of The New Jersey Historical Society is that by Jesse Talbot (1806-1879). Talbot was active in New York from about 1838 on, but from 1845 to 1847, and perhaps until 1849, he was living in Paterson where he had, of course, every opportunity to visit the Falls. His depiction of them is romantic and moody, with dramatic lighting and gathering storm clouds; in the foreground is a solitary Indian, and the picture conveys a sense of the passing of time, a relationship between man and Nature, and a sympathetic interpretation of the defeat of a vanishing race. A similar mood and the use of Indian subject matter can be found in other of Talbot's paintings.

One of the most colorful, controversial, and influential of all of New Jersey's painters and the one who may have painted the Falls most often, was Thomas W. Whitley (fl. 1835-1863). He was an Englishman who settled in Paterson, probably in 1835, and remained there until around 1839. It was at this time that he painted numerous views of the Falls and the Passaic River, and perhaps dating from this period are his two located pictures, both of the Falls, one in the spring and one in the autumn, now owned by The New Jersey Historical Society. There is a hasty, free brushwork and the interpretation of the Falls is much less romantic, more factual, than Talbot's. Various visitors can be seen in and around the site, which is much less grand and monumental.

From 1839 to 1842 Whitley was in New York and may have gone to Italy after that. In 1848 he went to Cincinnati to become superintendent on Edwin Forrest's farm at Covington, Kentucky, but returned East in 1849. At this time, like a number of other artists of the mid-century, he settled in Hoboken where he remained at least until 1860. He continued to paint landscapes, some of them reminiscences of his stay in the Midwest, some of England, but mostly views in and around Hoboken and Weehawken, including Charles Loring Elliott's country seat mentioned earlier. In addition, he was employed as art and drama critic of the *New-York Herald,* a critic on the *Home Journal,* and editor of the *Hoboken Gazette.*

One of the most fascinating developments in the history of the fine arts in America was the growth and popularity of the Art-Unions, subscription organizations by which engravings and original oil paintings were purchased or commissioned, and then awarded by lottery to some of the members. The Art-Unions grew up around 1839, beginning with the most successful of all of them, the American Art-Union, in New York City, and numbering sister organizations in Philadelphia, Boston, Cincinnati, Newark, and even Sandusky, Ohio. These organizations had great public support and seem to have contributed directly to the popularizing of art, particularly by native artists, in America. Scenes of everyday life especially were purchased and awarded since this type of subject was a favorite of all subscribers, and the growth of interest in this theme is usually credited to the Art-Unions.

Thomas Whitley, however, has the unenviable distinction of being the prime mover in the destruction of these organizations. Whitely's disenchantment with the Art-Unions began at the time he was working in Kentucky, when he submitted works to the Western Art-Union in Cincinnati, founded in 1847. During that organization's first year of operation, it purchased for distribution three of Whitley's work; but during the next year, he was rejected, and in retaliation he wrote a scathing criticism of the Art-Union. Meanwhile, Whitley began submitting works to the American Art-Union in New York and was at first successful in getting them to purchase his landscapes, due to the influence of William Cullen Bryant, who was a friend of his.

Gradually, however, after he returned East and settled in Hoboken, he grew more disenchanted and increasingly bitter with the Art-Union which recognized, in its Decem-

Thomas W. Whitley, "Passaic Falls in Spring"
Collection of The New Jersey Historical Society, Newark

ber, 1849, Bulletin, the existence of "enemies far more insidious and persevering . . . among the body of the artists themselves." Whitley may, in fact, have been a member of "The American Artists Association" formed in October, 1850, in opposition to the Art-Union which the Association accused of bullying and underpaying artists, and showing favoritism in their choices. Further diatribes against the organization appeared in the *New-York Herald,* of which journal Whitley was art critic, and succeeded in turning the public against it. Furthermore, Whitley even organized a lottery drawing of his own to mock the Art-Union, offering 30 paintings, chiefly landscapes. Attacks by Whitley and others continued and on June 11, 1852, the New York Supreme Court handed down a decision declaring that the American Art-Union lottery system was illegal and unconstitutional. It was Whitley and the *New-York Herald* that had constantly pointed the finger of immorality and illegality at the organization as violating anti-lottery laws, and it is Whitley, therefore, who may earn the dubious credit of having destroyed an organization popular among both artists and the public. His disappointments, lack of success, and fanatical temper accomplished this destruction.

In addition to resident New Jersey artists, other professional painters—such as William Guy Wall, the Irish-born landscapist of New York City, famous for his popular engraved and published "Hudson River Portfolio," and the German-trained Philadelphia artist Augustus Köllner—visited New Jersey to paint the Falls. Thomas Sully also painted three views of the Passaic Falls as early as 1807. Primitive and amateur painters of the State also painted here, including William Arthur Tipson (born 1846), a self-taught Newark artist who painted the Falls in 1872 before moving out to California.

The most illustrious of all the amateur artists who depicted the Passaic Falls was undoubtedly Charlotte Julie Bonaparte (1802-1839), known as the Countess de Survilliers, the daughter of Joseph Bonaparte, brother of Napoleon, former King of Naples and of Spain.

Joseph Bonaparte bought an estate on the Delaware River near Bordentown in 1816. Charlotte Bonaparte lived at "Point Breeze" with her father from about 1819 to 1828 and exhibited in the Pennsylvania Academy of the Fine Arts. In addition to a charming portrait of Cora Monges, painted in 1822, she is best remembered for a series of American views which were engraved in Joubert's *Picturesque Views of American Scenery*. There are five New Jersey scenes, two related to the Passaic Falls, one at Point Breeze, one in Hunterdon County, and one in Bergen County. In addition, three other views by her are known, another of the Passaic Falls, one near Tuckerton, and one at Schooleys Mountain.

Actually, Joseph Bonaparte's home was something of an artistic center, thus continuing a Bordentown tradition going back to the days of Patience Wright. Bonaparte had brought with him a distinguished collection of Old Masters from which he frequently lent paintings to the American Academy of the Fine Arts in New York. His "Rape of Europe," by Noël-Nicolas Coypel, which he gave to General Thomas Cadwalader, is now in the Philadelphia Museum of Art. Foreign artists such as the British naval officer, Captain Basil Hall, and the Swiss artist, Karl Bodmer—who accompanied Maximilian, Prince of Wied-Neuweid on a trip through the country in 1832-1834—came there. The finest depictions of the beautiful house at Point Breeze were made by a Bordentown-born artist, Charles B. Lawrence (fl. 1811-1864). He was a portraitist as well as a landscapist, and studied under Rembrandt Peale and supposedly under Gilbert Stuart. Lawrence's artistic life, until he abandoned painting around 1840, was connected with Philadelphia, but he was back in Bordentown in 1813 and 1821, perhaps painting Point Breeze in the latter year.

Lawrence's style is somewhat akin to that of the best-known of the early Philadelphia land- and seascapists, Thomas Birch. Birch worked in Philadelphia throughout his long life, and was noted for his marine pictures, naval battle scenes, and snow scenes. A number of the last are paintings done in New Jersey, and the Jersey side of the Delaware seems to have served Birch as a source for rural scenery, much as the northern part of the state did for New York artists. A somewhat later artist, George R. Bonfield, also of Philadelphia, specialized in both marine paintings and snow scenes. Bonfield, however, lived in New Jersey: in Beverly from 1853, in Bordentown in 1856, and in Burlington in 1857. A number of his coastal scenes were painted on the Jersey shore, and it is probable that he, like Birch, also found inspiration in New Jersey for his winter landscapes.

The finest landscapist of all to live and work in southern New Jersey, however, was Joshua Shaw (1776-1860). He was born in Bellingsborough, Lincoln County, England. After serving an apprenticeship, he became a signpainter. He practiced drawing and easel painting, however, painting pictures of flowers and fruit, cattle portraits, and landscapes, and also made copies of works by such artists as Berchem, Gainsborough, and de Loutherbourg. He began exhibiting in London in 1802, at one time showing his "The Deluge" at the same time that Turner was diplaying a similarly titled scene.

Shaw came to America in 1817, accompanying Benjamin West's picture, "Christ Healing the Sick." He settled in Philadelphia and frequently exhibited there, being instrumental also in the formation of the Artists' Fund Society. Shaw traveled through America, drawing the scenery and also depicting the life of the Indians and frontiersmen, and he was one of the first professional artists to do so. Dunlap met him in 1819 and 1820 in Norfolk, Virginia, on his return from South Carolina. Some of his works were engraved and published in his *Picturesque Views of American Scenery* in 1820, the engravings made by John Hill. At the same time Shaw was successfully established as the inventor of the percussion cap and made many improvements in firearms.

Shaw lived in Philadelphia for the first several decades of his American residence, but by 1844 he had crossed the river and was living in Bordentown. In 1847 he

Joshua Shaw, "English Landscape with Two Figures"
Collection of Henry M. Fuller

purchased a property on Farnsworth Avenue, which is still standing, and lived there until his death. The subject matter of the landscapes which he exhibited, however, was drawn from many regions of America, and he seems always to have continued to paint scenes in Italy and in his native Great Britain. In America, in addition to views in South Carolina, he must have journeyed to Pittburgh and beyond, and while he does not seem to have painted many scenes in New Jersey, he did a beautiful painting of the home of Bishop Doane at Burlington.

Shaw also painted many marine scenes, and these, like some of those of his nearby colleague, Thomas Birch, were also romantic pictures, bearing such titles as "Storm and Shipwreck" and "Sea Piece—Morning during a Heavy Storm." Stylistically, however, Shaw's painting was almost unique in the America of his time, although he shared with Birch a preference for the lighter, more silvery tonalities which seems to have been preferred in the Philadelphia area, as opposed to the hotter, more golden tones of the landscapists in and about New York. Shaw had after all been trained in England and practiced there before coming to America, and he brought to this country the pastoral landscape tradition which can be seen in the idyllic shepherds and shepherdesses of François Boucher, the French painter. The light and graceful rococo interpretations of such themes were brought to England by such an artist as Phillippe de Loutherbourg, whose work Shaw knew; an earlier Dutch equivalent of this is seen in the paintings of Nicholas Berchem, which were also familiar to Shaw. In England, landscape settings with peasants and rural cottages were painted by such artists as George Moreland and Julius Caesar Ibbetson, and Shaw brought this form to America. It can be seen of course most directly in some of his paintings based upon English scenery, but even in his Indian paintings there is a light, vibrant touch with dainty forms which reveal an indirect, French rococo precedent. A series entitled "The Progress of Vice," with its obvious relationship to the morality paintings of

William Hogarth, also suggests continuing English influence. Shaw does not seem to have any close followers, however, either in Philadelphia or in New Jersey.

The most significant, however, of all the pre-Civil War American landscapists to be associated with New Jersey was an artist of the northern part of the state, Asher B. Durand (1796-1886). The artist's grandfather came from Connecticut and settled in Newark in 1640. His son, John Durand, bought land and built a house in Jefferson Village, now Maplewood, in 1774, and brought his wife there, the former Rachel Post Meyer of Newark, in 1779. Asher B. Durand was their eighth child; eleven in all were born, of whom ten reached maturity.

John Durand was a watchmaker and silversmith, and in the process of his work naturally engraved monograms and other designs. Asher Durand became fascinated with this art, and also with the process of woodcut-making and engraving. With the encouragement of an Enos Smith, a frequent visitor to John Durand's shop, Asher Durand became apprenticed for five years to Peter Maverick in October, 1812. Maverick was one of America's most successful engravers in the early nineteenth century, and had then only recently removed from New York to Newark, New Jersey. Durand's first engraving task was a piece of lettering consisting of an old title-page to *The Pilgrim's Progress.* Successful at this, Durand was given a series of commissions by Maverick, the first of which was engraving illustrations to Calmet's *Dictionary of the Bible.* Durand was an extremely able engraver, doing vignettes for bank notes, diplomas, and other miscellanies. So successful was he that Maverick took him into partnership, an association that lasted three years. Durand's first original work, not copying the work of others but engraving directly from a painting, was the head of "Old Pat," the beggar, after a painting by Samuel Waldo. This was so greatly admired by the famous artist, John Trumbull, that he commissioned Durand to do the engraving of his painting "Declaration of Independence." Unfortunately,

Maverick himself wanted a share of the commission, and the disagreement that followed resulted in the dissolution of the partnership. The engraving which occupied Durand from 1820 to 1823 was highly successful and, admired as it was by Trumbull and others, established Durand's artistic position.

Meanwhile, Durand had moved to New York in 1821, after his marriage to the daughter of Isaac Baldwin of Bloomfield, New Jersey. He continued successfully there as an engraver, creating many portraits of well-known divines, famous theatrical personalities, and other illustrious figures. In addition he created many engravings for gift books and annuals after compositions by the leading painters of the period. In 1824 he formed the partnership of A. B. & C. Durand & Co., with his brother, Cyrus Durand, who had invented the geometrical lathe to produce bank note designs. In 1830, Durand was engaged in an enterprise entitled *The American Landscape*—a series of engravings after paintings of American scenery by native artists with text by William Cullen Bryant. The project was not a success and only one group of six landscapes was published, but the series was prophetic of Durand's later interest. One of the landscapes in the group was of Weehawken, after a watercolor by William James Bennett.

In 1835 Durand produced his engraving after John Vanderlyn's "Ariadne," probably the finest engraving to be created in the early nineteenth century in America, depicting a beautiful nude figure lying in a landscape. Successful though the engraving was, it represented the termination of Durand's career as an engraver. As early as 1826 he had begun to exhibit paintings at the National Academy of Design, starting with a series of biblical illustrations. He also painted numerous portraits including one of Colonel Aaron Ogden, Governor of New Jersey, and a series of Presidential portraits for Luman Reed, the principal art patron in New York City whose portrait Durand also painted. Later he turned to historical paintings, including "The Capture of Major

Asher B. Durand, "Portrait of Mrs. Durand and Her Sister," 1831

Collection of The Newark Museum

Andre" and "The Wrath of Peter Stuyvesant," the latter painted for Reed.

Durand went back to New Jersey briefly during his wife's illness, but after her death in 1830 he returned to New York City.

In 1840, in the company of the young landscapists John F. Kensett, Thomas P. Rossiter, and John William Casilear, Durand sailed for Europe, visiting England and the Continent. At about this time, Durand gave up portraiture and began to devote his time entirely to landscape painting. Indeed, even much earlier he showed an interest in this theme, and in some of his portraits, such as his 1831 "Portrait of his Second Wife and Sister," he portrayed his subjects in verdant landscape settings. During the next decades he spent his summers in the country, studying nature. He was particularly familiar with the Catskills and Lake George, and with the mountains of Vermont and New Hampshire. Surprisingly, very few of his landscapes depict his native state, probably because he sought wilderness subjects less pastoral than New Jersey afforded.

Durand was one of the leading figures of the New York art scene during the long period from 1821 to 1869, and in 1845 he became President of the National Academy of Design. Nevertheless, as he entered into old age, he decided to retire to the country, and returned to the family property in Maplewood. The old house having burned down, he built a new one with a larger studio. He had pleasant, agreeable society, for nearby lived his son-in-law, George Woodman, a fellow artist, Gaston Fay, and Dr. Alfred M. Mayer, of Stevens Institute. He continued to paint landscapes, including his "Primaeval Forest," painted in 1870 and now in the Corcoran Gallery of Art. In 1872, the landscapist Jervis McEntee, who had received some artistic advice in his youth from Durand, arranged a surprise party for the aged artist in Maplewood. To it came the painters McEntee, William Page, Thomas Hicks, Eastman Johnson, John F. Kensett, Christopher Pearse Cranch, John

Asher B. Durand, "Landscape," 1849
Collection of The Newark Museum

M. Falconer, George Hall, and Worthington Whittredge, the sculptors Erastus Dow Palmer, Launt Thompson, and John Quincy Adams Ward, and also William Cullen Bryant; surely, this was the most illustrious gathering of artists to assemble in New Jersey during the nineteenth century. Durand died at the age of ninety, tranquil and sure of a life of major achievement.

Durand has often been called the "Father of American Landscape Painting." That he was a major figure in its development there can be no question, but his artistic career began, actually, first with engraving and then with portraiture; he was an early historical, religious, and genre painter, and it was only later that he emerged as a truly significant landscapist. His early works have a grace and charm and a quaintness which identifies him still with the romantic style prevalent in his youth. This is true of some of his earlier landscapes, too, such as his 1840 series, "The Morning of Life" and "The Evening of Life." Without the grandeur and majesty of the contemporary series by Thomas Cole, such as "The Course of Empire" and "The Voyage of Life," Durand's early landscapes have the sentimental and emotional appearance of the age.

Durand's most important contributions to the development of American landscape painting occurred in the following decade and continued to his death. The term, "The Hudson River School," has been used to describe American scene painting from its beginning to the end of the nineteenth century. This oversimplification does not take into account the differences that occurred within the succeeding styles of the century, but certainly it is Durand who best illustrates the prevalent landscape style of the 1840's, 1850's, and 1860's, a style of great realism and truth to nature. There was an emphasis upon factual detail, clarity of form, and a timelessness in the effects of Nature. The artist's role was limited to choosing and occasionally ordering the elements of the landscape, but the interpretative, emotional, and idealizing effects of Nature of the preceding age were abandoned. Indeed, critics of the period preferred Durand to Cole because of his fidelity to Nature, and many younger artists of the mid-century looked upon Durand's work as a fitting model for emulation. From that point of view, then, Durand was a determining influence in American art of the mid-nineteenth century. His connections with his native state were never forgotten, and surely the influence of his rural upbringing upon the development of his art is indicated by his return to his homestead toward the end of his life.

Although Durand's influence was great, and although he had many pupils, his only New Jersey follower was a nephew, Elias Wade Durand (1824-1908), who worked in Newark from 1851 to 1857. Elias Durand's style is very much like that of his uncle in its sharpness, clarity, and detail; it differs in tonality, emphasizing often an interesting harmony of pale blues and orange-browns, rather than the hotter tones of the older painter.

There were, however, a number of local landscapists of note in the Newark area, although none of them ever achieved the fame of Asher B. Durand. One of these was Jacob C. Ward (1809-1891), was was born in Bloomfield, the son of the artist, Caleb Ward. He was active in both New York and New Jersey, painting among other works the scene of the Hamilton-Burr duel in Weehawken. He was also a pioneer photographer, joining his brother Charles V. Ward on a trip to Chile, Bolivia, Peru, and Panama to take daguerreotype likenesses. He returned to New Jersey in the late 1840's and spent the rest of his life in Bloomfield. Otto Sommer (fl. 1851-1868) lived in Newark and Belleville, painting and exhibiting landscapes of Essex County. He also painted copies of Thomas Cole's "The Voyage of Life"; his best-known picture was his large "Westward Ho!" The best of all these lesser landscapists was William Mason Brown (1828-1898), born in Troy, New York. He studied in New York City and was working in Newark from 1850 to 1858, painting landscapes. On August 17, 1852, there was a drawing of a group of twelve of Brown's landscapes and seascapes at the studio of George Ross, the portraitist, in Library Hall. Ross himself won one of the paintings, entitled "English Coast Scene"; a number of the others had romantic titles. Indeed, Brown's style was much more in keeping with an earlier generation, painted broadly and thickly, with brilliant color and idealized forms. In the 1860's, however, a thematic change occurred in his work, and he became one of the leading still-life painters of the period, in a hard and tight photographic style. By then, however, he had removed to New York City. He is not to be confused with the English landscape and genre painter, William G. Brown (fl. 1837-1861), who was living in Hoboken from 1856 to 1861 with his daughter, the painter Mary Ann Brown (fl. 1837-1873). Finally, Joseph Rusling Meeker (1827-1887) was born in Newark but his artistic life centered around St. Louis, where he achieved fame for his landscapes of the Mississippi Delta bayou country, and his New Jersey connection is therefore only peripheral.

Not all of the landscapists of the period, of course, were living in the Bordentown or Newark areas. De Witt Clinton Boutelle (1820-1884), for instance, lived at Basking Ridge around 1848 and 1849, where he sketched from nature landscapes which he later exhibited, including one of "Winter on the Passaic." Born in Troy, New York, Boutelle worked in New York City before and after his Jersey residence, and later painted in Philadelphia and Bethlehem. He is perhaps best known for having completed one painted set of Thomas Cole's famous series, "The Voyage of Life," and his work shows a combination of Cole's romanticism and Durand's more factual approach to Nature.

As with portraitists, a number of the landscape painters active in the more rural areas of the state worked in a more primitive style. John Jesse Barker (fl. 1815-1860) is one.

The *New Brunswick Times* for June 29, 1815, announced the opening of his school for instruction in drawing and painting, but he was spoken of in 1820 as

John Jesse Barker, "East Entrance to Rahway, New Jersey," 1843
Collection of Mrs. Carlos A. Hepp

having returned from Philadelphia to New Brunswick where he engaged rooms next to the residence of Bishop Croes. In the summer of the same year he was in Elizabeth and painted portraits of members of such local families as the De Harts, Chetwoods, and Woodruffs, from his rooms at the old Union Hotel on South Broad Street. At that time Barker was mentioned as a pupil of Thomas Sully in the *Elizabethtown Gazette* for August 8.

In 1824, Barker again opened a drawing school in New Brunswick on the corner of George and Prince streets, charging six dollars per quarter for instruction in drawing and painting in watercolors, and eight dollars for instruction in painting on velvet. From 1840 to 1843 he was at 246 Broad Street in Newark where he painted in 1843, his best-known picture, a landscape, "East Entrance to Rahway, New Jersey," and it is likely that he turned more and more to the theme of landscapes as its popularity increased. While Barker was in Newark, George Inness studied with him. In 1856 there was an exhibition of 15 of his works in New Brunswick, and a lottery drawing distributed the paintings among the 66 holders of three-dollar tickets. Among the works shown were landscapes of the New Brunswick area.

Another engaging semi-primitive landscapist who worked until the end of the century was Edward Kranich (1826-1891). Prussia appears to have been his birthplace, and family tradition has him a native of Essen; the family probably emigrated around 1848 and settled in Elizabeth, where his father manufactured Kranich and Bach pianos. Edward Kranich married Vashti Collins in Northfield, New Jersey, and his sister Amelia married Vashti's brother Sidney; the second couple moved to the outskirts of Morristown. Although Kranich lived in a town of some size, most of his landscapes were painted in the Morristown area and none seem to relate to Elizabeth. The most engaging of them are his "farm portraits"—depictions of rural homesteads, including out-buildings, grounds, figures, and animals. Kranich

Edward Kranich, "The Old Homestead"
Collection of the Colby College Art Gallery, Waterville, Maine

gave great care to the details of building structure, fences, and landscape elements. Although the figures were not individualized, they not only added scale and brightness to the scene, but gave a suggestion of man's activity. The mood was usually tranquil and idyllic. Other themes included distant views of Morristown, animal paintings—among which were several fascinating ones of numerous birds, all of different varieties—and some portraits.

The Kranichs had six sons, five of whom were artists. Lamentably, these five all appear to have died young at the end of the century. The father was, however, the only one who considered himself a practitioner of the fine arts, his sons engaging in sign, ornamental, fresco, and windowshade painting. Edward, the father, was the only painter of the period in Elizabeth whose works have so far come to light, though the existence of other painters is known.

There were several women landscape painters of the period who lived in New Jersey. One of these, Edith Cook (fl. 1864-1872), is listed as living in Hoboken in the 1860's and early 1870's, exhibiting in the National Academy of Design. Although little is known about her, she was a friend of many of the major landscapists of her time and accompanied them on their camping trips in the pursuit of native scenery. The life of a later artist, Julie Hart Beers Kempson (1835-1913), has been more fully documented. She was the sister of two well-known landscapists of the Hudson River School, James and William Hart. As Mrs. Julie Hart Beers she lived in New York City and exhibited there and in Boston. She later married Peter T. Kempson and was living in Metuchen by 1877. Her few known landscapes are competent work not unlike that of her brothers. She died at her home in Trenton.

Another landscapist who lived in New Jersey, one of national and even international fame, was Jasper Francis Cropsey (1823-1900). He was born near Rossville, on Staten Island, and began by studying architectural modeling. Lack of encouragement led him to undertake painting, but he never completely abandoned architecture. His most famous project in that discipline was the "master" station for the Sixth Avenue Elevated Railroad in New York, at Sixth Avenue and Fourteenth Street. He also designed houses in Long Branch, New Jersey, and his later home at Hastings-on-Hudson is not only a masterpiece of Gothic Revival domestic architecture but one of the most complete studios surviving from the nineteenth century.

When he began a career in painting, Cropsey was induced to visit Greenwood Lake. The large painting that resulted was so successful that it attracted the attention of Henry Inman who suggested that Cropsey send it to the National Academy of Design; he was soon elected an Associate of that institution. Cropsey continued to frequent that area, and in 1847 he married the daughter of J. P. Cooley of Greenwood Lake; after two years spent abroad he returned to America. He kept a summer studio at the southern end of Greenwood Lake, but made more than occasional use of it, however; in 1850, for instance, he proposed to remain there until December. During the next several decades Cropsey continued to paint New Jersey scenes, including views on the Passaic River, scenes of Lake Wawayanda, but above all, numerous views of Greenwood Lake—scenes from different parts of the Lake, paintings of different sizes, and works done at different times of the day or of the year. Even when he went abroad in 1857, staying in London in 1863, he continued to paint views of the American lake. Another New Jersey subject of which he painted several beautiful replicas was "Janetta Falls, Passaic County," the location of which has still to be determined. While in his New Jersey studio Cropsey painted at least one religious landscape, "The Good Shepherd" of 1855.

Cropsey's later career was spent first across the New York border at Warwick, and then across the Hudson at Hastings-on-Hudson. By the end of his life, the meticulous realism of the Hudson River School which marked Cropsey's style was long since outdated, and the artist's sense of structure, light, and clarity had begun to fail. During his heyday, however, at the time he painted his New Jersey landscapes, Cropsey was one of the most successful of American landscapists, a success which he was able to repeat during his London sojourn. At that time he exhibited his nine-foot-long "Autumn on the Hudson River" at the Great International Exhibition of 1862, which was highly praised as an outstanding American landscape.

Both at home and abroad, Cropsey was particularly noted for the brilliance of his color and in order to justify his coloristic interests, he specialized particularly in the depiction of autumnal landscapes. This aspect of his art was noted on both sides of the Atlantic, but the range of his pigments pervaded all his landscapes and can be seen even in his less numerous winter scenes. In this regard he differs greatly from Durand whose tonality was usually limited to the earth tones, although Cropsey adopted the sharp precisionism and meticulous detail of the older artist, after he abandoned Cole-like romanticism in the early 1850's. The new pastoral quality which was beginning to predominate in American landscape painting about 1850 can also be seen in many of Cropsey's landscapes, and the scenes depicted illustrate details of everyday life—boating, picnicing, haymaking—in tamed, bucolic settings. There was often also a dramatic setting forth of trees and other natural forms against a clear brilliant sky, or a dramatic use of light and shade in his earlier works, more diffused in the later ones.

Cropsey's one major pupil was the landscapist David Johnson (1827-1908), who began exhibiting in 1849. Johnson's studio was in New York City, but early in his career he often visited his former teacher at his summer studio, and some of his finest landscapes were painted at that time, including his masterpiece, "Old Mill, West Millford, New Jersey." John Bunyan Bristol (1826-1909)

Jasper Francis Cropsey, "Greenwood Lake," 1862
Collection of The Newark Museum

was a fine landscapist working in the style of Cropsey and Johnson whose earliest pictures were scenes of Llewelyn Park, New Jersey. Walter M. Oddie (c. 1808-1865) was another landscapist who, while never residing in New Jersey, visited the State for scenic inspiration about 1847, painting Somerset County subjects such as Chimney Rock. Edward Beyer (1820-1865) was a German artist who came to America about 1848 and remained here until about 1857. He traveled a great deal, doing views of American spas which were lithographed back in Germany and published as *An Album of Virginia;* he also exhibited panoramas. He was in Newark in the winter of 1852-1853, when the Passaic River froze over, and several delightful views of "Skating on the Passaic" are souvenirs of this visit.

Still another extremely talented artist who worked extensively in New Jersey was William Rickarby Miller (1818-1893). Again, there is no evidence of his having lived in New Jersey, but numerous views survive depicting scenes in and about Weehawken, Hoboken, and Jersey City. He was an English artist who came to America in the winter of 1844-1845, and made his home in New York City. An oil painter of note, Miller's best talents lay in the field of watercolor painting, and he was probably the finest artist to work in this medium before Winslow Homer; his New Jersey scenes were painted in both oils and watercolors.

The most important of all the visiting artists in New Jersey of the period was Martin Johnson Heade (1819-1904). Heade was one of that group of relatively advanced painters who have recently been grouped under the name "luminists." Although these artists—Heade, John F. Kensett, Sanford Gifford, Joseph Rusling Meeker, and others—continued the emphasis upon particularized realism which marks the Hudson River School, they exhibited a subtle concern with diffused atmospheric conditions and overall luminous light effects which gives the paintings of these men broader, more open effects, and a general haze which obscures distant detail. This interest, of course, is

William Rickarby Miller, "Weehawken Bluff on the Hudson," 1871
Collection of The Newark Museum

allied to the investigations in light and atmosphere which mark first the French painters of the Barbizon School, such as Corot, and later the Impressionists themselves. The American luminists, however, Heade included, never abandoned the specific and particular as did Corot, nor did they begin to explore color and painterly effects as did Claude Monet and his colleagues. Nevertheless, their investigations produced a series of remarkable landscapes and are part of the general scientific concern of the age.

Heade was born in Lumberville, Bucks County, Pennsylvania; his mother, Sarah Johnson Heed, came from Hunterdon County, New Jersey. Heade studied in Europe, painting first portraits and later landscapes and still life. He is probably best known for his 1863-1864 trip to Brazil to create a series of paintings of landscapes and hummingbirds ultimately to be made into chromolithograph. He became a great favorite of the Emperor of Brazil, Dom Pedro II, but the difficulties of the chromolithograph project led to its abandonment. Actually, Heade traveled perhaps more extensively than any other nineteenth-century American painter, not only to South and Central America, the West Indies and Europe, but to Canada, California and, finally, to Florida, where he settled.

Actually, Heade does seem to have had a New Jersey residence, for, in a document of 1854 concerning the purchase of some Illinois property, the artist gave his address as Trenton, New Jersey. Heade had worked in that city in 1844, and lived there again from about 1856 to 1859, the most important artist connected with the State capital. More significant, however, in the annals of American painting and in the history of New Jersey art, are Heade's interpretations of the Jersey Meadows. In his landscape painting, the artist seems to have been particularly interested in marshland, and among his favorite sources for scenic subject matter were the Newburyport, Massachusetts meadows, the salt marshes at Newport, Rhode Island, and various tropical marshlands in Florida and Latin America. But quite a number of

Martin Johnson Heade, "Jersey Meadows," 1877
Collection of The Newark Museum

paintings by him of the meadowland between Hoboken and Newark are known, and although the area is a subject which has attracted other nineteenth and twentieth-century painters. Heade is pre-eminently the interpreter of the region.

His preference for painting these meadows is not difficult to understand. Nearly all his landscapes emphasize broad, uninterrupted horizontal planes, and his canvases, almost always exceedingly horizontal, seem to depict limitless space, extended far beyond the segment actually shown. Except for minuscule figures and patterned haystacks which recall man's activity in the landscapes, these often small but panoramic canvases have little reference to the contemporaneous world. The wet marshaland, too, was ideal for the suggestion of sometimes rich, sometimes exceedingly subtle atmospheric effects, with silvery or golden light filling the canvas—especially since the invariable low horizons leave about two-thirds of the canvas as empty, open sky. The interpretations of the various geographic areas which Heade chose to paint differ among themselves very little, for all were ideal for the mood of poetic reverie which infused his landscapes.

IV

NEWARK AT MID-CENTURY

SINCE NEWARK WAS the largest city in New Jersey in the middle of the nineteenth century as it is now, it is important to understand the artistic currents in the city around 1850. Such a discussion is especially pertinent, since there are certain events and developments, of particular interest to this history which were unique to that city.

Some of the artists already discussed were, of course, at work in and around Newark at this time—the portraitists John McDougall and George Ross for example, and such landscape painters as William Mason Brown, Ed Beyer, and Otto Sommer. Undoubtedly the work of these artists was admired and appreciated locally. However, the most popular artistic events in Newark were the public exhibitions of panoramas and other large paintings which traveled from city to city, usually showing for a period of weeks, and accompanied by lectures and sometimes by brochures. These showings were open to the public at a fixed admission price. There had been a long history of this form of artistic "entertainment," going back to exhibition of Benjamin West's "Death on the Pale Horse" earlier in the century.

In 1848, one of the most famous of these mural-size paintings was exhibited with great fanfare in Washington Hall in Newark; this was Rembrandt Peale's "Court of Death," painted by the artist much earlier, in 1820, and owned today by the Detroit Institute of Arts. The huge picture, 11½ feet by 23 feet, 5 inches, called a "moral allegory" by its creator, was based upon a poem by the English clergyman, Bishop Porteus, and represents a dimly-lit cave in which Death presides over a gloomy assortment of figures representing such destructive agents as War, Conflagration, Famine, Pestilence, and a host of others.

The Newark newspapers of the period had many articles about the picture, mentioning its measurements and its valuation at $25,000. The admission charge was 25 cents, with a series of six tickets offered at 50 cents. Long descriptions and citizen testimonials appeared. G. Q. Colton, Peale's agent for the exhibition, gave numerous lectures on the painting. The exhibition was to close on June 9, but there appears to have been an extension, and the work remained open to the public until June 15.

More and more popular, however, in the period, were the panoramas, vast canvases not unlike the Cinerama motion picture productions today, which would be exhibited in circular form, the audience standing in the center and viewing the scene from all sides. Indeed, John Vanderlyn, the painter of America's most famous panorama depicting the palace and gardens of Versailles, built a rotunda in New York City, near City Hall, for the housing of this and other works. Most of the artists who painted panoramas, however, were more the equivalent of scene painters, working in a broad, decorative style, lush and dramatic but with little subtlety. Some of the panoramas were historic, and these would be composed of a series of chronological events, rather than one single, complete scene.

This was true, for instance of the panorama of the Bible, painted by John Insco Williams and exhibited in Newark at Washington Hall in August and September, 1850. It was completed in 1849 and included scenes from the Creation to the fall of Babylon. This panorama was also exhibited with success in Cincinnati, Dayton, Baltimore, Washington, and Boston, before its destruction by fire in Independence Hall, Philadelphia, in March, 1851.

One of the most famous of all American panoramas was on view in Newark early the next month: the "Panorama of the Mississippi River and Indian Life" by Leon Pomarede, a French artist who had studied theatrical painting in New Orleans and later moved to St. Louis in the fall of 1849, then in New Orleans, and subsequently along the Eastern seaboard. It opened in Newark in October, 1850, having first been seen in New York. It was to have been exhibited for only one week, but it was adjudged so far superior to any previously shown there, that it remained on view until November 19. At 3:00 A.M. on that date, the huge painting was destroyed by fire. Although it had been valued at $16,000, there was no insurance. After this loss, Pomarede returned to St. Louis.

Nevertheless, the popularity of this art form remained undiminished. On December 16, a "Panorama of a Voyage to California" opened in Washington Hall and the public was invited to visit it each evening at half-past seven; in addition, it was open on Wednesday and Saturday afternoons for children. On May 1, 1851, the "Panorama of Pilgrim's Progress" opened, although mechanical trouble kept it closed the following evening. The work was lauded both for its artistic quality and its moral value.

The taste for biblical panoramas continued. G. D. Beale, after exhibiting a panorama of California in October, opened a "Panorama and Diorama of the Creation and the Deluge" in December of 1851. It continued on view throughout the month, and its popularity prolonged its stay through the middle of January. Many ministers lectured on it, and one evening attendance reached two thousand.

Every year witnessed the showing of several panoramas. There were two shown in 1852. They were both probably by John J. Egan, one of Ireland shown in June and one of the Mississippi again, in August, after the designs of Professor Montroville Dickeson, who lectured on the presentation. In January of 1853 there was a "Diorama of Moscow" shown, and in April a "Panorama of General Taylor's Mexican Campaigns." In November, a "Panorama of Niagara Falls" was shown, painted by Godfrey Frankenstein, a member of a talented artistic family from Cincinnati. One New Jersey artist who exhibited a panorama in his native state was Samuel Waugh, whose "Italia" was shown in October, 1854, in Washington Hall. It was praised as being "most beautiful, accurate and altogether entertaining." In February, 1855, another panorama of the Bible opened in Library Hall.

Another popular event in the history of the fine arts in Newark was the annual fair of the Essex County Institute, which included a section on art. The one in 1848 introduced to Newark a young German artist named Fridolin Schlegel, one of many German and central European artists who came to New Jersey at the time, after the revolutions in their native lands. Schlegel lived in Newark but little of his production is known today. Other exhibitions were held in Newark also. Mention has already been made of the showing and lottery of the paintings of William Mason Brown. In January, 1854, William Henry Powell's famous painting of the discovery of the Mississippi River by De Soto was shown in Library Hall; this painting was done between 1848 and 1853 on commission to fill the last panel of the Rotunda of the Capitol. Although Powell is not known to have had a New Jersey residence, he painted many portraits of the family of New Jersey Governor Marcus Ward. Newark newspapers also reported the numerous exhibitions of the latest engravings which were available for sale at various bookstores in the city.

On January 3, 1852, the *Newark Daily Advertiser* had a special editorial, pleading for the establishment of an academy of design in the city. The writer stressed the industrial aspect of the project and the use it would have for various manufacturers. He asked for a night school with a professor and pointed out that such a school would also help to keep the young people off the streets. A vigorous attempt to form a school of design of a somewhat different nature occurred on October 13 of that year, when a number of young Newark ladies endeavored to bring over to Newark the well-known miniaturist and teacher, Thomas Seir Cummings of New York. Difficulties in traveling the distance to New York in winter prevented the ladies from attending his class there, but they hoped to offer sufficient enrollment to induce him to come to Newark. The project, however, appears to have been unsuccessful.

One of the most important events in the fine arts in America during this period, which had reflections in New Jersey and Newark, was the development of the Art-Unions. These were lottery organizations to which members were invited to belong, usually at a fee of five dollars. The money so raised was used by the Art-Unions to commission engravings after famous works of art and to purchase original paintings and sculptures. Each subscriber to these organizations would then receive the engravings, and a drawing would be made at the end of the year awarding to the lucky winners the works of art that had been selected for purchase. Many Art-Unions sprang up during the 1840's. The first, and always the most important, was the American Art-Union in New York City. This organization came into being first in an attempt to have a permanent picture gallery available to the public, where works by contemporary artists could always be seen. Nevertheless, the lottery increased in popularity over the years of its existence, numbering 814 members in 1839 and 18,960 in 1849; the number of works distributed in 1839 was 36; the number in 1849, 1010.

The plan for the Art-Unions originated first in Munich, in 1823; then in Berlin, in 1825. The London Art-Union was established in 1837 and similar institutions grew up in other cities in the British Isles. In America, a second such organization, the Western Art-

Union, opened in Cincinnati in 1847. Its subscription in 1849 had reached only 1407, but with the announcement that Hiram Powers' world-famous statue, the "Greek Slave," would be one of the prizes in 1850, the membership rose to almost five thousand. The next to appear in America was the Philadelphia Art-Union in 1848, and in 1850, the New England Art-Union, in Boston, but with both these institutions the winning subscribers could choose their prizes from accredited public galleries. Even after the demise of the American Art-Union, others such as the Chicago Art-Union sprang up, and one, the Cosmopolitan Art Association, eventually became a potent factor in American art in the 1850's. Also, some of the European Art-Unions had American subscribers, and one, the International Art-Union, of French origin, competed for popularity with the American organizations.

The Art-Unions had a strong influence upon the development of taste in America. In terms of sheer numbers, more Americans than ever before became interested in the arts and acquired works of art by some of the leading painters, sculptors, and printmakers in the country. Moreover, these organizations were of great importance in the furthering of interest in certain themes in American art. While portraiture had been the traditional form of art most greatly patronized in America, it is obvious that the managers of the Art-Union could not purchase portraits, and then award them to subscribers who might not have any knowledge of the subject of the likeness. Portraits, after all, were invariably commissioned works of art. The Art-Unions emphasized landscapes, occasionally still lifes, some historical subjects, and particularly genre paintings—scenes of everyday life. These could be counted upon to appeal to the widest audience, and these correspondingly were purchased in large numbers and distributed, and were also commissioned in the form of prints which were received by the entire membership.

The Art-Unions had the intention, also, of fostering a particularly national art form. To this end they advised young American painters to ignore the study of Old Masters and of foreign masters in general. Rather, American artists were enjoined to paint native subject matter and to cultivate native virtues of simplicity and freshness in their art. Here again, scenes of everyday life might well display purely American characteristics, and artists were also advised to pay more attention to historic art relating to American themes.

While Newark itself did not have an Art-Union during the 1840's, there were many subscribers from this city and state, and the Newark newspapers often presented notices relating to the Art-Unions—announcements of their distributions and news of the founding of new organizations. In 1848, the works of art awarded to local citizens by the American Art-Union were put on display in Olds Book Store in January: "The Park of St. Germain," by George Harvey, awarded to George B. Guerin; and a still life by Thomas Augustus Cummings, which went to George M. Spencer of Newark. On October 17 it was reported that there were three New Jersey winners at the Philadelphia Art-Union, including William B. Kinney of Newark. For 1849, 12 citizens of New Jersey received prizes at the American Art-Union.

With this much activity in the area, it is not surprising that a group of enterprising citizens should decide upon the formation of a New Jersey Art-Union. This occurred in January of 1850. About four hundred local citizens were members of the American Art-Union, and it was suggested that the two thousand dollars which they paid to that organization could be better spent in encouraging local artists by giving them preference. At the same time, it would allow for the establishment of a free picture gallery. The local artists who were singled out for special praise were Ross, McDougall, Pine, Schlegel, and Johannes Oertel and Rembrandt Lockwood, who will be dealt with shortly. It was also felt that a greater proportion of awards to subscribers could be made in a local art-union without lowering the quality of the paintings, particularly if the works were of smaller size by less nationally-known artists.

By the end of March, the organization had come into being and officers had been named. These included Abraham Coles, President; David A. Hayes, Vice-President; Thomas H. Stephens, Corresponding Secretary; Martin R. Dennis, Recording Secretary; and George M. Spencer, Treasurer. The walls of the Library Room were offered for the free gallery, which opened on April 29. The exhibition was open day and evening. New pictures were constantly added and the gallery was in sound financial condition.

In early December of the same year, a new gallery for the New Jersey Art-Union was completed, designed by John G. Hall and built by Kirk and Kirkpatrick. It was an addition to Library Hall on the current site of Bamberger's Department Store. Legally the Art-Union and Library Association were tied together; the assets of the Art-Union accrued to the Library Association, and the subscribers to the Art-Union found themselves owners of Library shares. The Library Association's contract required a regular exhibition program; when the exhibits did not materialize, the Library Association moved to take back the room. Various ministers from Newark and New York attended the opening of the gallery, and Professor Mapes gave an address on the relationship of the fine to the useful arts. The building was crowded to overflowing, and late trains ran from the suburbs for the opening. Among the paintings shown was one owned by the future governor Marcus L. Ward, "The Christian Maiden Converting Her Betrothed," which had been distributed by the International Art-Union, and also a "Portrait of Marie Antoinette" by the famous Swedish artist, Adolph Wertmüller, owned by the Reverend M. H. Henderson.

Newark was eagerly looking forward to the forthcoming drawing, especially after it was announced that the proportion of prizes to subscribers was one to 18, as opposed to the American Art-Union's one to 36. This could come to pass in part because the New Jersey organization distributed no engravings. At the drawing on December 31, there were 471 subscribers who were to be awarded 35 pictures and five busts of General Winfield Scott made by Thomas Dow Jones, a former resident of Newark. At the drawing were many notables including Governor William Pennington and General James Miller. Directors were chosen at the meeting for a two-year term; one was Marcus Ward. The cost of the purchase for the years was $1742.55, or an average cost of $43.56 per painting and sculpture. The cost of the gallery was given as over three thousand dollars.

The following is a list of the works of art awarded, the artists who created them, and the subscribers who won the awards, taken from the *Newark Daily Advertiser*, January 2, 1851:

1. "An Interior with Cattle," R. Lockwood—Miss Eleanor P. Stephens
2. "Landscape," R. Lockwood—William B. Kinney
3. "Sappho," R. Lockwood—T. H. Stephens
4. "Scene Near Munich," Kruger—William S. B. Clark
5. "Snow Scene with Deer," J. A. Oertel—J. Mix
6. "Fair Student," H. P. Gray—Caleb C. Garthwaite
7. "Landscape," W. M. Oddie—E. G. Faitoute
8. "Landscape," T. W. Whitley—J. P. Pennington
9. "Landscape," T. W. Whitley—William Shepard
10. "Luther and his Coadjutors," F. Schlegel—James Keene
11. "Madonna and child," F. Schlegel—A. N. Waters
12. "Friar Lawrence," E. White—Edwin Speer
13. "The Emigrant's Farewell," J. A. Oertel—J. B. Robinson
14. "The Young Artist," E. White—G. C. Ruckel
15. "Landscape," J. F. Cropsey—Charles L. Jones
16. "Capuchin Chapel," J. Barker—Hook and Ladder Co. No. 1
17. "Satiety," J. Barker—Mrs. Dolly Spanker, J. City
18. "The Bathers," Gignoux—J. B. Pinneo
19. "Landscape and Rapids," Lanman—B. F. Harrison
20. "Modesty," G. Barnwell—James L. Dickinson
21. "Devotion," G. Barnwell—C. N. Lockwood
22. "Landscape," M. Harting—J. D. Orton

23. "Girl with Fruit," R. Lockwood—David C. Dodd
24. "Healing of Jarius' Daughter," F. Schlegel—L. C. Grover
25. "Landscape," C. L. Heyde—J. C. Woodruff
26. "Landscape," C. L. Heyde—William P. Eastman
27. "Children Leaving the Forest," H. Dassel—J. P. Wakeman
28. "Landscape," T. W. Whitley—Louis C. Vogt
29. "Mariner's Wife," R. Boggs—C. C. Meeker
30. "Landscape," T. H. Richards—J. T. Garthwaite
31. "Landscape," F. A. Richards—Mrs. Catherine H. Thorn
32. "Still Life," J. A. Oertel—Bethud Dodd
33. "Shepherd Boy," F. Heinrich—J. M. Beach
34. "Bird's Nest," C. L. Heyde—David A. Hayes
35. "Road View," C. L. Heyde—B. McCormick
36. "Bust of General Winfield Scott," Jones—E. H. Wright
37. "Bust of General Winfield Scott," Jones—L. W. Badger
38. "Bust of General Winfield Scott," Jones—Charles Goodyear
39. "Bust of General Winfield Scott," Jones—Thomas W. Adams
40. "Bust of General Winfield Scott," Jones—Oscar J. Akers

It is interesting to note that the organization served the purposes for which it was formed. Not only did it enlist the subscriptions of even more persons than had previously joined the American Art-Union, but it did, indeed, patronize Newark and New Jersey artists. Besides the sculptor, Thomas Dow Jones, Rembrandt Lockwood of Newark and Charles Heyde of Hoboken were the most frequently purchased artists with four works; Johannes Oertel and Fridolin Schlegel of Newark and Thomas Whitley of Hoboken with three each; and John Jesse Barker of New Brunswick with two. Perhaps the best known artists, nationally, were Jasper Cropsey, the landscapist, Regis Gignoux, and Henry P. Gray.

During 1851 the New Jersey Art-Union again opened its gallery to public exhibitions a number of times. It was planned this year to issue an engraving and also to display and purchase works not only by local artists, but also by painters of national fame like Asher Durand and Thomas Cole. There were some signs that the Art-Union was not receiving sufficient support, although the newspapers spoke of their local institution as finer than its sister Art-Union in Boston, and equal to those in Cincinnati and Philadelphia.

The drawing in 1851 was again made on December 31. This year, the list of subscribers was much shorter than previously, only 261. President Coles spoke, decrying the lack of support, and mention was made of the contemplated school of design. Thirty paintings were purchased out of the recepits, at a total cost of $1598.66. The following awards were made:

1. "Partridge Hunting," A. F. Tait—R. Van Buskirk
2. "Grouse Hunting," A. F. Tait—D. D. Benjamin
3. "St. Paul," F. Schlegel—E. B. Stan
4. "Landscape," T. W. Whitley—E. Van Antwerp
5. "Sunset," R. Lockwood—Lewis M. Condict
6. "Interior, R. Lockwood—A. W. Canfield
7. "Guardian Angel," D. M. Carter—J. H. Stephens
8. "The Lovers," M. Harting—John R. Pierson
9. "Market Scene," Culverhouse—S. Sherwood
10. "Landscape," C. L. Heyde—John Hassel
11. "Landscape," C. L. Heyde—T. H. Stephens
12. "Landscape," C. L. Heyde—Thomas Kirpatrick
13. "Landscape," C. L. Heyde—Augustus M. Crane
14. "Landscape," T. W. Whitley—John P. Jube
15. "Landscape," W. Brown—A. Fitch
16. "Snowcape and Deer," J. Oertel—F. S. Thomas
17. "Landscape and Peasants," M. Harting—Wm. E. Layton
18. "Goats," J. Oertel—Mrs. John C. Miller
19. "Winter Scene," R. Gignoux—James Keene
20. "Goats," J. Oertel—C. N. Lockwood
21. "Autumn Scene," W. Brown—H. N. Peters
22. "Evening Scene in New Jersey," W. Brown—Geo. C. Ruckel
23. "Storm of the Prairie," J. C. Ward—Jacob Stuckey
24. "Landscape," A. B. Durand—Tho. W. Bedford
25. "Landscape," W. Brown—J. H. Muchmore
26. "Landscape," W. Brown—J. T. Garthwaite
27. "Landscape, J. F. Cropsey—J. B. Bemenover
28. "Comic Scene," Chappel—S. R. W. Houth
29. "Game Piece," S. Woodruff—F. H. Teese
30. "Landscape," Drake—F. T. Frelinghuysen

Again, many of the local artists of note such as Schlegel, Lockwood, Whitely, and Heyde were well purchased and awarded. In addition, William Mason Brown, the landscapist, had come on the local scene and his work must have been both popular and probably quite inexpensive, for the committee had purchased five of his landscapes for prizes, one of them at least, a New Jersey scene. Undoubtedly the most expensive item in the group was the "Landscape" by Asher B. Durand, although he may have let the Art-Union have it at a modest price, since it represented his home state. Other recognized names among the artists included Cropsey and Gignoux again, Johannes Culverhouse, a painter native to Rotterdam who had come to America only recently, and Arthur Fitzwilliam Tait, destined to become the leading painter in this country of sporting scenes and animals, was represented here by two works, among the first he had painted in this country.

Landscapes dominated the 1851 award of the Art-Union to a greater degree than in the previous year, when there had been a greater proportion of genre pictures and religious works. At this drawing, too, there were no sculptures, but sculpture was likely to be more expensive and, since one of the aims of the Art-Union was to encourage local artists, the relative dearth of sculptors in New Jersey might be a factor here.

On February 16, 1852, a meeting was held of the New Jersey Art-Union, at which an executive committee was elected, consisting of Coles, Marcus Ward, J. S. Quinby, Theodore Runyon, and John R. Wilson. The hope was expressed that the organization would be more successful than it had been in 1851, but this hope was not to be realized. Already in March there was discussions as to whether or not the art-unions infringed upon state lottery laws, and by the end of the year the parent organization in New York had suffered its demise, laudatory editorials in local newspapers notwithstanding.

In October, 1853, the local New Jersey Art-Union followed suit, and its dissolution was decided at a meeting of the board under its current president, Thomas H. Stephens, on the twenty-fifth of that month. At that time they relinquished their lease on the gallery built in Library Hall and suggested that the premises be used for some purpose relating to art or literature. The funds, $150, were divided between the Foster Home and the Orphan Asylum. An article in the *Newark Daily Advertiser* on October 28 gave a history of the organization. On November 26, 1853, a meeting of the Natural History Society called for the formation of a Museum of Natural History, with the suggestion that rooms be found by applying to the Library Association for the quarters of the old Art-Union, but they were eventually taken over by the Young Men's Christian Association.

It would be difficult to estimate the impact of the local organization upon the life of Newark and the surrounding area. The New Jersey Art-Union was active for only two years and in the second year there was a falling off of interest. Yet the Art-Union movement had great importance in the country as a whole, and Newark and New Jersey certainly and demonstrably shared in this. While the organization existed it kept the public informed of activities, and interest appeared to be quite keen. There was a free gallery open to the public much of the time, where works of art both European and American could be seen. Undoubtedly, too, local artists did enjoy additional patronage for these few years, and the homes of about fifty local residents and art patrons were graced with works of art which probably had some esthetic merit. It would be interesting indeed to be able to locate some of these paintings and sculptures; possibly some are still in New Jersey.

Another mid-century development, perhaps unique to Newark, was the growth of a short-lived school of religious painting. This group arose from among a number of German immigrant artists who had fled the turmoil of their native land. Fridolin Schlegel, already noted, was one of these. Another was Johannes Michael Enzing-Müller (1804-1888), a religious painter and engraver who was a native of Nuremberg. He came to America about 1848 and worked in New York City and Philadelphia as well as in Newark. One of his pupils in Germany was Johannes Adam Simon Oertel (1823-1909), who had studied painting and engraving with him in Munich and had come to this country about the same time, settling in Newark. Oertel taught art, painted, engraved, and designed ceiling decorations for the House of Representatives in Washington, D. C. In 1871 he became an Episcopal minister; and after his retirement in 1895 he was able to realize his ambition and devote the rest of his life to paintings of religious subjects.

The most important painter in this group, however, and perhaps the most acclaimed painter in the history of Newark, was American-born Rembrandt Lockwood (1815-after 1889). What led Lockwood to associate himself with the city of Newark is not known, but since he was studying and working in the field of religious painting in Munich at the time that Enzing-Müller and Oertel were there, it is very possible that he had known them then, and subsequently followed them to Newark where he was to attain at least momentary fame. Because of Lockwood's unique position in the history of art in Newark, let us examine his life and career.

Rembrandt Lockwood was born in 1815, the son of Millington and Jane A. (Cuisac) Lockwood. Nothing is known as yet of his early life or education, although his name suggests that his parents must have been sympathetic to the path which he pursued. In any case, he is mentioned in the Richmond, Virginia *Compiler* on January 1, 1841, which indicates that he had been active in Richmond's art life for a number of years, so it may be assumed that he began his art career there; he may even have grown up in that city. He painted many altar pieces for churches in Richmond but these were probably done at a later period.

By the end of the year 1845 Lockwood was in Munich studying, a period which was to have a decisive influence upon his career. Like many portraitists—American artists such as Copley, Trumbull, and Morse—in the generations before him, Lockwood, after exposure to European art and its traditions, began to hanker after "greater things." Although he continued portraiture, his vision expanded and he undertook subjects in varying fields, but particularly in religious art. It was during his Munich years that he conceived the idea of painting a great Last Judgment, which was to be the outstanding work of his career. The impetus, however, for his picture and for his choice of subject, was the versions of the "Last Judgment" he saw abroad, particularly Michelangelo's in Rome and Peter von Cornelius' in Munich itself.

It is not known how long Lockwood stayed in Germany. He had finished four small cartoons for the project and had begun a fifth when he left Munich. He went first to Harrisburg, Pennsylvania, where he finished the fifth cartoon, but he could not have been there long, for by 1847 he was in Newark which was to remain his residence for eleven years, years which were very fruitful in his career. From 1848 until his departure from the city he lived at 461 High Street, a street which was the residence of other Newark artists. In the *Newark Daily Advertiser* of November 25, 1848, is a note telling of Lockwood's plaster model of "Coleridge's Genevieve" which was to be seen at Olds Book Store. This is the only known suggestion that Lockwood had sculptural as well as painterly interests, and it confirms his growing preoccupation with literary subject matter during these years.

In 1848, giving his residence as Newark, Lockwood exhibited two paintings at New York's American Art-Union, an "Interior" and a "Sheepfold." In 1849 he showed a figure study entitled "Lily of the Valley." That he continued to practice portraiture is proved by his showing a male portrait at the National Academy of Design in that year, along with "A View on the Passaic River," both owned by Marcus L. Ward. These were the only works by him to be shown at the National Academy. That Ward owned these works is proof that

Lockwood was enjoying at least a modest patronage in his home city, for Ward was New Jersey's outstanding art patron, a postition which Ward may have "inherited" through his wife's uncle, Nicholas Longworth of Cincinnati, who sent Ward a number of artists whom he patronized. Lockwood may have been in Cincinnati just prior to going to Newark, and it may well be that Longworth encouraged Ward to patronize Lockwood and may even have been partly responsible for the painter's choice of residence.

On July 11, 1854, the *Newark Daily Advertiser* announced the opening that week of the exhibition of Lockwood's "Last Judgment" in Concert Hall, a room chosen because no other in the city could accommodate the painting. This work, begun in Munich and continued in Harrisburg, was finished in Newark, where Lockwood painted a sixth cartoon, a colored sketch, and finally the great work itself. The cartoons and sketch took Lockwood seven years and nine months to produce; the finished work itself took a year and three months, and it was 27 by 17 feet in size.

During the creation of the work other artists saw it and gave testimonials as to its merits. By 1852 the preliminary work had been sufficiently advanced for Asher B. Durand and Daniel Huntington to offer words of praise, and the Reverend Dr. Huntington, Daniel's brother, echoed their approval. A more important accolade, however, was that given on July 8, 1854, just before the exhibition of the work, by the Common Council of the City of Newark:

REMBRANDT LOCKWOOD, ESQ.

Dear Sir:—At a regular meeting of the Common Council of the City of Newark, held at this chamber on the 7th inst., the following Preamble and Resolution were adopted unanimously.—

"Whereas, Rembrandt Lockwood, Esq., a citizen of Newark, N. J., after toiling during nine years and the greatest discouragement, has at length produced a painting which, for the grandeur of its design, the difficulty of its subject and the

Rembrandt Lockwood, "Last Judgment," c. 1850
Collection of the Vose Galleries of Boston

felicity of its execution, in the opinion of men competent to judge in such matters, has never been equalled in this country; and Whereas, the said Rembrandt Lockwood thereby has forever connected with his memory the name of our said City of Newark, therefore be it

"*Resolved,* I. That the congratulations of the Mayor and the Common Council of the City of Newark, be tendered to the said Rembrandt Lockwood, on the recent completion of his great painting, entitled "The Last Judgment"; and that previous to removing it, as he contemplates, to the City of New York, he be requested to give our citizens an opportunity to see it, in this, its native place.

"*Resolved,* Furthermore, that a copy of this Preamble, with the Resolutions, properly attested, be presented without delay to the said Rembrandt Lockwood."

In accordance with the terms of the last Resolution, I have the honor to present to you the action of the Common Council, in regard to this matter.

Very respectfully,
Your obedient servant,
Isaac M. Tucker
Clerk of the Common Council.

Nor was this the only testimonial issued in Newark to Lockwood. On the day after the grand opening of the exhibition of the picture, on July 18, 1854, an opening to which the press and clergy were invited, the *Newark Daily Advertiser* reported a letter suggesting that the City of Newark purchase the work so as to keep it in its place of origin; on July 27 appeared another certificate and testimonial, this time one of appreciation from the citizens of Newark for Lockwood's great contribution. One of the gentlemen signing this document was the portraitist, George Ross. The newspaper also contained Lockwood's reply of thanks written by Joseph C. Hornblower, because Lockwood himself was ill. Indeed, the newspaper was constantly mentioning the great picture with laudatory comments through the date of closing of the exhibition, August 19.

Although the painting itself has not, so far, been located, a finished drawing of it has recently appeared.

This perfectly matches the line engraving of the painting which appeared as the frontispiece of the brochure published about the picture in 1854. It is undoubtedly a preliminary drawing by Lockwood himself. The drawing is full of excitement and movement, crowded with many figures. The great painting is known to have contained over fifteen hundred figures. Those in the drawing are painted in the idealistic, bland interpretation of Raphael which characterized the German Nazarenes; the composition is more reminiscent of Michelangelo.

Through the line engraving we can identify the various figures in the picture. God sits in judgment, of course, in the upper part of the picture. In the lower left are the races of Man, the Caucasian comforting the Malayan, representing, respectively, the highest and lowest levels of civilization. The Angel of Death sits with face hidden, right of center. George Washington in the lower center, is a symbol of Liberty, while Despotism lies at the bottom, vanquished. To Washington's left is the symbol of Slavery, a nude figure who has broken her bonds. Farther left is the Holy Family. Above this group are the "Good Deeds," and above them, the Crowning of Saints and Martyrs. Surrounding the figure of God are Prophets at the left, and the Apostles at the right. The largest angels in this group are the Angel of Life at the right, that of Justice at the left. Below the figure of the Lord is St. Michael who drives forth the evil spirits—from top to bottom: Hypocrisy, Lost Virtue, Pride, Lust, and Crime. Shielding his face from the light of God is Satan himself, and below him, Ambition, Despair, Drunkenness, Hate, Sloth, Procrastination, Envy, and Covetousness, the latter represented as a miser. Finally, the figures behind Washington, Slavery, and the Holy Family, represent the Sciences and the Arts: Galileo for Astronomy, Pascal for Mathematics, Erasmus for Belles Lettres, Plato for Philosophy, Dante for Poetry; the Fine Arts are represented by Michelangelo, Raphael, Titian, representing respectively the Epic, the Dramatic, and the Voluptuous, and at the far left are the Sacred Arts, in the figures of Fra Angelico, Fra Bartolommeo, and Plantella Nelli.

The undertaking of the painting was naturally an immense task and it is no wonder that the work impresses one as more melodramatic than truly epic. Partly, of course, this can perhaps be attributed to the fact that the artist was only thirty years of age when he began it; partly it was the period, which favored allegorical symbolism found in other works of the time such as Huntington's famous "Mercy's Dream." It was an age when religious painting was something apart from the main traditions of art and could find roots only in an eclectic appeal to the past; this is the reason that even so fine a painting as John LaFarge's "Ascension," in the Church of the Ascension in New York, is not a totally successful work.

Many of the encomiums of the painting had to do not with its esthetic qualities but with its moral significance. It was often compared with other representations of the scene—Orcagna's, to some extent—but mostly with Michelangelo's work in the Sistine Chapel, with Peter von Cornelius' painting in St. Ludwig's in Munich, and with the representation by John Martin. The general feeling was that these works were not successful because they constituted a partisan religious spirit—the Michelangelo as a symbol of Catholicism, the Martin as a symbol of Protestantism. Michelangelo's figure of God was criticized as being neither sacred nor merciful, and too full of the spirit of awfulness. Cornelius too was condemned for his Roman Catholic bias. Lockwood, on the other hand, "swept away the rubbish of mythology, paganism and indecency, that defiles the conception of Michael Angelo, and the sectarianism that disquiets one on the canvas of Cornelius and Martin."

The City of Newark failed to comply with the suggestion to purchase the picture, but subscriptions of ten dollars were taken for an engraving of the painting, to measure one-twelfth of the original: 27 inches by 17½ inches. This was undertaken by Johannes Enzing-Müller. Meanwhile, Lockwood made plans to take his picture to New York, although he continued to maintain his Newark residence. The exhibition of the work was begun in New York on September 11, 1854, in the Racket Court, and the opening ceremony included a eulogy by the Reverend Dr. Schroeder. On September 30, 1854, the *Morning Courier and New York Enquirer,* however, spoke at length of the defects of the picture—its esthetic inadequacies, its confused symbolism, and the borrowings from other artists. The article ends:

> In brief the 'Great Painting' is absurd and incongruous in conception, awkward in composition, puerile in sentiment, faulty in drawing, feeble in color, and indebted for its few merits to the memory rather than the imagination of its author.

Putnam's Magazine dealt no more kindly with the work, complaining that Lockwood had been overly ambitious in undertaking the picture. The periodical went on to praise the engraving, however, stating:

> It is being exquisitely engraved by Mr. Enzing Müller—who is correcting all its faults of drawing and also the blunders in anatomy. No true idea of the execution of the picture can ever be obtained from the engraving—and, indeed, it is not pleasant to think that so fine an engraver as Mr. Müller should be devoting his time to the perpetuating so poor a work. But we believe that the enterprise is a distinguished pecuniary success.

Newark critics came to the rescue of their fellow townsman and defended him, in the local newspaper, against his adversaries. Such a defense, however, was not necessary, for in February and March, newspapers across the country announced the sale of the work to the Roman Catholic Cathedral of Philadelphia for the munificent sum of $12,000! The artist, in addition, reserved the engraving rights to the picture, and four thousand individuals were said to have subscribed for an engraving at ten dollars each.

Unfortuately, however, the Cathedral does not have the painting today and no information is available as to its possible whereabouts. In fact, in 1855 the Cathedral was under construction and had difficulty enough in meeting costs, let alone finding $12,000 for a painting. Perhaps the work never was actually purchased. Another clue, but only a clue, to the fate of the picture is contained in an account of Lockwood which mentions that the painting was damaged by fire. It is not known whether this damage occurred in the Philadelphia Cathedral or elsewhere, nor when this fire occurred. Perhaps the damage was too extensive to be repaired and the picture was ultimately abandoned. This same account mentioned that the colored sketch of the work was in the possession of Courtland Parker.

By 1858, Lockwood decided to abandon his Newark residence and his studio was taken over by the well-known genre painter, Mrs. Lilly Martin Spencer, in that year. About the same time Lockwood also abandoned the profession of painting for that of architecture. No trace of his activity is found for the next five years, but in 1863 he is listed in the New York City directories with an office at 293 Broadway and a home at 240 Cumberland Street in Brooklyn. He seems to have maintained his Broadway office through 1876, although his home addresses changed. During these years his profession is listed in the directories as architect.

Although Lockwood changed his profession, he did not change his interests, and his important architecture, like his important paintings, was designed to serve religious purposes. This is proved in an interesting letter written by Lockwood to his early patron, Marcus L. Ward, from his office on Broadway, and dated December 16, 1867. In this letter Lockwood explained that he considered himself a failure as a painter, despite the encouragement given him by such friends as Ward. He therefore turned to church architecture, and his letter reveals an extensive list of buildings to his credit:

St. John's Methodist Church, Bedford Avenue, Brooklyn
Congregational Church, Jersey City
Catholic Church, 7th and Erie, Jersey City
1st Methodist Church, Newburgh
Catholic Church, Newburgh
St. Paul's Methodist Church, Peekskill
Catholic Church, Peekskill
Unitarian Church, 40th Street, New York City
St. Paul's Convent Church, 49th Street and Ninth Avenue, New York City
Congregational Church, Elm Place, Brooklyn
Universalist Church, Green Avenue, Brooklyn
1st Presbyterian Church, Middletown, New York

and smaller churches in Hyde Park, Sing Sing, Cornwall, Buttermilk Falls, New Castle, and Rhinebeck.

His buildings were not only ecclesiastic; he had sent a design to Albany for the State Capitol building, and he was writing to Ward for the latter's assistance in securing an appointment to design the new Post Office and United States Court Building in New York City.

Lockwood also gave Ward some family news. He mentioned that he now had a boy of eleven and that his daughter, Helen, had married a Mr. Colburn of Washington. Through other sources, it is known too that another daughter, a Mrs. Frances Brundage (1854-1937), born in Newark, became a painter and illustrator of children's books, and thus carried on that aspect of her father's career.

Nothing more is known of Lockwood's life or career. He seems certainly to have been successful as an architect, judging by the number of buildings to his credit in what was, after all, a short period of time. Although he seems no longer to have been in Brooklyn or New York after 1876 he is not found in obituary notices of that year and since the 1889 account of him mentions his date of birth but not his death, it may be presumed that he was still alive at the time.

Lockwood emerges from this story as an artist of sincerity, one whose failure lay more in the fact that he was not attuned to the demands of his time rather than in a lack of ability. Religious art was never less a part of the culture of a period nor less in demand than in the mid-nineteenth century in America. Yet, he was willing to gamble nine years of his life for his ideal and, even after he was forced to acknowledge defeat he continued, in a different vein, to offer his services to art and to religion. That he was able to do so is attributable partly to his ability and partly, certainly, to his amazing versatility. For this reason, as a solitary symbol of the religious artist in an alien period, he deserves to be remembered.

V

OTHER THEMES IN NINETEENTH CENTURY NEW JERSEY PAINTING

PORTRAITS AND LANDSCAPES were the subjects which were painted most often and which occupied more New Jersey painters than any other themes, throughout the nineteenth century. The landscape, particularly, due to the nature and geographic position of the state, was the pre-eminent theme in New Jersey art, but other subject matters gradually found their practitioners and specialists as the century developed. One of these was still-life painting.

Actually, still life was a subject which found its professional beginnings in America as early as, if not earlier than, landscape painting. In the Columbianum Exhibition of 1795 in Philadelphia, quite a number of still-life paintings were exhibited. These included several by a Doctor Foulke and, particularly interesting, four fruit pieces and a "Wood Duck, Still Life" by the eminent Boston portraitist, John Singleton Copley. Unfortunately, none of his works of this nature has yet come to light. This early show also contained works by both James and Raphaelle Peale, the former the brother of the well-known Philadelphia portraitist, Charles Willson Peale, and the latter one of his painter-sons.

The Peale family of Philadelphia, in fact, was dominant in the field of American still-life painting for many years, painting usually simple fruit compositions displayed upon a ledge or shelf. Raphaelle Peale was probably the finest painter of still life in the family and his Uncle James scarcely less so. Raphaelle's brother, Rubens, was a more primitive painter of this subject, and many of James' daughters were also proficient: Anna Claypoole Peale, Margaretta Angelica Peale, Maria Peale, and Sarah Miriam Peale. In addition, Mary Jane Peale, a daughter of Rubens Peale, carried the family's concern with still life into the third generation and into the twentieth century, since she lived until 1902.

Largely because of the interest of this painting family, Philadelphia remained the center of still-life painting in America throughout the nineteenth century. In mid-century it was the home of such notable artists of this theme as George Cochran Lambdin and John F. Francis. At the end of the century, the most eminent still-life painter in America, William Michael Harnett, lived there. By mid-century there were still-life painters in New York City too, George Henry Hall being especially noteworthy. Artists of Baltimore and even Charleston, produced still lifes of note, though, oddly enough, the subject seems not to have been popular in New England, with only occasional practitioners later in the nineteenth century in such relatively remote centers as Fall River, Massachusetts, and Bangor, Maine.

But while still life became popular in America in the early nineteenth century, New Jersey does not appear to have been home to a specialist in this theme until the 1860's. Previous to this time, William Mason Brown had, as we have seen, lived in Newark, but was then a landscapist and only turned to still life after he had left the State. In the middle of the 1860's, however, an artist named Paul Lacroix (fl. 1831-1870) lived in Hoboken, one more evidence of that town's attraction for the painters of the period. Lacroix is a fascinating painter for a number of reasons, not the least of which is the lack of information available about him. He was living in New York City in the late 1850's and remained there until 1866. From 1867 to 1869 he was in Hoboken; then he seems to disappear from record. Almost nothing is known of his life before 1856; nothing after 1870. Recently, however, a rather sentimental figure drawing has appeared dated "Mai 1831" and signed by Lacroix in Cincinnati. If this is indeed by the same artist it would suggest that he had just recently come over from France to America, and hence gives a little more information concerning his whereabouts, his dates, and his subject matter.

A curious element of the last is that he exhibited in New York exhibitions during the 1860's, showing landscape paintings, but, except for one example, the paintings so far known by him—and there are quite a few—are all still lifes. So the question arises as to the whereabouts of his landscapes and why he did not show his still lifes. All this speculation about Lacroix would be immaterial if he were not one of the better still-life painters of the period. Actually, the one landscape known by him—a view of New York City from Hoboken—is rather crude; but many of his still lifes show a delicacy and subtlety almost as fine as any of the period. His style is a quite distinct one and within the still-life genre he explored many subjects. Some of his paintings are quite simple works, particularly some of his pictures of flowers in a vase or lillies in a pond. He painted some vegetable still lifes which were never common in American art and, in one picture at least, he set fruit—in this case a bunch of strawberries—in an open field with trees, sky, and clouds behind, thus combining in an unusual degree still-life and landscape elements.

Many of his other fruit paintings, however, are typical of a rather special development which occurred in still-life painting in America in the 1860's; the "return" to a natural setting of these elements plucked from nature. Thus, instead of the common motif of a ledge or a table top to support the melons, apples, peaches, and grapes which he painted, rather incongruous arrangements of various fruits would be assembled and composed on a rocky ledge or grassy ground. While this may seem strange today, it was doubtless done in the interest of

Paul Lacroix, "Still Life with Grapes and Watermelon," 1866
Collection of James Ricau

avoiding an artificial background and giving the fruits their "natural" setting. In some cases the subject matter is even "alive," as when grapes are actually still attached to and growing on the arbor which produced them. Other artists such as William Mason Brown also used this motif and it was a phenomenon of the period. Lacroix also painted quite elaborate table-top still lifes too, in the manner of the flamboyant German-American still-life painter, Severin Roesen. In general, Lacroix's paintings have a rather brightly illuminated central area, with a somewhat dramatic contrast made between the accented fruit, flower, or vegetable subjects, and a gradually darker area toward the edge of the canvas.

Still life was a subject that attracted an increasing number of women painters during the century until, toward the 1880's and 1890's, the great majority of painters of this theme were women, usually specializing in somewhat sentimental flower pictures. In Philadelphia the number of women painters was particularly great, probably due to the example set by by the many female artists of the Peale family; it is interesting in fact that at mid-century about half the exhibitors of still life in Philadelphia were women, whereas they comprised only about 15 per cent of the New York exhibitors of the period. At this time there was a fine painter of still lifes in South Jersey, Mrs. E. B. Duffey (fl. 1860's) of Woodbury. Actually, even less is at present known about her than about Lacroix, although their brief New Jersey residences corresponded almost exactly. Mrs. Duffey was a Philadelphia artist, but she lived in Woodbury around 1866 and 1867, and perhaps longer. It is also believed that she lived in Brooklyn. She exhibited pictures of fruit and flowers at the Pennsylvania Academy of Fine Arts, and a number of her works have come to light. Some of these are attractively painted pastiches of Dutch seventeenth-century still lifes, combining flamboyant fruit and flower arrangements with ceramic and glassware of antique or pseudo-antique derivation. Perhaps the most interesting of her paintings, however, is one entitled

"October" depicting leaves and grasses in a landscape. It is rather crisply and tightly painted and again is typical of a subject that had particular appeal at the time. A number of painters did pictures not of elegantly composed flowers but rather of common everyday grasses, weeds, and leaves painted informally, as though they had been blown by the wind and casually arranged by chance.

Another woman adept at still-life painting in Bordentown at the end of the century was Susan Waters (1823-1900). She was born in Binghamton, New York, of a gifted family of artistic talent. At the age of fifteen she and her only sister, later Mrs. Amelia M. Pierce, attended a seminary at Friendsville, Pennsylvania, where she paid their tuition by painting copies of specimens for the class of Natural History. She was considered a prodigy by the teachers. At seventeen she was married to William C. Waters, by whom she was encouraged to develop her talent, and she became a portrait painter. A number of her early portraits, painted in upper New York State, are in a private collection in Convent, New Jersey. After her husband's health failed, Mr. and Mrs. Waters established themselves in the business of taking fine ambrotypes and daguerreotypes.

Afterwards they came to Bordentown, teaching drawing and painting there and in nearby cities. They built a cottage on Mary Street, which was afterward sold. They traveled in many states teaching until 1866, when they returned and purchased their former home. For twenty-seven years Mrs. Waters painted pictures in her quiet studio, encouraged by her husband. After his death in 1893, she devoted herself entirely to her art, living alone most of the time. For over a year she boarded at the Friends' Home, in Trenton, and faithfully attended the Friends' Meeting. She is buried in the cemetery in Bordentown.

Actually, Susan Waters had two specialties in later life—not only still-life painting, but the depiction of animals, too. Typical of late nineteenth-century still-life

Mrs. E. B. Duffey, "Lillies," 1866
Anonymous Collection

painting, some of her works depict objects hung on boards and doors, in a deceptively realistic manner. In several instances she combined traditional fruit subjects with such animals as squirrels.

Susan Waters' real speciality, however, was the painting of farm animals, cattle, and particularly sheep. She kept sheep in a pen behind her house. Her sheep paintings still adorn many homes in Bordentown and the Historical Society there as well. She also painted rabbits, and her cow pictures were well known too, particularly one of the prize Guernseys of Anthony Bullock of Chesterfield, famous throughout the neighborhood.

By the end of the nineteenth century there were many other women painters of still life from New Jersey exhibiting, but paintings by few of them have come to light. A flower picture by Matilda Browne of Newark, for instance, is known, and records reveal that she worked in that city in the 1880's, but otherwise her life is unrecorded. More interesting is the case of one E. N. Griffith, two of whose pictures have been known for some years, one of them with a false signature of the most famous still-life painter of the late nineteenth century, William Michael Harnett of Philadelphia, and both of them are close to the work of that master. Harnett had many imitators, admirers, and disciples during his lifetime and immediately afterwards; one of the Griffith paintings is dated 1894 but until recently there had been no reason to connect Griffith with New Jersey. However, an Ella Griffith is known to have been living in Orange at exactly that time, and recently a painting signed by Ella Griffith was located in a private collection in Verona. It is a painting also in the Harnett circle, and close enough to the two previously known Griffiths so that there can be little question that all three are by Ella Griffith. While there is still nothing known of her life, she was obviously an able practitioner of *trompe-l'oeil* painting *à la Harnett,* meticulously depicting the books, candlesticks, old pipes, and other homely objects which were the standard props of still-life painters of the period.

Susan Waters, "Still Life with Squirrels"
Collection of Ferdinand Davis

It was William Michael Harnett of Philadelphia who determined the character of the late nineteenth century still life in America, much as it had been the Peale family who had accomplished this several generations earlier. Obscure artists such as Ella Griffith and much better known ones like Jefferson David Chalfant of Wilmington were indebted to Harnett for the form and philosophy of their still-life painting. Gone was the emphasis upon fruit and flower subject matter, and gone too, the sense of the bountiful and the beautiful, with almost feminine sensuousness and sometimes sentimental overtones. Instead, the still lifes of Harnett and his circle were often masculine in feeling, with pipes, beer mugs, guns, and trophies of the hunt. Instead of a well-laid table, implying the good life of a prosperous family, the objects depicted suggest the solitary and sometimes the melancholy—worn books, musical instruments and sheet music, a pair of spectacles. Harnett himself tempered this somewhat, with an emphasis upon antique objects which might appeal to the newly rich in America, bent upon acquiring social and cultural prestige through collecting the very objects which Harnett introduced into his paintings. Finally, the dark, sometimes monochromatic tonalities of these intensely realistic paintings differ greatly from the bright, light colorful still-life paintings of the early and mid-nineteenth century.

By far the best-known still-life painter in New Jersey was the finest of all the artists in Harnett's entourage, John Frederick Peto (1814-1907). The story of his rediscovery is a fascinating one but need not concern us here. It involves the gradual recovery of Peto's *oeuvres* from under the forged signatures of Harnett, forged not by the artist but by the unscrupulous who realized that a work by Harnett, the leader of the school and well recognized during his lifetime and afterwards, would bring far greater financial rewards than works by an obscure painter whose very name was, until recently, all but unknown.

Peto himself, like so many of our leading still-life painters, was born in Philadelphia, the son of a merchant in fire engines. Like many artists, he was tremendously interested in music and played the cornet in the band of the Philadelphia Fire Department. He probably studied briefly at the school of the Pennsylvania Academy of the Fine Arts, where he exhibited between 1879 and 1886. The greatest influence upon Peto, however, was certainly that of Harnett himself. Harnett was quite a good friend of Peto's before the former left to go to Europe in 1880. Many of the individual elements and whole compositional approaches in Peto's paintings are related to works by Harnett, the older and better known of the two, and, according to Peto's daughter, her father talked constantly of Harnett, considering his paintings as the perfection of still life.

At about the time of his marriage to Christine Pearl Smith of Lerado, Ohio, in 1887, Peto began going to Island Heights, near Toms River, to play the cornet at camp meetings there. Religious revivals were held there at the Island Heights Camp Meeting Association and Peto led the singing. After traveling back and forth for some time, he built a house in Island Heights in 1889 and remained there for the rest of his life. Two maiden aunts came to live with Peto and his family, causing trouble in the family and making it impossible for him to go to Europe. The constant pressures of this situation may, in fact, account for the unevenness of quality of Peto's work at Island Heights, but most of his known production comes from these later years there, from 1889 to his death in 1907. Many of Peto's works were sold or given away locally, and his studio still survives with many of the "props" which he incorporated into his pictures.

Yet, while Peto's paintings are similar to Harnett's, they are in many ways profoundly different. Peto was never interested in the degree of meticulous realism which occupied Harnett. His forms are soft, his edges are blurred, and a luminous atmosphere of light fills his canvases and has led some critics to think of him as an "American Vermeer," after the great Dutch seventeenth-century artist. Nor did Peto ever adopt Harnett's interest in antique and precious objects. There is a deep sadness in Peto's still lifes, if still lifes can be "sad." Plaster is peeling, books are worn, pipes and matches are out, candles have burned down, and all these objects are rude and homely ones. A case may be made that the concern with discarded and rejected objects reflects the artist's own life of obscurity. This very factor is also one reason interest in him has revived at a time when the modern artist has been exploring the fascination of bits and pieces of everyday objects, incorporating them into collages, assemblages, and "junk" sculpture.

There were, of course, other still-life painters in New Jersey; Paul de Longpré (1851-1911), for instance, lived in Short Hills. He was born in Lyons in France, and worked in Paris before coming to this country in 1890. He settled first in New York, and the end of his life was spent in Los Angeles and Hollywood. He was well known for his flower paintings: large, lush watercolors vividly but meticulously painted. Two other still-life painters in the Harnett-Peto tradition who had New Jersey connections are William Keane, who is supposed to have been working in Camden in the 1880's and 1890's, and John Califano, who is recorded as living in Trenton at the same time. Almost nothing is known about either artist, however, and few of their works have so far reappeared. Others, too, will gradually emerge who are today only vaguely remembered names. The activities of these isolated figures in New Jersey art life—Peto above all, of course—add greatly to the flavor and variety of the art of the State.

Another category of painting in America which had its own specialists is that of the animal painters. There were not, of course, many of these, but during the nineteenth century there were some extremely able artists in this field, the work of some of whom has fallen into unjustified neglect. Thomas Hinckley of Massachusetts,

John Frederick Peto, Still Life
Collection of The Newark Museum

for instance, was well known for his cow and sheep pictures in the middle of the century. The brothers James and William Beard both specialized in anecdotal paintings in which the follies of man were caricatured in animal guise. Arthur Fitzwilliam Tait, an artist who exhibited at the New Jersey Art-Union, was famous for his paintings of farm animals and, particularly, sporting scenes involving birds, deer, and other game; there were even artists who were renowned for particular animals—John Henry Dolph was especially fond of painting cats, and William Jacob Hays was noted for his dogs, although he is best remembered today for his paintings of western animals such as buffaloes.

Earlier specialists in the painting of birds and animals in America were more artist-scientists; only later did the anecdotal and the sentimental approach to the subject prevail. One of the earliest ornithological artists of note in America was Alexander Wilson (1766-1813), whose book *American Ornithology,* is a classic study. He was originally a peddler and a weaver from Scotland and he taught in New Jersey and Pennsylvania. Wilson had a school in Bloomfield in 1801 near the Presbyterian Church. Perhaps the most interesting result of Wilson's sojourn, however, was not his artistic creations but the poem "The Dominie," which he wrote in Bloomfield and which was published in the Newark newspaper, *Sentinel of Freedom,* on September 8, 1801. In 1813, the year of his death, he was in Newark. More significant in the artistic life of the State was the appearance here of Wilson's successor, and the nation's most famous painter of birds and animals, John James Audubon (1785-1851). Audubon settled in America in 1806. He was a portrait painter, but his greatest interest was natural history and, from about 1820 to his death, he occupied himself with painting and writing about this subject; the fruits of this study were his *Birds of America, Quadrupeds of America,* and *Ornithological Biographies.* Naturally, in his search for birds of America on the Eastern seaboard, he passed through the rural state of

New Jersey and has left an account of his visit in Great Egg Harbor where he stayed for several weeks looking for birds known as "Lawyers," and doing many drawings of birds. He also took permanent lodgings in Camden in 1829, on his return from Europe, when he was studying the migrating warblers in New Jersey and Pennsylvania.

Wilson and Audubon add luster to the roster of names of artists who worked in New Jersey, but they were primarily "passing through" the State and cannot be said to have affected the nature of the cultural life of New Jersey in any way. On the other hand, Susan Waters has already been mentioned as an animal painter of note at the end of the nineteenth century. Another painter, even less known today, who specialized in animal subject matter was William D. T. Travis (1839-1916) of Burlington. He was born in Virginia, and in his adolescent days migrated to the West where a strenuous life in the open restored his impaired health.

With a talent for drawing he decided to become an artist, and contributed both in that capacity and as a writer to *Harper's Weekly* and the *New York Illustrated News.* In 1888 he bought a house on the Burlington-Jacksonville Road. Here he was able to indulge in his great love of horses—some horses he kept in his house. As a most unusual adjunct to his studio he built an elevator in a square tower, the machinery and platforms of which were capable of raising three horses to the third-floor level. Thus Travis was able to model live horses in the spirited action which was very often a major element in his paintings. These were sometimes simple depictions of horses and donkeys, and sometimes great allegorical canvases of huge dimensions, such as his "Aftermath of War" and "The March of Mortality."

Even when Travis was painting works on other themes, white horses in forceful action occupied the backgrounds of his works. He declared that if he were inspired to paint a picture of Heaven the angels would be mounted on white horses. He was a devout churchman and a militant member of the Burlington Presbyterian Church, a fact reflected in the religious aspect of much of his painting and in the sketches which he published. He is a forgotten artist in a neglected branch of the fine arts, but an interesting and unique figure.

Another artist to be considered at this time is Gerard Rutgers Hardenbergh (1856-1915). He was an ornithologist who spent his whole career in New Jersey as an illustrator of bird life. He was born in New Brunswick and was living there in 1886, but shortly afterwards moved to Bay Head where he died in the early years of the present century. He lived in a houseboat and was well known locally for his coastal scenes as well as for his depictions of birds of the region.

The most significant thematic development in American art, however, to occur around mid-century was the rapid growth of genre painting—the depiction of scenes of everyday life. In the eighteenth century, American paintings of this nature were well-nigh non-existent. A few examples can be dated from the early nineteenth century, when the scope of art was expanded to include landscapes, still lifes, and other subjects, stimulated undoubtedly by growing patronage. Occasional genre pictures were painted by Asher B. Durand and Henry Inman. Inman is considered the first artist to paint such subjects successfully, although almost all of these were done late in the artist's career, in the early 1840's. Earlier, in 1810, the artist John Lewis Krimmel had emigrated to the United States from Germany and settled in Philadelphia where he became the first specialist in genre painting in this country. His career was an exceedingly brief one, however, since he returned to Germany for several years and died in 1821.

It was only in the 1840's that genre painting grew in popularity and the growth was exceedingly rapid. It was allied to the growing democratization of a country which was discarding its ideological ties with Europe and its cultural dependency at the same time. In this change there arose a great interest in the presentation of scenes depicting the casual activities of the common man, presented with "honesty" and "truth to nature." Involved here also was the discarding of romantic and ideal interpretations of subjects, whether in portraits, landscapes, or genre, and the substitution of direct, straightforward realism. Parallel with this was a growing and sometimes militant nationalism, in which artists were not only advised to shun European teaching but to choose subject matter typically American. The roster of genre paintings of the time abounds with Yankee peddlers and newsboys and shoeshine boys who suggest the humble origins of youths who might yet grow up to become President.

Nor is it surprising, therefore, that the artist who was extolled at mid-century as not only the finest American genre painter but also the finest artist at work in the country, was William Sidney Mount of Long Island. Mount was, indeed, a first-rate painter, but this adulation was due more to his complete embodiment of the new ideal. His paintings exhibit an easy-going naturalism with overtones of humor; they are all rural American scenes without any of the taint of European influence which could be found in the larger cities in America; and Mount himself had never been to Europe. His work was popular, too, with the Art-Unions, and these organizations were partially responsible for the interest in and growth of genre painting, for scenes of everyday life were sure to appeal to the random winners of the lottery drawings. In addition, lithographs after his pictures, published in Paris and London, were widely circulated in this country.

The first major genre painter to work in New Jersey was William Tylee Ranney (1813-1857). He was the son of a sea captain and was born in Middletown, Connecticut. Ranney grew up in Fayetteville, North Carolina, where his uncle, William Nott, was a merchant, but his artistic development appears to have begun on his return to the North when he studied painting and drawing in Brooklyn. Perhaps the most significant event in Ranney's career, however, and one which was to influence much of his painting, was his joining the Texas Army in 1836, just six days after the fall of the Alamo. Ranney supposedly was in the guard placed over Mexican President President Santa Anna after his capture at the battle of San Jacinto.

Ranney remained in the Texan army until November 23, 1836, and then he returned to Brooklyn, continued his artistic studies, received his first commissions, and exhibited his work for the first time. In 1843 he opened a studio in New York City and advertised himself as a portrait painter. By 1847, however, Ranney had moved to Weehawken, and in the following year he married. He and his wife appear to have moved back to New York City for a short while around 1850, but later settled permanently in West Hoboken (now Union City).

Ranney was thus another artist to join such painters as Charles Loring Elliott, Paul Lacroix, and Thomas Whitley in the artistic community of Hoboken, and undoubtedly there was much lively exchange of ideas among these residents. Lacroix, of course, did not settle there until about a decade after Ranney's death, but he must have known the other painters there. The Ranneys, too, were friendly with the leading family of Hoboken, the Stevenses who were chiefly responsible for developing the town, making it available by steamboats which they owned and which plied between Hoboken and New York; they also owned the most beautiful house in Hoboken.

The Ranney house at Thirteenth street and Palisades Avenue was a large building of about 14 rooms and a large, glassed-in studio, two stories high. There were spacious grounds with many trees, and a summer house, and also a stable for the horses which the artist painted in many of his pictures. Henry T. Tuckerman, in his *Book of the Artists,* gave an interesting description of Ranney's studio:

. . . it was so constructed as to receive animals; guns, pistols, and cutlasses hung on the walls; and these, with curious saddles and primitive riding gear, might lead a visitor to imagine he had entered a pioneer's cabin or border chieftain's hut: such an idea would, however, have been at once dispelled by a glance at the many sketches and studies which proclaimed that an artist, and not a bushranger, had here found a home. Yet the objects around were characteristic of the occupant's experience and taste. He had caught the spirit of border adventure, and was enamored of the picturesque in scenery and character outside of the range of civilization; and to represent and give them historical interest was his artistic ambition.

Ranney was also something of a sportsman, fond of duck hunting, which is reflected in some of his paintings on this theme. He was also one of the founders of the New York Cricket Club which met at the Elysian Fields in Hoboken, playing with the group in 1854. After that date he may have become ill, for he died three years later of consumption at his West Hoboken home. The funeral took place at St. Mary's Catholic Church in Hoboken, and Ranney was laid to rest in Bergen cemetery; Charles Loring Elliott attended the funeral. The following year, the Ranney Fund exhibition and sale was held in New York. Works by Ranney were borrowed for exhibition at the National Academy of Design, and many of Ranney's fellow artists, including Inness, Cropsey, and Durand, donated paintings to be sold for the benefit of his widow and two sons. Over seven thousand dollars was netted, some of which was necessary to pay off a lien on his house.

Ranney's work falls into several categories. He began his artistic career as a portraitist but relatively few of these have been identified and they are perhaps the least significant aspect of his production. He painted and drew a number of landscapes; one of these depicted the often-painted Hackensack Meadows, and this work is owned by a descendent who still lives in Union City. His best-known works, however, are genre paintings. Some of these, "The Old Oaken Bucket" and "The Match Boy," for example, were straightforward presentations of everyday subjects, not overly sentimental. More interesting were his scenes of duck shooting, with solidly constructed figures, almost sculpturesque in their posed attitudes, somewhat dramatic, and rather stiff and formal. A concentration upon details of costumes, rifles, and game contrasts with a breadth and freedom in the treatment of landscape. Ranney was also noted in his own time as an historical painter, depicting scenes of the Revolutionary War, but these concentrate not upon heroic moments of battle but upon incidents affecting the lives of the populace.

The great bulk of Ranney's art, however, deals with the prairie and the West. These are not great dramatic landscapes such as those painted by Albert Bierstadt, nor exciting paintings of Indian life akin to those created by George Catlin, Seth Eastman, and others. They are what could be called Western genre: scenes of the lives of the trappers, the guides, and the settlers, undoubtedly inspired by Ranney's experiences in Texas. They relate the daily occurrences and hazards on the prairie, the meeting of scouts, halts around a campfire, the floods and fires threatening the settlers, and death on the prairie. They are unexciting paintings in which theatrical gestures and expressions are only occasionally introduced. Ranney's work does not have the liveliness of that of Mount, who completed some of the work left unfinished at Ranney's death. Nor does it have the humor of the Pittsburgh genre painter, David Blythe, not the anecdotal quality of that of Richard Caton Woodville; nor the complex construction and vigor of the paintings by George Caleb Bingham. But his work may be considered typical of the general level of American genre at mid-century, with the additional distinction of a unique regional interest. It is amusing, in fact, to think of the life of the West being pictorially reconstructed in West Hoboken, New Jersey.

The year after Ranney's death, New Jersey was graced

William Tylee Ranney, "The Pipe of Friendship," 1857
Completed by William Sidney Mount, 1859
Collection of The Newark Museum

by the activity of another genre painter, Lilly Martin Spencer (1822-1902), the most famous woman artist in America in the third quarter of the century. She was born Angélique Marie Martiné in Exeter, England to two Breton French school teachers. In 1830, her parents came to New York City and opened a school. The young girl had several lessons at the National Academy very early in her life, but the family moved to Marietta, Ohio, in 1833, where her father was a teacher of French. Lilly is supposed to have covered the walls of her home with drawings in charcoal as a child, a sign of her artistic precociousness. She was taken under the tutelage of two Marietta painters, Sala Bosworth and Charles Sullivan, and in the summer of 1841 an exhibition of her work was held in order to raise funds for her further artistic education.

The exhibition brought the young artist to the attention of Nicholas Longworth, the leading art patron in the Midwest, who lived in Cincinnati and who offered to assist her. In November of that year she went to Cincinnati and continued her studies there under the animal painter, James Beard. There she married Benjamin Rush Spencer, and by 1846 Mrs. Spencer had become one of the leading artists of the Midwest. She exhibited at the Western Art-Union, and the first engraving award of that organization was taken from Mrs. Spencer's "One of Life's Happy Hours."

The Spencers moved to New York City in 1849. In the following decade, Mrs. Spencer became a special favorite of the Cosmopolitan Art Association, an organization originally in Sandusky, Ohio, and then moved to New York, a successor to the defunct art-unions. The Association commissioned and purchased many of her works, and Mrs. Spencer's paintings were often reproduced, particularly in the form of colored lithographs. Undoubtedly because of her growing family—which eventually numbered 13 children—Mrs. Spencer moved to Newark in 1858 where she took the studio recently vacated by Rembrandt Lockwood. Perhaps, too, she chose Newark because Nicholas Longworth's niece who married Marcus L. Ward was there. The governor-to-be became one of Mrs. Spencer's patrons, renting her a house on High Street at the corner of Orleans Street in return for the painting of a portrait of his children, a portrait of Mrs. Ward, and a "fancy piece"—probably one of her genre paintings. The agreement was drawn late in 1857, to take effect the following April. Mrs. Spencer had a two-year option to purchase the property but did not do so, and instead moved in 1860 to 294 High Street where she and her family remained for nineteen years. Her studio was at the foot of her garden, a large building with sketches covering the walls and casts filling the room. It is said that she allowed each of her children to decorate his or her room with paintings, and her son Angelo did a creditable job with ships, pools, and lily pads.

The portrait of the four Ward children, which appears as the frontispiece, must certainly have been one of Mrs. Spencer's most ambitious works, a painting 10 feet high by an artist who did not measure half that height. It is a solidly constructed group, centering about a large Gothic Revival chair, brilliantly lighted and colored, and with a touch of sentiment. Mrs. Spencer's portrait of Mrs. Ward is not known, but she painted at least one other portrait for the Ward family, an appealing posthumous likeness of the young Nicholas Longworth Ward. The Wards also owned a number of Mrs. Spencer's animal paintings.

She was well known in New Jersey and exhibited extensively at this time, her pictures winning three medals, a goblet, and a diploma at the 1860 New Jersey State Agriculture Fair in Elizabeth in three classes of painting: figure, still life, and animal. In May, 1866, three of her pictures were on exhibition at Campbell's frame shop in Newark and were described in the local newspapers. In the following month a fourth painting was put on display, "The War Spirit at Home," which depicts a group of children reveling at the news of the fall of Vicksburg. It is typical of genre painting of the

Lilly Martin Spencer, "The War Spirit at Home—Celebrating the Victory at Vicksburg," 1866

Collection of The Newark Museum

time with its emphasis upon prettiness and growing sentimentality. The motif of news and newspapers can be found in many an American genre picture and it is indicative of a recognition of America's newness, a concern with immediate events, and of a lack of tradition in the young republic. Some of the finest American "war" pictures relate the effect of war news upon the home front, as in the present example; the mother depicted in the painting may be the artist herself.

Another of her well-known pictures painted in the

1870's in Newark is "The Picnic on the Fourth of July—A Day to be Remembered," a large canvas about 5 by 7 feet. It was one of the artist's works which was lithographed. Family tradition reports that the setting for the picnic scene was near Newark, and was thus, in all likelihood, along the Passaic River. The central figure in the composition, a gentleman who has just fallen from a broken swing, is a portrait of Mr. Spencer, and the artist herself appears with arms outstretched toward him. The other figures in the painting are very probably friends and members of the Spencer family.

Mrs. Spencer's most famous painting was a large allegory entitled "Truth Unveiling Falsehood," which was painted in Newark. It was awarded a gold medal at the Philadelphia Centennial and was also exhibited in France. John Wanamaker is supposed to have offered Mrs. Spencer $20,000 for the painting, and Senator William Sprague of New Jersey also offered to purchase it. Most of her other popular pictures, however, were frankly sentimental, as their titles—"Day Dreams," "Grandpa's Prodigies," "Jolly Washerwoman"—testify. The *Cosmopolitan Art Journal* spoke of her as doing much to popularize art, and the following verse, written by John Frankenstein in his *American Art: Its Awful Attitude* of 1864 typifies Mrs. Spencer's painting:

> Let not my justice, gallantry and wit
> A Lilly Martin Spencer here omit;
> The humor of the lower life she shows
> Wherein but few superiors she knows.

More and more toward the end of her life, Mrs. Spencer turned to portrait paintings, and the list of her sitters includes General Grant, Washington Irving, William Cullen Bryant, and Mrs. Benjamin Harrison. In 1880, the Spencers moved up to Crum's Elbow, where Mr. Spencer died in 1889. On his death, his widow returned to New York City to establish herself again as an artist. When she died, nearly ninety years old, she had painted over one thousand canvases. An exhibition of her work at The New Jersey Historical Society in 1960 commemorated the best-known woman artist of New Jersey in the nineteenth century.

The best-known nineteenth-century artist in Red Bank was the genre and portrait painter, Charles D. Sauerwein (1839-1918). He worked in Baltimore before studying in Paris in 1860 under Charles Gabriel Gleyre; after ten years abroad he returned to Baltimore. Ten years later he moved to Red Bank where he remained until his death. His address at one point was actually recorded as Phalanx, the site of a comparatively successful experiment in communal living, based on the principles of Fourierism. His son, Frank Paul Sauerwein (1871-1910), lived in Red Bank from 1880 until the late 1890's. Most of his painting was done in the Southwest, however, where he first went because of respiratory ailments in 1893; in 1906 he bought a house in Taos, New Mexico. The younger Sauerwein died in Stratford, Connecticut. He was a painter of American Indians, not in the somewhat romantic and dramatic tradition of the Indian painters of the early part of the century, like George Catlin (who died in Jersey City) and Alfred Jacob Miller, nor in the exciting illustrative style of Frederic Remington, but rather as one who objectively depicted the costumes, way of life, and racial characteristics of this ethnic group. A large collection of his work is at West Texas State College.

Another painter of Western life was Ferdinand H. Lungren (1859-1932). He was born in Hagerstown, Md. and lived in Nutley when in the East.

Genre specialists as well as landscapists who were not residents of the State occasionally visited New Jersey in search of appealing subject matter. Probably the best known and most individual of these was Edward Lamson Henry (1841-1919). Henry's artistically productive years were spent almost entirely in New York City. His style was unique in America, hard, meticulous, very colorful and anecdotal, but mercifully avoiding the excesses of sentiment of so much genre painting of his time. His paintings are invaluable transcripts of the life of the

Edward Lamson Henry, "Station on Morris and Essex Railroad," c. 1864
Collection of The Chase Manhattan Bank
Photograph by Lee Boltin

time—the costumes, the house furnishings, the village life of the second half of the nineteenth century, painted in a technique which is akin to that of the English Pre-Raphaelite painters. Henry was at Sparta, New Jersey, as early as 1862. His best-known works done in this State —and among his finest paintings—are a number depicting railroad stations which include large crowds of people and animals, various kinds of coaches and the buildings surrounding the stations. These include stations on both the Morris and Essex Railroad in Orange and/or South Orange, and the Camden and Amboy Railroad, at Bordentown, and a depiction of the Camden and Amboy train, "Planet"; the paintings were created in the 1860's and 1870's. One of Henry's numerous Civil War scenes also depicts a New Jersey subject, his "Departure for the Seat of War from Jersey City."

There were also painters in New Jersey who aspired toward the creation of canvases with noble themes—scenes of allegorical, historical, mythological, or classical content. Actually, many of America's most important painters, like Washington Allston and Samuel F. B. Morse, painted pictures of this nature, but few found adequate patronage for such work, John Trumbull, the artist of Revolutionary scenes, being an exception. One such artist was Henry Sanderson (1808-1880), who painted historical and literary scenes, besides portraits, landscapes, and genre pictures. He was born in Philadelphia but settled permanently in New Brunswick about 1830, except for a period of study in London about 1841. Sanderson was active in New Brunswick town life; he served as postmaster from 1857 to 1861 and was a member of the board of education.

Sanderson seems to have been impressed by the moralistic series of paintings done by Wiliam Hogarth in England in the eighteenth century, for on his return to America he exhibited pictures in New York from a series entitled "The Drunkard's Progress," obviously based upon the English master's "Rake's Progress." His best-known work is a large copy of Emanuel Leutze's

"Washington Crossing the Delaware," owned by Rutgers University today. In addition, Sanderson did illustrations after Shakespeare's plays, especially *Hamlet* and *The Merry Wives of Windsor.* He made an attempt also to get a commission for a painting for the Newark Senate Chamber.

An artist of much greater significance nationally was Robert Walter Weir (1803-1889). Like Sanderson, he was an artist of many interests who did portraits, fine landscapes, attractive genre paintings, and also historical scenes. He was associated with New York City in his youth, but he is remembered best today as instructor of drawing at West Point, a position which he held for forty-two years. It was early in his career there that he painted his most famous picture, "The Embarkation of the Pilgrims," on commission from the United States Government, which hangs today in the Rotunda of the Capitol.

Weir retired from the Army with the rank of colonel in 1876. For the next few years he lived in a small cottage at River and Sixth streets, Castle Point, in Hoboken, before moving on to New York City. Though his stay in Hoboken was a brief one, late in his life, it is interesting to note Weir's residence there, somewhat later than the Hoboken artists with whom this book has previously dealt. Also, some of Weir's most famous historical pictures were painted in Hoboken, including his "Columbus Before the Council of Salamanca," one of his best-known works. An article entitled "An Artist at Home" in the *New York Evening Post* for October 1, 1877, gives a picture of Weir in Hoboken:

The professor received me in his charming studio at Castle Point. On the easel was his latest work almost finished, "Columbus Before the Council of Salamanca." On the walls in the studio were "The Belle of the Carnival," "Titian in His Studio," "Portia at the Palace of Octavia," "Virgil and Dante Crossing the Styx," "Out in the Garden."

Here is a view I took from my window in Hoboken! It is evening and you see the gleam of lamps on the opposite side of North River. It is a dim light and a sombre picture but those coal barges are typical of that particular wharf. Many other paintings stood about the studio. There was an air of charming disorder in their half-hidden appeal—as if the mind had been too alert to more than suggest the theme, the hand only slowly bringing it to the finish.

Weir is noteworthy also as the father of two famous painters, John Ferguson Weir, the earliest American painter of industrial genre scenes, and Julian Alden Weir, one of the first American Impressionists. Neither of these artists, however, had New Jersey connections.

One of the finest and most individual of all the painters to work in New Jersey in the nineteenth century was William Page (1811-1885). He is also one of the most difficult artists to define. The bulk of his work was portraiture and he was certainly one of the best portrait painters of his age but, particularly in the early and middle years of his career, he was equally absorbed in paintings of other themes: genre, classical, and religious subject matter. Actually, he might best be thought of as a figure painter, one who was concerned primarily with the expressive qualities of the human form rather than with the narrative and anecdotal interests of the genre painter.

Page's work was quite distinct from that of his contemporaries in both form and interpretation. Instead of the direct, vigorous paint treatment associated with Charles Loring Elliott and others, Page used ever-increasingly subtle glazes of thin paint applied over a middle tint, so that glowing color seems to illuminate his static, monumentally conceived figures, all of which earned him the nickname of "The American Titian," after the great Venetian artist whom Page so greatly admired. Page was extremely influenced by the great religious writer, Emanuel Swedenborg, and he developed a theory of creativity in art in which he conceived of his figures as complete entities, based upon nature but embodying a divine spark of life.

The early part of Page's career was spent in New York and Boston, and during his middle years he was one of the foremost American painters in Italy, an intimate associate of the Brownings and other expatriates there. On his return to this country in 1860, he arrived in New York with the purpose of re-establishing himself in the major artistic center of the country. However, by 1862 he had taken a studio in Eagleswood, New Jersey, a section of Perth Amboy that was to bring together a group of artists at this time and which will be discussed more fully in connection with George Inness. By staying in Eagleswood, Page was able to remove himself from the wartime environment of New York, and in September he began to record his procedure of painting in a journal that Mrs. Page kept. Since Page's painting technique was conscientiously thought out in great detail and was quite distinct from that of his contemporaries, it is regrettable that it was never published as its author had meant it to be.

While much of Page's stay in Eagleswood was given to theorizing, several of his important paintings were also created there. One of these was a copy of Titian's "Venus of Urbino," Page's demonstration piece upon which he worked while his wife recorded his procedures. It was made from a tracing of the original. The last of the artist's major figure compositions was also painted there, the third version of his "Venus Guiding Aeneas and the Trojans to the Latin Shore." The artist had previously painted versions of this subject in 1857 and 1859; while Page did make changes each time, the paintings were almost identical. Only one is known today which may be the picture painted in New Jersey. It is one of the most important nudes painted by an American in the nineteenth century. The face itself is not unlike the Titian which the artist admired so much and which he copied. The drawing is somewhat naïve and the color, which was greatly praised in its own time, has now darkened, a fate which has sadly overtaken many of the artist's works.

After the last "Venus," nearly all of Page's major paintings were to be portraits. In Eagleswood he began

William Page, "Venus Guiding Aeneas and the Trojans to the Latin Shore," 1862

The Page Collection
Courtesy of The Detroit Institute of Arts

a series of "hero" portraits, major figures of the Civil War. The first of these was of the young colonel, Robert Gould Shaw, who had died in 1863. Page had no aversion to painting portraits from photographs and in this case, of course, it was necessary. It was followed by a portrait of General Winfield Scott, which was presented to General Ulysses S. Grant at a reception at the Union League in New York; it, too, was painted largely from a small *carte de visite* likeness. The third in the series, and the most monumental, begun when Page was still in New Jersey, was his "Admiral Farragut in the Shrouds of the Hartford at Mobile Bay," 114 by 77 inches! Attempts were made to have the work purchased for the Nation; when this failed, it was presented to Grand Duke Alexis of Russia in the name of the Tsar, as a tribute of gratitude for Russia's support of the North during the Civil War. Presumably, then, this work begun just outside Perth Amboy is somewhere in Russia today.

By the time the Farragut portrait was finished, Page had re-entered the active art world. He had built himself a house in Staten Island and had a studio in New York City. His New Jersey years were few, but the State had offered him a retreat where he could still find a stimulating environment of other painters, and where he was able to develop his esthetic ideas, both in theory and in a series of major canvases.

There was a sentimentality about Lilly Spencer's work which was saved from mawkishness by an effervescent cheerfulness and a lively quality, but as the century neared its end, American genre painting became more and more saccharine. The artist who is usually associated with this development and embodied its ideals best was John George Brown, a New York City artist, well known in his own time for his well-scrubbed newsboys and street urchins, meticulously painted in a highy finished technique. Actually, Brown was capable of beautifully painted landscapes and rather fascinating genre scenes, but his tendency toward the sentimental was unfortunate.

His equivalent in New Jersey was Karl Witkowski (1860-1910). Witkowski was born in Austria and studied in Cracow, painting many portraits there. After coming to America he lived in Irvington and Newark. He was a capable portraitist who painted a number of the leading citizens of the area, and his "Portrait of Monsignor Doane," who had been painted as a young boy by Henry Inman, is owned by the Newark Museum. His genre paintings are perhaps more interesting today, and are extremely similar to those of the better-known Brown, with beautifully rendered forms and textures, overly sweet, with perhaps a glistening silvery quality somewhat different from Brown's golden tones. Another artist of similar bent was Cyrus Durand Chapman (1856-1918), who was born and died in Irvington and had a studio or lived in Newark. Chapman had been a student of Brown and also of Lemuel Everett Wilmart, who was a professor in charge of the schools of the National Academy of Design in New York and a popular genre painter. Chapman later trained in Paris under Benjamin Constant. He was a painter, illustrator, architect, writer, and teacher. Painting in a style not dissimilar from that of Witkowski, and also living in Irvington, the two artists must have known each other quite well. Chapman's works are also sentimental and quite in the vein of the illustrator. This is typical of many of the genre and figure painters of the end of the nineteenth century.

There were other painters of this nature working in New Jersey at the time. One of the best-known locally was H. August Schwabe (1843-1916). He was born in Obersweisbach, Germany, studying first in Munich and then in the United States under William Merritt Chase. He was extremely active in Newark art circles, as President of the Newark Art League and as a member of the Newark Sketch Club. He was a figure painter and a portraitist of note and was perhaps even better known as a designer of stained glass, for which he won a gold medal at the St. Louis Exposition of 1904. A contemporary who also painted portraits and characterful figure paintings was Lawrence C. Earle (1845-1921). He spent a good deal of time in the Midwest, in Grand Rapids and Chicago, before settling in Montclair in 1890, at a time when that town was becoming popular with painters and sculptors.

Another category of painters are those who specialized in the depiction of war scenes. Except for John Trumbull, this country has never had any major artist who devoted his talents primarily to this subject, although both Winslow Homer, early in his career, and Eastman Johnson, in a few of his paintings, essayed such subjects, based upon the Civil War. That conflict, naturally enough, attracted a number of artists, some of whom actually participated in the conflict and others who were illustrators and reporters of the armies and their battles.

A painter best known for his Civil War scenes whose talents have just recently been rediscovered was Edwin Forbes (1839-1895). In 1861 he accompanied the Army of the Potomac as staff artist for *Frank Leslie's Illustrated Newspaper,* and his sketches of camp life and battlefields appeared throughout the War. After the War he continued to paint from sketches he had made, and in 1876 etchings from these sketches were published and received an award in the Philadelphia Centennial Exposition. In 1891 he published his own reminiscences. Forbes' connection with New Jersey was brief; he lived in Hoboken in 1860 and 1861. He had then studied under the animal painter Arthur Tait and concentrated first upon his master's subject matter, and subsequently on genre and landscape. Since his Hoboken years were before the Civil War, they do not figure importantly in his career, but this period of his life deserves being recording—especially since it provides one more example of the popularity of Hoboken among our nineteenth-century artists.

A New Jersey painter who devoted almost his entire career to Civil War scenes was Julian Scott (1846-1901). Scott was born at Johnson, Vermont, and served as a volunteer in the Army of the Potomac from 1861 to 1863.

As a patient in a military hospital, he had drawn a soldier's figure on the wall which was judged to indicate unusual talent. Brought to the attention of a New York merchant, he was enabled to pursue an artistic education at the National Academy and later with Emanuel Leutze. He settled in Plainfield in 1876 where he lived until his death, the most significant artist to reside there in the nineteenth century. Although he painted some portraits, most of his work consists of war scenes: "Battle of Cedar Creek, "Rear Guard at White Oak Swamp," "In the Cornfield at Antietam," "Blue and the Grey." These, of course, are Civil War scenes which constitute the bulk of his production, but his paintings occasionally relate to other conflicts, as his "Capture of André," his "Molly Pitcher," and his "Prussian Soldiers at the Time of Frederick the Great" testify. His best works combine a nobility of bearing and solid construction with direct realism, sometimes quite vigorous, and the lack of recognition his work has received compared to other Civil War artists rediscovered in recent years is puzzling.

One other New Jersey artist deserves to be mentioned in this regard, Thomas Buchanan Read (1822-1872). He was born on a Pennsylvania farm, but ran off first to Philadelphia and then to Cincinnati where he became a ship and sign painter. In 1841 he was in Boston in the circle of Washington Allston and Henry Wadsworth Longfellow, and in 1846 he was in Philadelphia. In 1850 he went to Europe. During the Civil War he was on the staff of General Lew Wallace as a lecturer and propagandist. He returned to Italy after the war where he made his home in Rome and Florence almost until his death.

The extent of Read's connection with New Jersey is not known, but he did live in Bordentown for some time in a large and beautiful old mansion at 15 Farnsworth Avenue. He also painted portraits of some of the family of Governor Marcus L. Ward in 1846. Actually, however, Read was even better known as a poet than as

Julian Scott, "Scene of the Civil War," 1872
Collection of The Newark Museum

a painter, and the poem acknowledged in his lifetime as his masterpiece was his "Sheridan's Ride," recounting the famous 20-mile ride made by Sheridan between Winchester and Cedar Creek to take command of the Union troops. The popularity of the poem probably inspired Read to paint the same subject. It is a composition of General Philip Sheridan on horseback which the artist often repeated, while living in Rome, in different sizes for patrons such as Governor Ward. It is a rather stagey, melodramatic picture, and, without it, Read probably would not be thought of as a Civil War artist, but it remains his best-known painting. William Gilbert Gaul (1855-1919), who was a well-known illustrator of Civil War scenes, was born in Jersey City and grew up in New Jersey, but since his mature years were not spent in the State, he cannot really be considered a New Jersey artist.

VI

LANDSCAPE AND SEASCAPE PAINTERS OF THE LATE NINETEENTH CENTURY

THE NUMBER OF ARTISTS in New Jersey in the second half of the nineteenth century naturally increased along with the size of the general population. Communication with and transportation to the more remote parts of the State became increasingly easier, so that artists could be found living not only in the larger towns but in smaller settlements conveniently situated within a ferry ride of the larger metropolises in adjoining states. Professional painters at this time essayed all possible themes, as we have seen. Yet, one subject stands out most prominently in New Jersey painting at the time and that is landscape painting. A plurality of the State's leading artists gave their attention to this theme, increasingly so, perhaps, as the areas adjoining New Jersey became more and more built up.

Furthermore, this thematic interest and the stylistic direction it took were greatly influenced by the art of one painter who was intimately associated with New Jersey, George Inness (1825-1894). Inness may be considered the most important artist in the history of New Jersey, one whose style helped change the course and character of American landscape painting. His influence upon his contemporaries was profound. This influence was by no means limited to artists in New Jersey but, because of his associations with the State, that influence was proportionately greater here than elsewhere, and might be said to represent a distinct element in New Jersey painting.

There were three periods of Inness' association with New Jersey and these three periods correspond to three different stages of his artistic development. To characterize Inness' art within these categories as "early," "middle," and "late" is, of course, an oversimplification; more than many others, Inness' career exhibits a logical development in which quality remains a constant factor, whatever the personal preferences of the observer and collector. Not only in aspects of his daily living but also in the progress of his art, New Jersey played a most important role, one that should be elaborated in some detail.

Inness was the fifth of thirteen children, the son of a wealthy business man who retired early in life and bought a farm near Newburgh, New York, where George was born. When the future artist was four the family moved to Newark where George Inness spent his boyhood. The Inness home was on a high hill near farmland, what today is the intersection of High Street and Central Avenue. Inness attended Newark Academy but made little progress and was finally withdrawn from school. He was something of a dreamer, and when he saw an artist sketching in a field, decided that he also would become a painter.

This desire did not at first meet with the approval of Inness' family, and so, at the age of fourteen, his father put him to work as proprietor and owner of a small grocery store on the corner of Washington and New streets in Newark. Even here, however, Inness continued to paint, keeping his canvas, paints, and brushes behind the counter and hiding them when a customer entered. This did not, however, lead to great financial success, and after about a month, young George closed the shop and turned away from the commercial world, a decision which his father finally, if reluctantly, approved.

At this time, around 1840, he was placed in the studio of John Jesse Barker, who was then in Newark. Inness remained with Barker for a few months, copying the older artist's pictures until his teacher declared that the boy had learned as much as Barker himself knew. Later, Inness went to work in an engraver's office, but soon abandoned that branch of the arts because of epilepsy, which afflicted him all of his life. He next studied in New York City with Regis Gignoux, a French landscapist who had just recently come to America. Gignoux was an able artist, best known today, perhaps, for his lively winter scenes. From him, Inness learned the use of color and theories of composition.

Inness' real inspiration, however, came from studying prints after works by the Old Masters, which were grand and monumental compared to the works of art that he saw around him. Among the American landscapists, however, he admired certain qualities of Thomas Cole and Asher B. Durand. He liked the lofty idealism of the romantic Cole, and the more intimate aspect and technical sureness of Durand. It became Inness' goal to combine these two approaches to nature. From 1844 on, Inness started exhibiting his work in national exhibitions. While his studio was now in New York, he returned to New Jersey to visit during and after his first marriage. His wife, Delia Miller of Newark, died soon after their marriage. Many of Inness' early paintings, done while he was in New Jersey, had titles such as "View near Newark," "View on the Passaic," and "View at the Foot of Newark Cemetery." In style, those of his early works which are known indicate that he was partially successful at creating the amalgam that he sought. While some of these are obviously youthful productions, they have a breadth of treatment and a grandeur which obviously derive from Cole's romanticism, but they are rather meticulous and intimate rural studies in a way which relate his early work to Durand and the Hudson River School.

At first, Inness was not financially successful as a

painter, perhaps because of his youth, perhaps because he was little known, or possibly because his style varied somewhat from that of the better-known landscapists of the time. His brothers, who had entered the business world, helped him whenever they could by buying his work. However, Inness was fortunate in finding a patron in Ogden Haggerty, a prominent New York auctioneer, who not only bought his work but, after the artist's remarriage in 1850, sent the couple abroad to study at his expense.

They remained in Italy for two years, while the artist studied the Old Masters. In 1852 they returned to America, but two years later they were back in Europe, this time in Paris. This may be considered the most significant aspect of Inness' art education, for at this time he became acquainted with the work of the artists of the Barbizon School, such landscapists as Camille Corot, Theodore Rousseau, and Charles François Daubigny. These artists and others were presenting a new form and a new interpretation of landscape, concerned with Nature's moods, with monumental and even dramatic forms, with conditions of weather and changes of time. Inness admired Rousseau's work particularly, and many of the American artist's pictures of this period contain dark and massive oak trees as major compositional elements which are similar to the way such trees figure in Rousseau's paintings. But Inness was anxious to eliminate the emphasis upon detail which characterized so much of American landscape painting and which he found a defect even in Rousseau's work, preferring Corot's pictures in this regard. Also, in some of Inness' pictures can be found a banding of successive light and dark areas receding into space which is typical of Corot's early paintings. He admired the works of Turner and particularly of Constable, whose interpretations of Nature were especially close to Inness' goals. On his return to this country he settled in Brooklyn for a few years, without achieving recognition, but with Haggerty's assistance things improved, and the Inness family took up residence in Medfield, Massachusetts, where they remained from 1859 to 1864.

At this time, of course, Inness' connections with New Jersey had temporarily ceased, but that state had assumed a place of large importance in the artist's development and as a source of subject matter. Undoubtedly too, the rural and even country environment it provided must be partially responsible for the direction which his art took and perhaps for the basic inspiration itself. Indeed, even after his return from Europe, he continued to paint the New Jersey landscape from the Hackensack Meadows to the Delaware Water Gap. The Medfield period, in turn, was the era in which Inness' art completely matured; some of his finest and most dramatic and impressive works were done at this time, often of the area around Medfield itself. Inness did a good deal of painting out-of-doors in the area.

In 1864 began the artist's second New Jersey period. He was persuaded to go to Eagleswood, a suburb of Perth Amboy. There, Marcus Spring, a cultured art patron of the period and a friend of Margaret Fuller, had established an artistic colony which revitalized the cultural climate of Perth Amboy, which had been dormant since John Watson's residence there in the eighteenth century and William Dunlap's in the early nineteenth century. Spring built Inness a house there, "Eagleswood Eyry," receiving in part payment the picture which is the most famous of all the artist's works, his "Peace and Plenty," which Inness had painted in Medfield and which is now in the Metropolitan Museum in New York. Spring also acted as Inness' manager and agent.

The Eagleswood period was a significant one in Inness' life. Another well-known artist who had established himself there two years earlier was William Page (1811-1885), who has previously been discussed as a figure painter. Page and Inness had known each other in Florence, where they had occupied studios in the same building, but their friendship ripened during their stay in New Jersey. Particularly significant was Inness' introduction to the teachings of Emanuel Swedenborg to which Page had in turn been introduced by the sculptor, Hiram Powers; those teachings became both artists' dominant religious faith. Inness wrote a good deal about Swedenborgianism later in his life, although most of these essays were not published. Page united his religious and artistic beliefs in one philosophy, and his belief that a painting as a whole must radiate one sentiment undoubtedly appealed to Inness and strengthened his conception of landscape as an entity rather than a multitude of small parts and details. On the other hand, Inness disagreed with the theory on "the middle tone," which was Page's discovery; namely, that the horizon should be the half-way between the lightest light and the darkest dark in a picture. This much Inness agreed to, but the two painters could not agree on precisely what constituted the middle tone. Both artists, at one point, took a strip of tin and painted it white on one end and black at the other, grading them in stripes until a gray tone was reached in the center, as the middle tone. When the two were compared there was no resemblance between them. Actually, this disagreement led to many heated arguments after which the two painters would not speak to each other for days; later they would resume the argument. The disagreement continued for two years until Page left Eagleswood and built a large octagonal house at Tottenville, Staten Island, which he painted white and then glazed down to a middle tone. According to George Inness, Jr., the sun faded the tone out and his father then declared that there was no such thing as a middle tone, and that Page was a fool! Page does not seem to have had any interest in the work of the French Barbizon painters whom Inness admired so much.

Inness and Page were the two leading artists at Eagleswood, but there were others. One was the landscape and genre painter, William McEwan (fl. 1859-1869), who also lived in New York City and Brooklyn, and another was a landscape painter, Elisha W. Hall

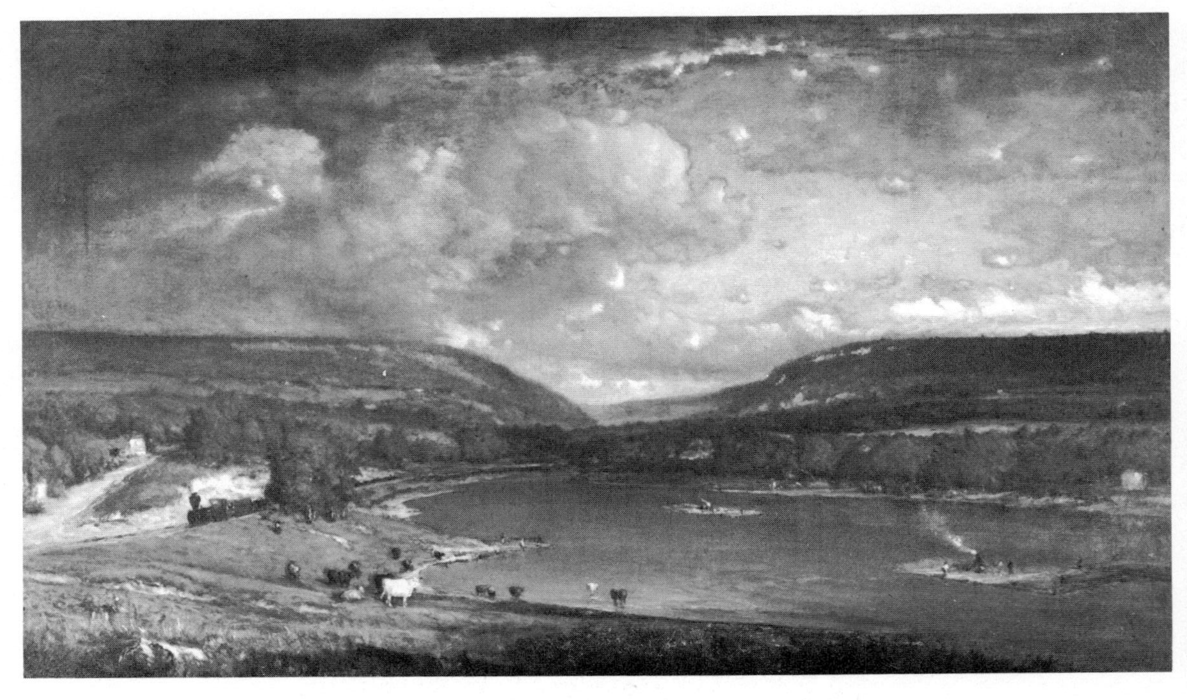

George Inness, "On the Delaware River," c. 1861
Collection of The Brooklyn Museum

(1833-1903). Hall was of Scottish descent and was born in Liberty Corner and died in his farmhouse in Lyons. The most important aspect of his career was his association with George Inness at Eagleswood; one painting exists which was a joint work by the two artists, but in Hall's other landscapes Inness' influence is abundantly clear. Hall's association with the Perth Amboy area may have initially begun through contacts with William Hall, his influential uncle of that city, and most of Hall's scenes depict the landscape either around Eagleswood and Perth Amboy or around the family farm at Liberty Corner; in addition, Hall was a capable portraitist and a number of family portraits have survived. In his own time Hall was quite successful and received between $250 and $500 a work, quite a respectable sum for a painting in those days. Among other commissions, he painted four panels for the President of the Rome, Ogdensburg and Watertown Railroad. Hall never married and became something of a recluse; he lived with two of his sisters who persuaded him to remain at home, despite the urging of Inness that he go to Europe. Hall's last work was painted about 1890; his failing eyesight forced him to abandon painting and devote himself to farming during his last years. McEwan and Hall shared a fine studio building in the Eagleswood settlement with Page, and McEwan also had his home there. In addition, the settlement contained a large stone edifice occupied by a military school, a fine mansion, and the residence of Marcus Spring.

Inness' most distinguished pupils studied with him at this time: Louis Comfort Tiffany (1848-1933) and Carlton Wiggins (1848-1932). Tiffany is, of course, far better known for the superb *art-nouveau* glass which he originated and which is called by his name; it is less well known that he was originally a painter of high quality. He came to Eagleswood in 1866 to study with Inness, in preference to a college education. However, his interest in watercolor painting and his love of pure earth tones in his paintings seem to suggest greater debt to another of his teachers, Samuel Colman, and he was also influenced by his French master, Léon Belly. Wiggins lived most of his life in Brooklyn and studied there with the Hamburg-born artist, Johann Hermann Carmiencke, but also with Inness at Eagleswood. Inness' influence on Wiggins was quite great, although the latter turned more and more to animal painting and became the leading painter of cattle and sheep in the United States. His landscapes and landscape backgrounds always acknowledge his debt to his famous teacher. Neither Tiffany nor Wiggins maintained any further connection with New Jersey; however, one of Tiffany's best-known paintings is a depiction of the Palisades, and his rich color harmonies which so markedly characterize his later achievements in the decorative arts undoubtedly were partially inspired by his study with George Inness.

Inness painted a number of scenes in and around Eagleswood, but his most important works done there were a series of large pictures painted on commission for a syndicate of men including Fletcher Harper, Chauncey Depew, and Clarke Bell. These were subjects from Bunyan's *Pilgrim's Progress.* These were not typical works by Inness, but rather allegorical landscapes tinged with an idealism which harked back to his early admiration for Thomas Cole. They included such subjects as "The Delectable City" and "The Valley of the Shadow of Death," the latter a painting about which Walt Whitman composed a poem entitled "Death's Valley." Inness had always been an intensely religious man and perhaps the inspiration attendant on his conversion to Swedenborgianism led to his interest in painting these moralistic landscapes.

In 1867, Inness ad his family left Eagleswood for Brooklyn, and thus ended the artist's second New Jersey period. In 1868 he became a full National Academician, and in the spring of 1870 he left once more for Europe. Much of Inness' time was spent in Italy where, in Rome, he had a studio supposedly once occupied by Claude Lorrain. His admiration for Titian as the greatest colorist who ever lived may indicate a continuing influence of his colleague, Page. On his return, Inness worked first in Boston and later took a studio in New York. Then, in the summer of 1878, Innes moved to Montclair, where he spent the rest of his life.

At this time, Inness rented a little cottage on Grove Street, and he and his son, George Innes, Jr., used two little outbuildings on the place for studios. Also, at this time, Inness began to achieve increasing success and recognition, his work being purchased by Thomas B. Clarke, Benjamin Altman, and other important patrons of art of the period. He was able to purchase the old Mapes homestead on Grove Street, in Montclair, and built a studio there. Inness continued to prosper and to paint many canvases of the local area which are still highly prized there, as well as other areas in New Jersey, such as Sparta and Oak Ridge. He was also able to travel and made trips to England, Canada, Florida, and California. It was on a trip to Scotland in 1894 for his health that Inness died at the Bridge-of-Allan. His body was returned to this country, and an imposing public funeral was held at the National Academy of Design; eulogies came from both fellow artists and the press.

Inness is known almost completely as a landscape painter and this certainly was the major interest during his life; for a while, however, he was deeply interested in the figure and painted many nudes, although these are not known today. In landscape, his reaction against French Impressionism was intense and he felt that the artists of this movement were shams. Yet, in a curious way, the works of Inness' last period, his Montclair years, share certain elements in common with the Impressionists. During this period, Inness abandoned the solid forms of his middle years and concentrated upon broad, diffuse tonalities and soft mist and atmosphere. His color was glowing but—faithful to a tradition which was not only derived from Corot but owed something also to his knowledge of the work of his friend, William Page, and the Old Master, Titian—he made use of rich

George Inness, "Winter Morning, Montclair," 1882
Collection of the Montclair Art Museum
Photograph by Jean Lange

transparent glazes over middle tones, and his work of this period may well be called "tonalist" rather than "colorist." Here, of course, his work was radically unlike that of the Impressionists, and in his motivation, more than ever before, his painting seems to embody his religious concepts, rather than the scientific interpretations of the advanced French artists. The soft atmosphere in which his forms dissolve into generalities suggests a unity of concept which is essentially Swedenborgian; no strident discords are introduced and each element in the painting unites with the other to form an overall harmony and serenity. Natural phenomena are the bases of Inness' art, but these are transcended to create great appeal to the emotions of the observer and to create Nature anew. The tranquil scenes which he painted in later life were intimate in scope, and he shunned the huge panoramas of Frederic Church and Albert Bierstadt; broadly painted as Inness' canvases are, they do not have the topographical value of the more meticulously painted American landscapes. They record an everyday, natural world which, through the artist's interpretive powers, is made enduring.

It was at the beginning of Inness' career in Montclair that large sums of money began to be paid for his works, and the history of the artist's reputation in this respect is a fascinating subject itself. Furthermore, about this time—or even earlier—Inness began to have both pupils and followers. Some of these were quite noted artists, while others have not achieved major reputations. Many of these painters, however, lived and worked in New Jersey and some notice, therefore, should be taken of them here.

Mention, of course, has already been made of the training that Louis Tiffany and Carlton Wiggins received from Inness during the Eagleswood period. Naturally enough, Inness' closest pupil was his son, George Inness, Jr. (1853-1926), who was born in Paris. He shared studios with his father, first in New York City and later in Montclair, where he worked much of his life. His father was often very critical of the younger man's work, and the younger Inness, who was his father's biographer, admired his father's painting so much that he came almost to imitate it: he used the same glazing techniques, the same color and atmosphere effects. The son was more the animal painter than his father and, perhaps, more the draftsman, which may be due to his study with Léon Bonnat in Paris. He was a member of the National Academy in 1899 and of the French Academy in 1902. About 1890, Inness, Jr., built a beautiful home known as Roswell Manor in Montclair; later it became the nurses' home of Mountainside Hospital. The artist had a winter home in Florida and died in Cragsmoor, New York. A friend of both Inness and his son was the well-known illustrator and wood engraver, Harry Fenn (1845-1911), one of the founders of the American Water Color Society, who lived in Montclair.

Inness' influence on several generations of American artists was strong, and it is impossible in most cases to say how direct it was. The influence of the work of his middle period was increasingly strong toward the end of the nineteenth century, extending even to California in the painting of his friend and associate, William Keith. At the very end of the century his influence was again felt, when a whole school of landscape painters arose who emulated his late frail and poetic works, artists such as Dwight Tryon, Bruce Crane, and above all, J. Francis Murphy.

In New Jersey both periods of Inness' art had their influence, but the connections between the master and the followers have so far not been ascertained. Indeed, the work and lives of many of these artists has yet to be studied. James Crawford Thom (1835-1898) was born in New York, the son of James Thom the sculptor. He studied with Inness as well as with a number of French Barbizon painters and resided and exhibited in London from 1864 to 1873. He lived in Old Bridge, New Jersey, from 1884 on and died in Atlantic Highlands. He was a landscape and genre painter, often including well-painted figures in broadly painted landscape settings not unlike Inness'. Joseph Jefferson (1829-1905) was a famous actor of the late nineteenth century, best known for his interpretation of the role of Rip Van Winkle. He was also a major collector of contemporary art, owning works by members of the Barbizon School and their Dutch equivalents. He was an admirer of George Inness and was a landscape painter of professional ability. In 1878 he was living in Hohokus, New Jersey.

Albert B. Insley (1842-1936) was a landscape painter of the period who had long New Jersey connections but about whom very little is known. He was born in Orange and lived in Jersey City from 1863 on. By 1883 he was in New York City and appears to have spent his last years in Nanuet, just over the border in New York State. His known paintings, so far, to show some similarities to Inness' style. Somewhat better known is Thomas Bigelow Craig (1849-1924), who lived in Rutherford. He was a landscape and animal painter who usually combined the two themes. His development is quite interesting; most of his paintings seem to be landscapes with cattle, the animals appearing as minor elements in his landscapes early in his career, and becoming more and more prominent in time, so that his late paintings are often primarily depictions of cows with subordinated landscape backgrounds. A later painter specializing in rustic landscapes with cows and sheep was Henry Rankin Poore (1859-1940), who was born in Newark and lived in Orange.

Julian Walbridge Rix (1850-1903) reversed the process of most Western painters; though he was born in Peacham, Vermont, he began his career in San Francisco, working in a paint store and painting scenes of the California coast. After establishing a reputation in the West, he was induced by William Ryle of Paterson to come East. He was living in Paterson as early as 1885 and had a summer studio on Ryle's estate in North Caldwell. His work displays strong atmospheric interest, relating both to the luminist tradition of Heade and other mid-century landscapists and to the broad, painterly tradition of Inness. Joseph Tubby (1820-1895) was a landscape painter who worked in the Hudson River School tradition in Kingston, New York. In the last decade of his life he was living in Montclair, where he knew Inness and appears to have adopted a more painterly and more dramatic style relating to the work of that artist. He painted seascapes and landscapes, some of the finest of the latter category being scenes of Montclair. Another Montclair landscapist, often called in his own time the "Dean of Montclair artists," was Thomas R. Manley (1853-1938), also an etcher of distinction. He was born in Buffalo, grew up in Richfield Springs, New York, and moved to Montclair in 1893.

A whole school of painting grew in the late nineteenth century out of the more fragile and delicate painting of Inness' last period. Reflections of this in New Jersey art, however, despite Inness' residence in Montclair at the time, seem less marked than the influence of the work of the 1860's and 1870's. George Herbert McCord (1848-1909) lived and died in New York City, but he did reside in Morristown between 1885 and 1891 at least. He painted landscapes and seascapes and his early work is, like Tubby's, in the Hudson River School tradition. His later paintings, however, have a poetic quality which relate to Inness' pictures of the period; a number of them are rural subjects, sometimes snowscenes, of frail trees along a path, often at sunset. He found his subject matter in New England, Canada, Florida, and the West, but he also painted New Jersey scenes, one well-known one depicting the Whippany River. Albany-born Charles Warren Eaton (1857-1937) was a later painter of evening scenes. He had a studio in New York early in his career, next to that of George Inness, who purchased one of Eaton's paintings and then became a close friend and the greatest influence on Eaton's life. Eaton was the leading artist of Bloomfield, where he lived from the late nineteenth century on, although many of his works are depictions of Bruges in Belgium. Bruce

Crane (1857-1937) was another landscapist of distinction who followed the Barbizon tradition, sometimes with a greater flair for color which bespeaks some knowledge of Impressionism. He had resided in Elizabeth early in his life; later he studied under Alexander Wyant, and he maintained a studio in Summit.

The work of all these artists of the late nineteenth century is still in need of study and evaluation. This is true also of the career and painting of Andrew W. Melrose (1836-1901). He was a native of Scotland, and was a landscape painter and an etcher. The subject matter of his landscapes indicates a great deal of travel, for he painted scenes of England, Ireland, and the Tyrol, South America and the American West and South, as well as New England and the Hudson River Valley. His studio, however, was in New Jersey, in West Hoboken, from 1868 on; in Guttenberg from 1879, and ultimately in West New York, where he died. The quality of his work was uneven; some of his landscapes are quite bland and others, such as his Western scenes, could be very melodramatic. Probably his finest paintings are those depicting the region along the Hudson, the heights around Union City and Jersey City, and the Valley of the Hackensack. In these paintings he exhibited a panoramic sweep, a control of light, and an ability to unite informally but charmingly figures and landscape which suggests a real understanding of Inness' art.

Not all of the painters who shared certain stylistic characteristics with Inness are little known or unknown, however. Probably the most famous of these artists was Thomas Moran (1837-1926). Moran's reputation rests principally on his late romantic interpretations of the American Far West, and he shares with Albert Bierstadt the honor of drawing the attention of the American public to the beauties of this region. He was also the principal American painter to be influenced by the art of the Englishman, J. M. W. Turner, as Moran's Venetian scenes with their brilliant color and all-pervading sunlight testify.

Andrew Melrose, "Valley of the Hackensack from the Estate of J. Becker, Esq., Union City, New Jersey"

Collection of The Newark Museum

Moran was born in Bolton, England, but was brought to America in 1844. His home was in Philadelphia until 1872, although he made several trips to Europe during the 1860's, and made his first trip West in 1871, accompanying the Hayden Expedition to the Yellowstone. In 1872 he moved to Newark, where he remained for a decade. However, during this period he made several additional Western trips, in 1873, 1874, and 1879. The most important pictures he painted during this period were based on his travels. The best known of these was his "Mountain of the Holy Cross," an inspiring canvas sketched near Denver, for which he was awarded a gold medal and diploma at the Centennial Exposition in Philadelphia in 1876. The painting was exhibited in London in 1879, the year in which Mt. Moran in the Tetons in Wyoming was named for him. While few of Moran's works of this period relate to New Jersey, his work in this decade culminated in his "Lower Manhattan from Communipaw" of 1880, one of the finest American paintings of the period. The painterly treatment and expressive interpretation of the scene is far in advance of most painting of the day, and it is one of the earliest industrial landscapes to be painted in America. The brushwork and the treatment of the heavy atmosphere recall Inness' style again. Actually, however, the similarities to Inness' work are more striking later in Moran's career, not so much in his almost visionary Western and Venetian scenes as in the quiet and informal pictures painted at his later studio at Easthampton, Long Island, and those based upon his Mexican travels.

The Moran family included an extraordinary number of talented artists, including Thomas' brothers, the seascapist, Edward Moran, and the animal painter, Peter Moran. These artists, however, did not live in New Jersey. One other talented member of the family, however, was his wife, Mary Nimmo Moran (1842-1899). She was born near Glasgow, but came to the United States as a child. She married Thomas Moran in 1863

Thomas Moran, "Lower Manhattan from Communipaw," 1880
Collection of the Washington County Museum of Fine Arts, Hagerstown, Maryland

and was working in Newark with him in the 1870's. She accompanied him on his western trip in 1874. She painted principally in watercolor until 1879 and then became one of the leading printmakers in America, a specialist in etching. However, she painted landscapes in oil occasionally, and her "Newark from the Meadows" of about 1880 is a small but beautifully painted view, emphasizing the vast, flat meadowland and contrasting it with the industrial aspect of Newark, smoke rising from the smokestacks in the distance. Stylistically, the scene is broadly painted in alternating bands of light and dark and might well pass for a sketch by Inness of the same period.

Another landscape painter whose work has affinities with that of Inness, and an artist of major reputation, was (Thomas) Worthington Whittredge (1820-1910). He was born in Springfield, Ohio, and began his career in Cincinnati before going to Europe for ten years to study in Düsseldorf and then in Rome. He worked in New York City on his return, except for a western trip in 1865-1866; he was President of the National Academy of Design in 1865, and again from 1874 to 1877. In 1880 he moved to Summit, where he lived until his death. In 1905, Whittredge wrote an autobiographical sketch from "Hillcrest," his Summit home, and the short section dealing with his life in New Jersey is worth reproducing here:

> . . . my love for the country together with a family of children growing up around me induced me at length to leave the city as a place of abode (though for a time I still kept my studio at 51 West 10th Street) and fix my dwelling place among the hills of New Jersey. Summit was a region which had many attractions for me. There were wide stretches of forest land bordering on rich meadow lands along the Passaic, and from the hills glimpses of the far-off Kill van Kull and of the great city could be obtained. In 1880 I bought a small piece of land, at that time quite out of the village, and built a house upon it in which we have lived up to this time; not always observing the Sabbath in the strict manner of my

forefathers, but, after church in the mornings and while my children were small, devoting my Sunday afternoons to walks with them, spring, summer and autumn—walks on which we picked a chrysalis and brought it home and hung it up, and watched for the butterfly to escape as the warm days of spring gave it life.

Twenty-five years I have lived in Summit. That I had made friends, almost without a thought and certainly without ever thinking that my life had made any impressions on my neighbors, was made very clear to me on the occasion of my eightieth birthday. I then had the unspeakable pleasure of seeing all the old residents of the place and many new ones congregate one evening to do me honor. I was taken by surprise and felt like a wild animal just caught in the woods and caged and put on show. But there was no levity in this cordial greeting. It was all heartfelt, and has passed into my remembrance with a glow of warmth about it to make it sacred.

My neighbor, Mr. Hamilton W. Mabie, presided and another dear friend, Mr. William J. Curtis, presented me with a beautifully wrought loving cup; while there were present many of the artists from New York and other old friends from the city. How much pleasure my friends may have derived from this meeting their own hearts can alone attest; but for myself to be awakened as it were from a dream, for I had scarcely thought that I was eighty years of age, and find so much affection and respect, was a moment in my life which I shall never forget.

The artist's daughter, Euphemia Whittredge, also a painter, added that another dinner was given on her father's eighty-eighth birthday, to which a number of New York painters, among them Frederick Dielman, F. Hopkinson Smith, and John W. Alexander, came.

Whittredge's art has often—and somewhat erroneously—been included in discussions of the paintings of Durand, Kensett, and other painters of the Hudson River School. It is perhaps not surprising that this should be so, for his early work done in Ohio shows the meticulousness of mid-century landscape, and Düsseldorf imparted to Whittredge's German landscapes—as it did to the art of all painters who studied there—an emphasis upon minutiae and exactitude which went beyond even the hard detail practiced in America. Yet in his later work there came into Whittredge's painting a poetry, a luminosity, and a softer brushwork which bear kinship with the Barbizon School and its American followers. Whittredge seldom exhibits the panoramic quality that can be found in some of Inness' canvases, and he never followed the Montclair painter so far as the hazy, almost visionary interpretations of his last years. Where the two artists do share a similar approach is in an emphasis upon the informal landscape. Many of Whittredge's canvases, particularly his smaller ones, are casual rustic scenes, not at all "artful," and his woods interiors, if compared with those of Durand, seem far less self-conscious, less precise, and more atmospheric. Whittredge worked in many areas of the country, particularly in New York and along the Passaic River.

There were a number of other capable landscapists working in New Jersey in the late nineteenth century whose art was not related to that of Inness and the circle around him. A number of members of the Hartwick family lived in Orange and Jersey City: Christian Hartwick, a portraitist, and George Ginter Hartwick (d. 1899), and his son, Herman Hartwick (1853-1926), both of whom painted landscapes. The father, who moved to New Jersey from New York around 1855, worked more or less in the style of the Hudson River School; Herman Hartwick, better known, was a contemporary of William Merritt Chase. He painted portraits, landscapes, animal pictures, and genre scenes. Much of his life was spent in Munich where he had studied, where he was patronized by the Prince Regent, and where he died. He lived part of his life in Jersey City and painted the Hackensack Meadows; much of his work is European in flavor, however, allied to the rustic realism popular then in Germany and Holland. The leading landscapist in Jersey City at the end of the nineteenth century was John M. August Will (1834-1910), who was also a crayon portraitist and illustrator. He was a native of Weimar,

Thomas Worthington Whittredge, "Millburn, New Jersey"
Collection of The Newark Museum

Germany, and was in New York City as early as 1855. He was a capable oil painter and a sensitive draftsman; the Jersey City Museum has a collection of fine local scenes fully documenting the appearance of the town during the many years of Will's residence there.

Perhaps due to the growing urbanization of communities near New York—the large ones such as Newark and Jersey City, and the smaller towns such as Hoboken, Weehawken—artists seeking a rural retreat went a bit farther into New Jersey. Montclair was, by the end of the nineteenth century, the most important "art colony" in the State, with not only painters such as Inness and Tubby resident there but, as we shall see, a number of important sculptors as well. Second to Montclair was Nutley, where such artists, already mentioned, as Frank Fowler and Ferdinand Lungren lived. Probably the best known of the Nutley painters of the period and certainly the most important landscapist was Arthur Hoeber (1854-1915). He was born in New York City and studied there at the Art Students League with J. Carroll Beckwith, and later under J. L. Gérôme in Paris, where he exhibited at the Salon. He was interested in the effects of light, and his landscapes often depict twilights and sunsets; his palette showed traces of the inflence of Impressionism at times, not surprising for an artist of his era. By and large, however, Impressionism found little sympathy in New Jersey, steeped as landscape painting in the State was under the influence of Inness. What Impressionist influence did occur seems to have come late.

One other major landscapist was also working in New Jersey in the late nineteenth century, a very solitary figure, one of the group of late romantic artists. This was Ralph Albert Blakelock (1847-1919), whose name is usually linked with those of Albert Pinkham Ryder, George Fuller, and Robert Loftin Newman among the more individual artists of the century.

Blakelock was born in New York City on October 15, 1847, and much of his creative life was spent there. Yet he was almost always a landscapist—a few very beautiful portraits and still lifes by him are known—and the countryside not only seems to have always attracted him but his happiest moments appear to have been spent there. Even those relatively few paintings which depict towns and cities, such as several paintings of shanties in New York, are poetic and idyllic views which are basically rural in character and do not at all reflect the growing urbanization of the country. Most influential in his life was the trip—or trips—he made West around 1869. While Blakelock never became a painter of Western scenery like Albert Bierstadt, poetic associations through a vision of the uncivilized, romantic land of the Indian remained in his art.

Details of Blakelock's life are even more hazy and incomplete than the exact nature of his art, though the latter is obscured by the amount of uncertainly attributed pictures and outright forgeries. The facts of his early life, particularly, have seldom been published. Blakelock was one of three children of Dr. Ralph Blakelock, one of the outstanding homoeopathic physicians of New York City, who had intended that his oldest son follow him in his profession. However, young Blakelock often spent his summer vacations with his uncle, James A. Johnson, who was an artist and musician of ability, and from his uncle, Blakelock derived the strong interest in both painting and music which was decisive in the shaping of his career.

Johnson had a summer home in Arlington, Vermont, and it was there that Blakelock first found inspiration in painting and also received his first instruction from his uncle, although it would probably be too much to say that Johnson was Blakelock's teacher. Johnson was a gifted painter and a friend of the professional landscapists, Frederic Church and James Renwick Brevoort, who himself had had no training. He worked in the meticulous style of the Hudson River School, with a dry, rather heavily-loaded brush, a style akin to that of the well-known landscapist, William Louis Sonntag.

James Johnson had married Blakelock's aunt Emily,

and the family lived in East Orange, New Jersey. On February 2, 1877, Blakelock married Cora Rebecca Baithe, and a few years later moved out to East Orange. Blakelock lived there, along with his brother George, a young doctor who followed his father's profession, perhaps taking the place of Ralph who had become an artist much against parental desire and advice. In these years Blakelock spent much time at his uncle's house. Johnson was more interested in music than in painting, and he both sang and taught voice. Blakelock himself was a fine pianist and, like his uncle, combined the two art forms; his paintings have often been likened to music in their emphasis upon mood and emotion.

Financial hardship always was to be an oppressive element in Blakelock's life and his residence in East Orange was, in this respect, no different from the years to come. These were hard times, and he was employed painting plaques and panels for an "art" factory in Newark in an attempt to make a living. Even here he was the "star" workman among the dozen men who were employed to do the same sort of work, meanwhile painting some of his typical romantic moonlight scenes during his free time. Dr. George Blakelock, the artist's brother, was physician to the family of Franz Assmann in East Orange. A daughter, later Mrs. Earl LeRoy Wood of Newark, remembers Dr. Blakelock's coming to her father's home and appealing for financial assistance for his impecunious brother. Her father took paintings and lent Blakelock money. Eight or ten canvases hung on the second-floor landing of the Assmann house until Blakelock could retrieve them or until there was a prospective customer for them.

Eventually almost all of them were taken back. One picture, however, has remained in the possession of Mrs. Wood, a circular composition in pen and ink, entitled "Moon Rise, Adroscoggin River," signed with an initial-monogram. It is a simple drawing, but charming and mysterious; concern with a moonlight scene is often present in Blakelock's works, paintings and drawings alike.

Mrs. Wood recalls having seen the artist once with her father, but she never met him.

Another associate of the painter was Ernest H. Bennett, who lived on Pulaski Street in East Orange. Blakelock's father was the Bennett family doctor, and Ernest Bennett, a rug designer for Sloane's in New York, used to accompany the painter on sketching trips. One of the most charming of Blakelock's pictures in his painting of Bennett's two sons, Alfred George and Ernest H. Bennett, in a landscape, painted in 1883. Bennett gradually accumulated a number of Blakelock's paintings, in part to assist the artist out of financial difficulties.

Blakelock exhibited landscapes including scenes of New Jersey, early in his career at the National Academy of Design in New York. Few paintings from his stay in New Jersey, however, are known. One particularly impressive work, known only through a photograph, is entitled "The Artist's Garden, East Orange, New Jersey," which went directly from the artist to Lewis Bloomington Slocum. It was auctioned at the American Art Association–Anderson Galleries on October 29, 1931, as No. 62; but its present whereabouts is unknown.

Several East Orange pictures remain in the hands of descendants, owned by the Babbage family of Montclair. One is a large pen drawing of a woodland scene, signed and dated "South Orange May 21 1877 Blakelock." It is a dramatic landscape dense on both sides and open toward the center with an impressive vertical emphasis upon elements and a rich variation of pen strokes of different thicknesses and intensity. Another is a small oil painting of a young girl, back to the spectator, holding down the branch of a tree. It was painted in the East Orange garden of James Johnson, and depicts Grace E. Washburn, one of Johnson's daughters. It is a small sketch, broadly painted, and typically informal in the manner which relates Blakelock's art to that of the French Barbizon School.

After Blakelock's early period in New Jersey, he stayed in various places, particularly in New York City

Ralph Albert Blakelock, "Grace E. Washburn in Her Garden"
Collection of Laurence Babbage

and Brooklyn until a mental breakdown led to his confinement in 1899. Toward the end of his life, Blakelock once again returned to New Jersey. For a while in 1918, after doctors had decided that he was well enough to leave the mental hospital at Middletown, where he spent most of his life, he lived in a private sanitarium in New Jersey, where a studio was fitted up with a piano. Here he painted, though the works produced were crude and childish in comparison with his pictures painted before he was committed. Toward the end of that year he was returned to Middletown and he was discharged only a month before his death, in 1919.

Solitary romantics like Blakelock seldom have many direct followers. Three other romantic artists deserve to be noted at this time, though they are not strictly landscape painters. One is Frederick Ballard Williams (1871-1956), the leading painter of Glen Ridge, where he lived all his life after coming to New Jersey from Brooklyn at the age of eight. Williams studied in New York and early in his career painted landscapes with rich, broadly laid-on pigment. He soon began introducing figures into his scenes, women attired in beautiful gowns of brilliant color, usually eighteenth-century costumes. The paintings thus bear superficial similarities to the works of French rococo artists like Watteau, Pater, and Lancret, but the mood of Williams' pictures is that of idyllic reverie. Although less lushly painted and more solidly constructed, they remind one more of the pictures of the French nineteenth-century romantic, Adolphe Monticelli. There is a tapestry-like effect in the rhythmic compositions of his paintings which also are akin to the work of the early twentieth-century artist, Arthur B. Davies, who had great influence on Williams. Later in his life, Williams returned to painting landscapes.

A better-known romantic artist who is usually linked with New Jersey is Louis Eilshemius (1864-1941). He was born at Laurel Hill Manor, in Kearny, the family having previously lived in Hoboken and Jersey City. Eilshemius attended kindergarten in Newark, but after that went to school in New York and then in Europe; and his artistic career really has little relationship to his native State. Eilshemius' earliest works may bear some slight relationship to the landscape tradition already discussed, but the greater part of this prolific artist's work consists of idyllic nudes in very simplified landscapes which again bears some relationship to the painting of Arthur B. Davies. Both Williams and Eilshemius were active primarily in the twentieth century but their work has its roots in the previous era.

A third among this group of more imaginative landscapists, one who must also be considered as a figure painter, was George Arthur Williams (1875-1922). He too was more of the twentieth century than of the nineteenth, although many of the roots of his art lay in the earlier period. Williams was born in Newark and early in his career became an instructor at the Drawing School there, one of the first of the many distinguished artists to be associated with that institution. His first achievements were in the field of illustration, where he was recognized for his depictions of figures and scenes from English eighteenth- and nineteenth-century writers, especially Dickens. He was also noted for his illustrations for Richard Le Gallienne's libretto for the Wagnerian opera, *Tristan and Isolde.*

Just prior to the outbreak of World War I, Williams almost completely abandoned illustration to become a painter, working in both oils and watercolors and later in pastel. His landscapes and seascapes are noteworthy for their sense of mood and mystery. In the later paintings, particularly, he depicted a panoramic vastness and a sense of the all-inclusive scope and power of Nature, far from a literal transcription of the scene. The concern with time—time of day and time of year—characteristic of late nineteenth-century landscape painting, also is a major aspect of Williams' landscapes.

Perhaps even more interesting are Williams' figurative paintings, symbolic pictures of larger numbers of figures in weird landscape settings, cave- and grotto-like. These works bear titles such as "The Drama of Life," "The Drama of Nature," "The Drama of the Spirit," "The Seekers," and "The Marginal Way," the last in the collection of the Art Institute of Chicago. These are painted broadly and impressionistically, figures and surroundings merging together. Williams lived in Summit, New Providence, and Chatham until, toward the end of his life, he spent a summer in Ogunquit and then moved to Kennebunkport, Maine. The largest collector of Williams' art was Dr. E. Z. Hawkes of Newark, who bequeathed his collection to Union College, Schenectady.

It is not surprising that a state with a relatively long coastline and convenient to New York and Philadelphia should attract artist-specialists in seascape and marine painting among her visitors, and this was particularly true toward the end of the nineteenth century. Nearly all the leading painters of such themes seem to have visited the State, though they did not take up residence here. The seascapists came as often from Philadelphia as from New York—which was not the case among landscapists; this is understandable enough considering the proximity of south Jersey resorts to Philadelphia. Actually, since many of the New Jersey coastal towns were prominent resorts which artists might visit purely for leisure and relaxation, care must be taken in making claims for a relationship between painters found in this area and the history of the art of the State. For instance, the Philadelphia animal painter, Newbold Trotter, died in Atlantic City, and the Philadelphia portraitist, Edward Marchant, died in Asbury Park, but it would hardly be appropriate therefore to call them New Jersey artists!

Another Philadelphia painter, however, who made more use of the natural beauty of the New Jersey shore was James Hamilton (1819-1878). He was born in Northern Ireland and came to Philadelphia at the age of fifteen. He traveled a good deal, but Philadelphia remained his home throughout his lifetime. In the third quarter of the nineteenth century he was that city's leading marine painter, and the Jersey coast inspired many of his paintings. He interpreted this subject in a wide variety of moods, from haunting, desolate views which suggest a spiritual kinship with the later Albert Pinkham Ryder, to gay and airy scenes of bathers at Atlantic City. His canvases often caught the power of the sea, her mystery and her vastness, and he is an artist who is gradually being accorded the recognition he deserves. He was a major influence on the leading painters of the Moran family, Thomas—who has already been discussed—and Edward Moran (1829-1901), who emulated Hamilton and became one of this country's leading marine painters, first in Philadelphia and, from 1872 on, in New York City. Edward Moran made at least one visit to the New Jersey shore, to Sea Girt, and undoubtedly visited other coastal resorts as well.

A third Philadelphia seascapist of note was William Trost Richards (1833-1905), who was born in that city and lived there until 1890, when he moved to Newport. He was primarily a landscape painter until 1867, when he began to specialize in marine pictures. He first visited Atlantic City in the summer of 1870 and revisited there many times, painting usually broad and serene, unpeopled coastal scenes. These are often very horizontal paintings, composed only of successive planes of sand, water, and sky, painted in great detail which suggests a justification for his association with the English Pre-Raphaelite painters.

The most famous visitor to the New Jersey coast—indeed, the most famous artist-visitor to New Jersey in the nineteenth century—was Winslow Homer (1836-1910). The fruit of this visit is one of that artist's finest early pictures, his 1869 "Long Branch, New Jersey," now in the Museum of Fine Arts, Boston. In this painting, figures are admirably related to an open, airy coastal scene in which Homer demonstrated his sureness of control of air and sunlight. At least one wood engraving also relates to this visit to New Jersey.

Homer changed the character of seascape painting in

William Trost Richards, "Twilight on the New Jersey Coast," 1884
Collection of The Newark Museum

America, particularly with his large late oils depicting the power and struggle of natural forces, as waves beat against rocky shores. Many artists folowed the lead that Homer set but none so successfully as Frederick Judd Waugh (1861-1940). He was born in Bordentown, the son of the portraitist, Samuel Waugh. He studied under Thomas Eakins in Philadelphia and, after his marriage, spent much time in England, France, and the Channel Islands. On his return to America he settled in Montclair and used a studio which had formerly belonged to George Inness. His American seascapes were painted primarily at Bailey Island and Monhegan Island, Maine, and later in Gloucester, Massachusetts. After his Montclair residence he moved to Kent, Connecticut, where he bought a large farm, and finally, in 1927, he moved to Provincetown, Massachusetts. His paintings of pounding surf are sharper and more detailed than Homer's, but the best of them are dramatic and monumental works.

Several of the leading marine painters in this country in the nineteenth century lived permanently in New Jersey. Two of these were specialists in what can be called "ship portraiture," and both lived in what was then West Hoboken, now Union City. The earlier of the two was James E. Buttersworth (or Butterworth) (1817-1894), who was born on the Isle of Wight, England, and who may have been related to the English marine painter, Thomas Buttersworth. James Buttersworth came to America about 1850 and may have settled in New Jersey immediately, for his death certificate states that he had been in New Jersey for forty-five years. He became well known particularly through the lithographs after his works published by Currier & Ives. He specialized in the painting of sailing vessels and yachts, often in New York or Boston harbors, and he was the leading marine painter in the New York area at mid-century.

As steam replaced sail, so Buttersworth's successor in West Hoboken was a specialist in the painting of steamships. This was Antonio Nicolo Gasparo Jacobsen (1850-1921). He was descended from a long line of Danish

Winslow Homer, "Long Branch, New Jersey," 1869

Collection of the Museum of Fine Arts, Boston

violin makers, and was named appropriately enough after the great instrument makers, Antonio Stradivarius, Nicolo Amati, and Gasparo da Salo; the violin virtuoso, Ole Bull, was responsible for the choice of names. Jacobsen left Copenhagen in 1871 and eventually settled in West Hoboken, at least as early as 1886, where he spent the rest of his life. He painted ship portraits for the Old Dominion Line and later for the Fall River Line. His works are rarely inspired, and his approach was a matter-of-fact one with the sea serving only as a background, but he understood his vessels and painted them with keen observation and understanding. Another marine painter of the period was Henry Reuterdahl (1871-1925), who was born in Malmö, Sweden and came to America in 1893 for the Chicago Columbian Exposition He lived in Weehawken and painted steam yachts for the Astor and Vanderbilt families, as well as pictures of vessels in the United States Navy. In addition he taught at the Art Students League in New York.

Both Buttersworth and Jacobsen are fairly well known, and numerous paintings survive. There were also a number of other New Jersey painters who specialized in marine scenes who are all but forgotten. The earliest of these was William C. A. Frerichs (1829-1905), who was born in Ghent. He came to America in 1852, settling in New York City, but lived in Greensboro, South Carolina from 1854 to 1863, and later in Tottenville, Staten Island. By 1880 he was living in Newark. He was a portrait painter, but the works by him which are known today are nearly all seascapes, dark and powerful romantic paintings in the tradition of Joseph Vernet. He was also a teacher of note. Frerichs later returned to Tottenville and died there. One of the earlier artists to make up the art colony in Nutley was Harry Chase (1853-1889), who lived in the Stockton House there for several years. He was born in Woodstock, Vermont, and studied in Munich, The Hague, and Paris before returning to America. He was a noted marine painter and died at an early age in Suwanee, Tennessee.

James E. Buttersworth, "New York Harbor Scene"
Collection of The Newark Museum

Francis A. Silva (1835-1886) was a self-taught marine and coast painter who lived in New York City. He turned to these themes after serving in the Civil War. His subject matter ranged from the Chesapeake Bay to the New England coast and included scenes around Atlantic City and the Monmouth County coast. In 1882 he was living in Long Branch. The one resident seascapist in Atlantic City was George Essig (1838-1919?) who was born in Bavaria or Austria. He studied in Philadelphia under both James Hamilton and Edward Moran and thus continued the tradition of Philadelphia marine painters working on the Jersey coast. He was a dentist and lived and worked at Ventnor for many years.

VII

NINETEENTH CENTURY SCULPTURE

A CHAPTER ON SCULPTURE of the nineteenth century in New Jersey must necessarily be a short one, for New Jersey has never been the residence of many sculptors, well known or otherwise. There is probably no basic reason for this. If New Jersey does not offer particularly suitable stone for artists whose basic inclination is or was toward marble carving as, for instance, Vermont does, this would not justify the appearance of major American sculptors in the cities of Baltimore and New Haven. If the existence of foundries only in the very largest of cities might account for a concentration of sculptors of bronze statues in New York, it must be remembered that sculptors have in the past and continue in the present to ship their casts over many miles, and no New Jersey studio could be too far from the foundries of New York.

The history of sculpture in New Jersey started off rather auspiciously. It has been pointed out that Patience Wright, the first professional sculptor in America, began her career in Bordentown. While by the very nature of her wax sculptures and the short period of time that she produced them in New Jersey, she could not have been expected to establish a "tradition," one of the earliest of nineteenth-century sculptors, one of the first carvers of monumental marble pieces in America, and unquestionably the finest of such sculptors, was also a New Jersey artist, John Frazee (1790-1852).

Frazee was born in Rahway and was early apprenticed to a bricklayer named Lawrence. In the summer of 1808, Lawrence contracted to build a stone bridge over the Rahway River. The master bricklayer wanted to commemorate his achievement with a tablet bearing his name and the date; when it seemed that he would have to send to Elizabeth to have a tombstone cutter do the job, Frazee offered to try his hand at it. This inscription, BUILT BY WILLIAM LAWRENCE A. D. 1808, was the first carving that the budding sculptor ever did. It was from this inscription and from the opportunity for watching stonecutters from New York at work with mallet and chisel that Frazee's artistic imagination was first fired.

Frazee's next experience came in 1810 when John Sandford of Newark contracted to do the masonry for the New Brunswick Bank. Lawrence let Frazee work for him and the young man met Ward Baldwin, the stonecutter for the bank, who had received his training when working on New York City Hall. Baldwin encouraged Frazee toward a change of profession and the adoption of stonecutting as a trade, and allowed him to work at making some steps of stone. A third opportunity was provided during the following summer when Lawrence was building a house for Judge DeWitt Smith of Haverstraw. Judge Smith desired corners and door jambs of rusticated stone, as well as an engraved stone over the door, and Frazee prevailed upon both Lawrence and the Judge to allow him to undertake this. Frazee also worked on Queen's Hall, Rutgers College.

That winter, Frazee decided to undertake gravestone carving; he had Lawrence's aid and support, and was provided with rough slabs from quarries at Newark as well as board and lodging. Without previous training and with disdain for the rather outmoded forms of lettering and ornamentation which were currently utilized by local gravestone carvers, Frazee carved vines of flowers and ivy on his stones which won him immediate admiration. As he said in his autobiography: ". . . I can truly say that there was not at that time (what may have been done since) at Rahway nor at any of the neighboring cemeteries, any monumental work that could in neatness, propriety and beauty be compared with these, even my first simple and untutored efforts."

Frazee realized that Rahway alone would not furnish him adequate patronage and therefore, in August of 1813, he moved to New Brunswick. Unfortunately, due to the war, there was no building requiring cut stone, and hence his business was limited to plain tombstones. In 1815, the artist's first son died, and Frazee ornamented the tombstone with a figure of Grief leaning on an urn, his first attempt at the human figure. While purchasing marble in New York, Frazee saw samples of Italian marble carving of fruits and flowers and acquired a discarded piece of Italian marble on which he carved a relief of a basket of grapes and peaches.

In 1818 Frazee opened a shop in New York City, in partnership with his brother. Once there, appreciation of his skill at carving letters brought him much praise and at the same time he had far greater opportunities to study and learn more of the art of sculpture. Several New York churches, St. Mark's-in-the-Bouwerie and Trinity, have cenotaphs by Frazee, and the 1824 monument to John Wells, formerly in Trinity Church and now in St. Paul's Chapel, is surmounted by the bust of Wells, Frazee's first marble likeness. This had been preceded by a clay model of the artist's three-year-old son, and one of Lafayette.

The bust of Wells was indeed a difficult commission for Frazee. Wells was deceased and the sculptor had never known him. The basis for the bust was a posthumous portrait painted by Samuel Waldo. The clay model was successful, but Frazee had never had any experience in transferring such a conception to the more permanent medium of marble. To assist him in this process, Frazee invented a pointing machine with which he successfully completed the commission.

By the 1830's, Frazee's fame as America's leading por-

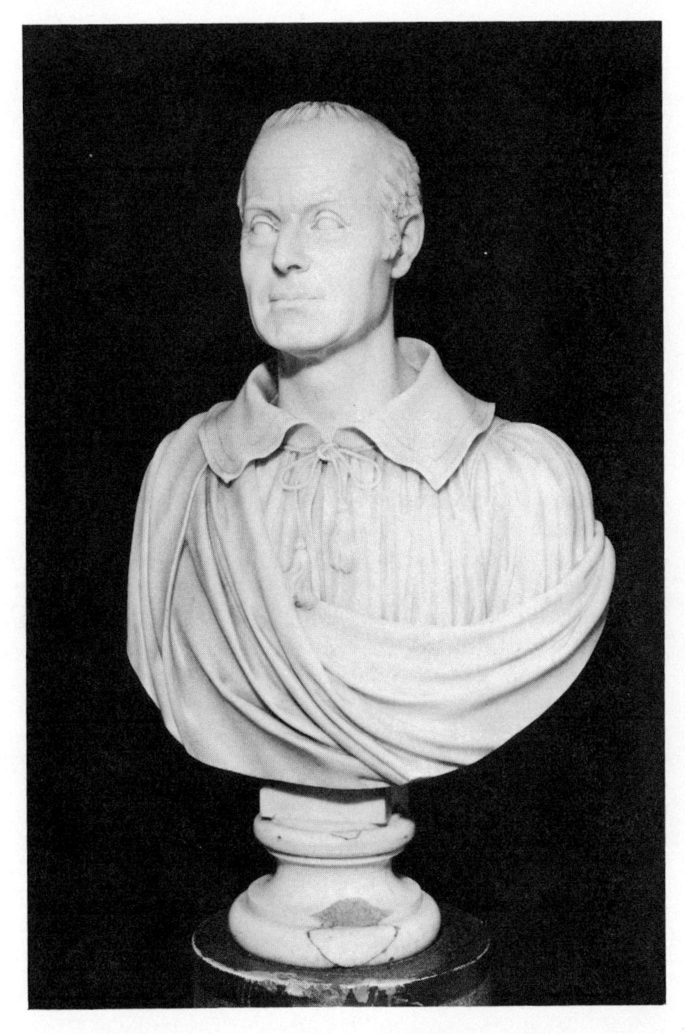

John Frazee, "Bust of Judge Story," 1834
Collection of The Boston Athenaeum

traitist in marble was secure, and in 1831 Congress commissioned him to do the bust of Chief Justice John Jay. Soon after this came several Boston commissions, busts of Nathaniel Bowditch and Daniel Webster for the Boston Athenaeum. These were finished in 1834 and were eventually joined at the Athenaeum by busts of John Marshall, Joseph Story, William Prescott, John Lowell, and Thomas S. Perkins, making that institution the major repository of Frazee's work.

By 1829, Frazee had parted from his brother to devote his time more completely to statuary, and during the following decade he was in partnership with the sculptor Robert Launitz. From 1834 to 1841 he was architect of the New York Custom House. In addition, he created other busts and reliefs, as well as chimney pieces and funeral monuments. Frazee did not study in Europe and condemned the Italian neo-classic school there as having betrayed the ideals of the ancient Greeks, to which Frazee subscribed. The costumes, poses, and general techniques of Frezee's art are certainly indebted to antiquity and his ability at modeling and differentiating textures suggest a sculptor of far more sophisticated training than that which was available to the Rahway artist. His portraits betray a remarkable combination of intense and detailed realism with a sureness, serenity, and nobility of countenance which are classical in origin. While most of Frazee's monumental carving was done in New York, his early training occurred in New Jersey which can rightly claim him. Frazee returned to New Jersey during the cholera epidemic of 1832, when he moved to Washington (now South River). His wife, Jane, died there on April 6, and in the graveyard there he erected to her memory a beautiful Grecian urn. Frazee is the one sculptor of his day who acts as a link, in the history of marble sculpture, between the visiting European artists who came to this country just before and after 1800, and the neo-classic school.

Strangely enough, however, none of that very numerous group of sculptors, involving two generations, had

New Jersey origins. That these artists, following the leads of the Italian, Antonio Canova, and the Dane, Bertel Thorwaldsen, worked in Italy rather than in their own land is not surprising. They joined sculptors from almost every country in Europe, living and working in Florence and Rome, turning out realistic portrait busts and ideal, often nude, figures of classical, religious, and allegorical origin. They formed the first "school" of American sculpture, and they came from many states, from Maine to Virginia, and from Ohio and Kentucky. But there were no New Jersey representatives.

There is, in fact, practically no record of sculptural activity in New Jersey from after the time of Frazee until the end of the century. The one other sculptor of the first quarter of the century who was working in New Jersey was William John Coffee (c. 1774–c. 1846). Coffee was born in England and worked there for pottery works. He moved to London about the turn of the century and modeled and exhibited in terra cotta. By 1816 he was in New York City, modeling portraits and animals and painting as well. In 1818 he visited Thomas Jefferson in Virginia and what brief fame Coffee ever achieved arose from this meeting, resulting, as it did, in the sculptures he made of Jefferson, his daughter, and granddaughter, and subsequent commissions attendant on this visit, particularly for ornaments for the Rotunda of the University of Virginia. Until 1827 Coffee gave his residence as New York City; thereafter, with Jefferson's death and a decline in his fortunes, he resided in Albany where he executed reliefs for the City Hall.

In the early 1820's Coffee was in Newark several times, as correspondence with Jefferson shows. On September 1, 1820, he was in New York City, but a week later he was writing from Newark, having left New York to escape the yellow fever. He closed up his New York studio and crossed the river with only the tools of his trade and the molds for the ornaments of the buildings upon which he was working for Jefferson: Bedford House and the University Rotunda. He worked upon these in

William John Coffee, "Bust of a Man," 1824
Collection of The Detroit Institute of Arts

Newark, as well as on other sculpture and painting, on into the winter, complaining about the rigors of the weather meanwhile. He was back in Newark again in October, 1824, from which visit a signed and dated portrait bust of an unknown man remains. This sculpture, now in the Detroit Institute of Arts, is a small, vivacious terra-cotta bust, typical of the best of Coffee's known work, and utilizing the medium in which, apparently, he was most comfortable.

The next sculptor in New Jersey's history was a resident over a long period of time rather than an occasional visitor, the only resident sculptor in the State, in fact, until the later decades of the century. This was James Thom (1799-1850), the father of the painter James Crawford Thom, already mentioned. He was a native of Ayrshire, Scotland, and was primarily a stonecutter in his native country, although he did exhibit sculpture also. He was in America by 1834, and was living in Newark in 1836. He does not appear to have remained there long, however, and was later in Paterson and in Little Falls. Toward the end of his life he built himself a house across the border in Ramapo, New York.

Before coming to this country, Thom's work was enjoyed by Sir Walter Scott, and much of the sculpture he did in this country was based upon the writing of Scott and his fellow author, Robert Burns. Thom chose to have a place at Little Falls because it was near the freestone quarries, from the material of which he created a gigantic statue of George Washington exhibited in New York, Philadelphia, and Washington. His most famous sculpture was a group of "Tam O'Shanter," two figures of which later flanked the doorway of the Colt mansion in Paterson. From the Little Falls quarry was also made the sculpture of "Old Mortality and His Pony" which was purchased by the Laurel Hill Cemetery in Philadelphia for the entrance thereto. Another of Thom's famous works was his statue of Robert Burns. He was also engaged in architectural carving and did the stonework for Trinity Church in New York.

The one other mid-century sculptor who worked in New Jersey was Thomas Dow Jones (1811-1881), who was born in Oneida County, New York, and is usually associated with Ohio, where he worked most of his life. He began in Cincinnati as a stonecutter and from about 1842 began to produce portrait busts, including likenesses of Presidents Zachary Taylor and Abraham Lincoln, of Henry Clay, and Generals Harrison and Scott. He traveled a great deal in the East and Midwest and is known to have resided for a few years in Newark, probably during the 1840's, although the dates of his stay are uncertain. Undoubtedly his Newark residence was responsible for the interest paid to him at the first drawing of the New Jersey Art-Union.

It was only at the end of the nineteenth century that New Jersey numbered among her inhabitants more than an occasional sculptor. At this time, Montclair, particularly, was the home of a group of major American sculptors, as much of a sculptor's colony, actually, as the State has ever had. These, together with the painters, Inness and his son, Tubby, Manley, and the rest, made Montclair an exciting artistic center.

Probably the most important sculptor in Montclair then was Inness' son-in-law, Jonathan Scott Hartley (1845-1912). He was born in Albany, New York, and, after working in a marble monument yard, had the good fortune to enter the studio of one of the finest neo-classic sculptors in America, Erastus Dow Palmer of Albany, one of the few and certainly the most important sculptor of his period *not* to have studied and worked in Italy. Hartley himself did study and work in Europe, though he spent more time in London, Berlin, and Paris than in Italy; he returned to New York in 1875. He catapulted to fame through a work entitled "The Whirlwind" which appeared in 1878. His most famous monument afterwards was the statue of John Ericsson on the Battery in New York City.

Hartley married Helen Inness, George Inness' daughter, in 1888 and moved to Montclair. The Hartleys lived next

Jonathan Scott Hartley, "Portrait of George Inness," 1894
Collection of the Montclair Art Museum

to the great landscape painter in a reconstructed farmhouse, connected to the Inness house by a covered passage. There was a large studio on the grounds which was used by both the painter and his sculptor son-in-law. At this time Hartley was more and more drawn to the production of portrait busts, including many stage figures in their roles. He was in his own time considered one of the finest portrait sculptors in the country, technically superb, with an emphasis upon virility and character and yet a great deal of sympathy towards his subjects. Among his portrait busts of note are those of Nathaniel Hawthorne, Washington Irving, and Ralph Waldo Emerson in the Library of Congress; of William T. Evans, who donated the first group of paintings to the National Gallery of Art; and of Hartley's father-in-law, George Inness. Toward the end of his life, Hartley moved back to New York City.

An even more famous American sculptor, one of the previous generation, who also lived in Montclair was Thomas Ball (1819-1911). However, it would be misleading to identify him too closely with New Jersey, and his usual appellation of "Thomas Ball of Boston" is well founded. Ball grew up in Boston, gaining experience as a wood engraver and painter, as well as a singer and violinist, before turning to sculpture. Immediately after his marriage in 1854, he went to Florence for several years and then returned to Boston, where he produced his most famous sculpture, the équestrian "Washington" for the Public Gardens. He worked on it from 1860 to 1864; it was finally installed in 1869 and the following year Ball returned to Florence. Among Ball's other major sculptures was his "Emancipation Group" in Washington and a statue of Daniel Webster for New York's Central Park. Although some of his works were in the neoclassic vein, he was one of the foremost sculptors of the realist movement in America. With his own work and that of his distinguished pupils, Martin Millmore and Daniel Chester French, he largely shaped the monumental art of New England.

Ball came to Montclair only in 1897, very late in his life. In this period, Ball turned back to painting. Although less active in his old age he must have served as an inspiration to the other artists in this active New Jersey town. Like George Inness, he furthered the cause of sculpture in Montclair another way: his son-in-law was a sculptor of note there also. This was William Couper (1853-1942) who, like Ball, lived on Mountain Avenue. Couper was born in Norfolk and spent much of his life in Florence, where he studied with Thomas Ball and married Ball's daughter. Couper did not return to America until 1897, when he established himself in New York City. From 1913 until the year before his death he lived in Montclair.

Couper's work is essentially a continuation of the neoclassic tradition far beyond the days of that movement's greatness. While Italian sculpture itself changed in the direction of emphasis upon baroque detail and clever carving, Couper continued the more refined and ascetic tradition of early neo-classicism. Idealization is an element in his work which differentiates it from the more realistic tendencies of his time in American sculpture. Nevertheless, Couper created many historical monuments, one of which remains in New Jersey: the statue of John A. Roebling in City Park, Trenton. His most famous works are probably those in the American Museum of Natural History in New York City.

Montclair thus establishes itself as the first city of the arts in New Jersey at the turn of the century, but as has been pointed out, Nutley takes only second place among the State's smaller localities. The one sculptor of note to reside there was Ralph Bartlett Goddard (1861-1936), a member of the National Sculpture Society who was best known for his portraits. Probably the best known of the women sculptors of the period was Caroline Peddle Ball (1869-1938), a pupil of Augustus Saint-Gaudens, who lived in Westfield for many years. Outside of the sculptors in Montclair, there were two other artists of national importance in the State at this time. One

Charles Schreyvogel, "The Last Drop," 1903
Collection of The Newark Museum

was Charles Schreyvogel (1861-1912) of Hoboken. Actually, like his even more famous contemporary, Frederic Remington, Schreyvogel was both a painter and sculptor of western Americana, creating rousing and sympathetic illustrations of life in the old West. He lived in Hoboken at least as early as 1890. He had been born in New York City and began life apprenticed to a gold-beater, and later worked with a die sinker and lithographer. He was a pupil of August Schwabe in Newark, and at the age of twenty-five he went to Munich to study for three years under Frank Kirschbach and Carl Marr. On his return to America he went West, and lived the life of the plains, the mountains, the Indian agencies, and the army barracks. He was fascinated by the life of the frontier and devoted himself to studying horses, Indians, and troopers in action.

On his return he was often engaged in making sketches for lithographs as a means of earning a living. One of his paintings, "My Bunkie," was offered to a lithographer who needed an illustration for a calendar, but the painting was rejected because it would not fit the necessary dimensions. After attempting to get other publishers, Schreyvogel tried to get it hung in a restaurant, but even that did not succeed. Finally, as a last resort, the artist submitted the painting to the National Academy of Design, where it won the Thomas B. Clarke prize, and Schreyvogel became famous overnight. From then on he continued to paint and sculpt subjects of Indian and army life of the frontier, full of action and sentiment. To gain further fame, the artist made an arrangement with a nearby photographer for issuing fine platinum prints of his works. After his death at his Hoboken home, the National Academy of Design hung again the artist's most celebrated painting as a memorial to him. Until recently, Schreyvogel's art has been overshadowed by that of his two most famous contemporaries who specialized in Western life, Frederic Remington and Charles Russell, but his work has recently regained great popularity.

The other major sculptor of note in the period was Karl Bitter (1867-1915), who lived near Schreyvogel in Weehawken. Actually, in his own time, Bitter was the more famous of the two, well-known as a builder of public monuments. He was born in Vienna, and in his youth attended schools of fine and applied art in his native city. In 1889 he came to America, landing in New York City. Bitter owed early success to employment by one of the leading architects of the time, Richard Morris Hunt, who gave him the commission for the bronze gates of Trinity Church. This was followed by a series of decorative sculptures for the residences of George W. Vanderbilt.

Meanwhile, from 1896 on, Bitter had chosen as his residence the town of Weehawken, which became even more important to the artist after his marriage in 1901. His home was one of the most lovely spots in New Jersey, overhanging the Hudson River at a height of 270 feet. Behind a high stone wall, Bitter had his house, a studio, a stable, and a stoneyard; the studio, once a famous suburban restaurant, was as large as a church. The artist loved to ride and was often seen on horseback and, later, behind a runabout with his family on the Jersey Palisades.

Gradually, after the beginning of the new century, Bitter turned from decorative sculpture to more monumental memorial work; this work culminated perhaps in the Carl Schurz Memorial overlooking Morningside Park in New York. In 1909 he regretfully agreed to move to New York for the sake of his family, but, while renting his house and garden, he kept his spacious Weehawken studio. In 1915 he was engaged on a figure for the Plaza fountain in New York, when he was run over by an automobile while crossing Broadway after the opera. Nevertheless, his achievement was considerable, and several of his monuments can be found in New Jersey, including an early fountain of 1899 for Jacob H. Schiff in Seabright, and the later 1911 Prehn mausoleum at Cedar Lawn Cemetery in Paterson, and the 1912 statue of Senator

John Fairfield Dryden in Newark. Bitter's work is the finest expression of the late nineteenth-century Renaissance Revival style in New Jersey, typical of the aspirational ideal approach that marks the work also of such artists as Daniel Chester French, Frederick MacMonnies, and others. Historical and monumental in nature, Bitter kept a light, fluid quality to his forms which may derive from his early decorative practice. Among his New Jersey works, the most important is probably the Prehn memorial, a mausoleum adorned with a procession of children in panels, some gay, some sorrowful. It was a memorial to three children who died early, and in its suggestion of della Robbia-like reliefs, it honors the style of the Renaissance era with intelligence and sincerity.

VIII

ART IN THE EARLY TWENTIETH CENTURY

THERE WAS AN INCREASE in overall interest in art and art activities around 1900 in New Jersey, particularly in terms of the formation of art organizations. In the last decade of the nineteenth century, the Newark Sketch Club was an active organization in the State's largest city, including among its members George Inness, Jr., several artists each of the McDougall and Schwabe families, and some painters, like Woodhull Adams and Charles A. (Gus) Mager, who were to become well known in the twentieth century. In Newark, too, the Fawcett School, formerly the Drawing School, which eventually became the Newark School of Fine and Industrial Arts, provided encouragement to students entering the fields of commercial, industrial, and fine arts, and produced some outstanding artists working in New Jersey and elsewhere. At this writing, the school is eighty-one years old and the oldest municipally-supported art school in the country.

Equally important a force for the development of the arts in New Jersey in the twentieth century was the formation of two major public museums: the Newark Museum and the Montclair Art Museum. The Newark Museum was founded on April 25, 1909, by John Cotton Dana, Director of the Free Public Library in Newark. Dana and his successors thought of the museum not only as a treasure house of works of art but as a vital force in the cultural and educational life of the community, the guiding principle being that of service to the public. Included in the program of the museum has been and continues to be the inclusion of contemporary art in the museum's collection and the presentation of it in the exhibition program. It was one of the first public institutions in America to patronize contemporary artists, and included among its earliest acquisitions paintings by Ernest Lawson and Bruce Crane, both very modern painters at that time and both with New Jersey connections. Thus, the museum began early to foster the development of art in the State, a policy which has been continued and enhanced in recent years through the triennial exhibitions, beginning in 1952, which have not only presented the work of outstanding New Jersey artists but which have led as well to the patronage of painters and sculptors of the State through purchases made from these shows.

For its maintenance, the Newark Museum depends upon appropriations from the City of Newark administered by the Newark Museum Association. The Montclair Art Museum, on the other hand, was opened in 1914 as a private organization designed primarily to serve the citizens of that town. The painting and sculpture collections of this institution, like that of the museum in Newark, are devoted primarily to the work of American artists, and there is a representation of New Jersey art, particularly of work by Montclair artists like those already discussed. The Montclair Art Museum further serves the public and artists of the State through the New Jersey State annual exhibitions inaugurated in 1931.

Not only through institutions but through private patronage as well, has contemporary art been encouraged in the State. One of the nation's leading art patrons of the late nineteenth century and early twentieth century was a New Jersey resident, William T. Evans. He was a friend and patron of many of the leading painters of his period, and in his collection were works by George Inness, George Fuller, Homer D. Martin, Ralph Blakelock, and others. He is best known, perhaps, in this avocation, as the first donor to the National Gallery of Art, but his original offer of a collection of American paintings for a Montclair Art Museum was the basis for the foundation of that institution, and his final gift of 54 paintings and two sculptures still remains the nucleus of that institution's collections. Among other patrons of American art of the early twentieth century in the State were Arthur Egner, J. Ackerman Coles, Joseph Isidor, and Louis Bamberger, all of whom contributed to the growth of the Newark Museum and all of whom patronized artists connected with New Jersey.

Art activity in the State, meanwhile, remained great and varied, but it was at this time that it took on a basically conservative character that has remained with it until very recent years. The reason for this is not difficult to find and it is a natural outcome of the directions that art in this country took in the first decade of the twentieth century. Around 1900, American painting and sculpture generally had begun to lose much of the vitality which had characterized their development throughout the previous century. Some of the nation's most advanced painters were expatriates, and the most vital artists in the country, such as Winslow Homer and Thomas Eakins, had already developed a solid, realistic art form which, in the hands of followers, was turning into an academic formula. The revival of Renaissance forms and motifs had led to the creation of a great many public sculptured monuments and the flowering of a vast but rather pallid mural art, one major and beautiful monument of which was created by Edwin Blashfield for the Prudential Insurance Company of America in Newark and only recently destroyed.

Meanwhile, genre painting had developed more and more toward coy and sentimental interpretations of themes that were sure to be popular, and landscape painting had taken on those frail, intimate characteristics assocated with Inness' late work. Probably the most vital forces at work in the art of the time were those that had been brought over from Europe by American artists who had gone there to study and work: the vigorous and dramatic approach of the painters of the Munich School and the new coloristic interpretations of the French Impressionists. The former was introduced into America by such artists as Frank Duveneck and William Merritt Chase. Through Chase's teaching, both at New York's Art Students League and at his own home on Long Island, the Munich School approach greatly strengthened American art. It had little influence in New Jersey, however, except for the activity of Herman Hartwick, already mentioned.

As has been pointed out, the strength of the landscape tradition deriving from George Inness may have retarded the acceptance of the more revolutionary developments of Impressionism. Nevertheless, one of the earlier and chief American Impressionists, Theodore Robinson (1852-1896), had a brief residence in New Jersey. Robinson had spent much of his short life in France and was a close friend of Claude Monet. His art, however, stemming from a basically realist tradition of solid draftsmanship and structure, is a kind of modified Impressionism, lyrical in mood, not brilliant in color. In 1894 Robinson was in New Jersey, teaching a summer class of eight to ten students at Evelyn College in Princeton. The stay was not very fruitful in terms of Robinson's painting, however, for he found the landscape not so exciting as in other areas where he had painted. After a return to Cos Cob for a few weeks, however, he came back to New Jersey and lived in Brielle between early September and the middle of November, teaching a class of four pupils. Several of his works painted at this time are known: sweet and charming representations of young women in landscapes.

Robinson's short stay in New Jersey had no lasting effect, however, and Impressionism never became a significant aspect of the art of the State as it did in New England, for instance. Edmund Greacen (1877-1949) of Oak Ridge had studied with William Merritt Chase and had then worked in France, living in the town of Giverny where Monet had painted. He was a figure and landscape painter who adopted an exceedingly soft and muted palette, painting landscapes reminiscent of James McNeill Whistler's "nocturnes" and "symphonies"; Greacen applied his tones in the broken brushwork of Impressionism. He was the organizer and first president of the Grand Central School of Art. His daughter, Nan Greacen (1908-   ), also of Oak Ridge at one time, is a noted still-life painter.

Probably the best-known New Jersey Impressionist was Van Dearing Perrine (1869-1955). He came east from Kansas as a youth and studied in New York City, where he lived for about fifteen years. Then he moved to New Jersey, where he had a home at the foot of the Palisades, close to the shore. He was one of a group of well-known artists of the period who made the area around Fort Lee something of an art colony, with painters like Walt Kuhn and "Pop" Hart there. Here Perrine painted many scenes of the Palisades, one of which was bought for Theodore Roosevelt by John LaFarge. Later Perrine moved to Maplewood. Many of his landscapes were painted with a vigorous Impressionist technique, utilizing a high-keyed, exciting color scheme, and he experimented with the depiction of light so brilliant as to negate form and with color sequences in autumn leaves and sunsets.

Still, despite the contributions of Munich and Paris, American painting around 1900 was in need of revitalization, and this did indeed occur, in two quite separate ways, in the years immediately following. One group of painters left this country and went to Europe to study and work, particularly in France. These artists, Max Weber, Joseph Stella, Marsden Hartley, Arther Dove, Alfred Maurer, and others, were in Europe at just the time that many of the outstanding twentieth-century modern art movements were beginning, and all of these American painters were receptive to one or another of these movements: Cubism, Futurism, Orphism, and the like. They admired and studied the work of such European painters of their own generation as Pablo Picasso and Henri Matisse and eventually brought the styles and techniques they had learned back to an unaccepting America.

The other major movement of the period was more in the direct realist tradition which has always been a part of the American art scene, but it was a movement that found contemporary criticism no less hostile than did the European-influenced painters. This group, centered around Robert Henri, was "The Eight" or "The Ashcan School," whose members interpreted contemporary urban life—the everyday street scene, the shops, the elevated railroads, the breadlines, the children playing on the sidewalks—in a dashing and vigorous manner which can trace its history back to the Munich School. It was a movement, however, that was markedly different from and markedly condemned by the academic idealism then enthroned in official art circles.

If New Jersey had prospered artistically as a rural retreat and had served particularly as a haven for landscape painters, her role in these exciting years was necessarily a somewhat limited one. Neither for the more modern painters who found their inspiration abroad, nor for the new realists who analyzed the life of the great cities, particularly New York, could New Jersey offer much. Nevertheless, for the new realists, the State had a role of some significance; it was the more populated and active areas of the State, close to the Hudson River, which enjoyed new popularity with the painters as well as the rural areas in which painters could settle quietly and work.

The painters of the "Ashcan School"—Robert Henri, George Luks, John Sloan, and the others—for the most part did their major work in New York City. One of this group, Everett Shinn (1876-1953), was from Woodstown, New Jersey. His art education, however, took place in Philadelphia, where he then did newspaper illustra-

Everett Shinn, Murals, Commission Chambers, Trenton City Hall, 191

Courtesy of the Department of Parks and Public Property, Trenton

tions before going to New York City to work on the *Herald* and the *World*. It was at about the turn of the century that Shinn began painting; many of his works, both in oil and in pastel, have the character of reportorial illustrations, and he also specialized in scenes of the theatre, vibrantly depicted with overtones of the French rococo style. His most ambitious works, though not his most successful, were the 1911 murals for City Hall in Trenton. These were painted in a vigorous realist tradition; the artist preferred to depict the industrial present rather than the historical tradition of Washington crossing the Delaware. He spent much time in Trenton studying the Roebling Steel Mills and the Mattock Kilns for use in his murals. Shinn was not able to imbue the works with the monumentality which such a subject deserved and which the mural art required, but they were the one major example in mural painting of the use of contemporary subject matter realistically treated. They differed markedly from the typical allegorical treatment among mural painters, but they found no followers in New Jersey or elsewhere. As one might expect, it was Ernest Lawson (1873-1939) of "The Eight" who spent most time in New Jersey, for he was the one landscape painter of the group. Never a New Jersey resident, he nevertheless painted a number of his canvases around the Palisades, the Hackensack Valley, Hoboken, and Caldwell, all in his somewhat Impressionist "crushed-jewel" palette.

New Jersey thus remained primarily a State for landscapists. Perhaps Lawson was in the Caldwell area because of Hayley Lever (1876-1958). Lever had been born in Australia and went to England in 1899, spending some years in St. Ives. He decided to come to America in 1912 and had such success in this country that, under Lawson's influence, he was persuaded to remain. He painted in New Jersey during the first year of his stay, but it was only from about 1925 to 1930 that Lever actually lived in Caldwell. Since he and Lawson were good friends and made painting trips together, it is very likely that Lawson's visit to Caldwell was partially due to Lever's influence. Lever did many scenes in and around Caldwell, landscapes painted in a brilliant tonality, with broad, sweeping brushwork and a vitality that links his work to that of "The Eight." His best-known subjects were probably harbor scenes and he was a vigorous still-life painter as well.

One of the most famous of all American artists of this period, never a member of "The Eight" but associated artistically with the group, was George Bellows (1882-1925). Bellows was born in Columbus, Ohio, and studied in New York City with Kenneth Hayes Miller and Robert Henri. In 1909 he spent a few weeks in a little town between Princeton and Flemington, Zion, with painter Edward Keefe and the famous playwright, Eugene O'Neill. They went there to experience the almost primitive ruggedness of life of the area and the beauties of the landscape. Bellows did nine landscape paintings of the area.

In 1910 Bellows returned to New Jersey, this time to Lakewood, probably in April, and two paintings of polo scenes derived from that visit. He was courting Emma Louise Story of Upper Montclair, who became Mrs. Bellows on September 23, 1910, and in the following two years visited the Story family often. In 1911, he painted three small sketches in Montclair, and in 1912 two major circus scenes there. Then the Story family moved into New York with their daughter and son-in-law and Bellows' connections with the State came to an end. Nevertheless, it deserves to be recorded, particularly as a number of fine, early works by this major artist were painted in New Jersey.

Another painter who followed a vigorous realism was Henry Glintencamp (1887-1946), who shared a studio in Hoboken with Stuart Davis and Glenn O. Coleman at one time. Hoboken was an ideal community for these painters, not only because of its proximity to New York City, but because it combined easy access to rural subjects with a concentrated urban and industrialized appearance. The three friends toured the metropolitan area extensively, including the music halls at Hoboken, Weehawken, and Fort Lee, and many establishments in Newark: canal boats under the public market, the Negro saloons, and the candy store of Gar Sparks (1888-1954), an artist of a somewhat visionary and individual style whose works are still too little appreciated. Stuart Davis has written:

> I first met Gar Sparks in a Negro saloon on Arlington Street in Newark, N.J. on April 12, 1912. He was drinking celery tonic. I remember the date because I had found a new friend. And a good friend is hard to find. It seems that Sparks was inspired by some paintings by Glenn Coleman, which he had seen in Columbus, Ohio. Since Coleman was my best friend, we found it easy to talk. Sparks told me about his own paintings and shortly afterwards I saw them. They were portraits of people he had seen while running an elevator in New York City. They had the quality of authentic art. In some way, probably by an inner image, (certainly not by instruction) he knew that a shape had a shape. He also had some paintings of people standing around in an expanse. A river was involved in some cases. I never inquired into the psychology of these things. They looked good. At that epoch Sparks was the director of a Nedick's Orange Juice stand. I used to meet him at midnight and we would go to the Arlington Street saloon to listen to real music, or to Childs restaurant to talk about art.

In Hoboken, Glintencamp organized an art club for the local residents, and one of his finest paintings depicts the Lackawanna Ferry terminal.

Stuart Davis (1894-   ), the most famous of all these artists, was born in Philadelphia where his father was the editor of the *Philadelphia Press.* In 1901 the family moved to East Orange, and Davis entered high school there in 1909; he remained only one year. In 1910 he went to New York to study under Robert Henri, but he also joined Glintencamp and Coleman in Hoboken. Glenn O. Coleman (1887-1932) was five years older than Davis and his artistic mentor. He had studied art in

Stuart Davis, "Hoboken," 1915
Collection of the Downtown Gallery, New York

Indianapolis before coming to New York in 1905, where he studied under Henri and Shinn. He supported himself by working as an usher at Carnegie Hall and as a policeman. Stuart Davis has described the visits he made with Coleman to hear the Negro piano players in Newark dives:

> These saloons catered to the poorest Negroes and, outside of beer, the favorite drink was a glass of gin with a cherry in it which sold for five cents. The pianists were unpaid, playing for the love of art alone, and many of them were very fine. In one place the piano was covered on top and sides with barbed wire to discourage lounging on it and to give the performer more scope while at work. But the big point with us was that in all of these places you could hear a tinpan alley tune turned into real music for the cost of a five cent beer.

Neither Davis nor Coleman, perhaps, did their finest or best-known work in New Jersey, but in both cases their experience in the State was important to the formation of their art. For Davis, with his love of jazz rhythms which he was later to represent in electric, semi-abstract and Cubist form, the New Jersey inspiration was great. And Coleman found in New Jersey the shabby aspects of urban living which were to be the subjects of his finest paintings.

There were other New Jersey painters, too, who were more or less concerned with the urban scene and the new industrialization. Chief among these was Frederick Dana Marsh (1872-1961) who was born in Chicago and studied there before going to Paris. He returned to America in 1900. In 1902 he took over the Nutley studio of the portraitist, Frank Fowler, where he chose to depict the life of the great industries—the laborers at work in building and bridge construction or the miners underneath the ground. He was also a figure painter of note. Fred Marsh's fame, however, has been eclipsed by that of his son, Reginald Marsh (1898-1954), perhaps the finest artist to portray the urban life of the average American in the generation following "The Eight."

The younger Marsh was born in Paris and attended school in Nutley. He grew up in a home filled with his father's paintings and a big studio filled with models—in clay and occassional live—art books, reproductions, and a general artistic atmosphere. Like so many artists who were born in New Jersey, Reginald Marsh left at an early age. After going to Lawrenceville School, he left the state to go to Yale. After graduation in 1920, he went to New York to work on newspapers and magazines, but around 1922 he attended the Art Students League, moved to Greenwich Village, and started painting in earnest.

In his work, Marsh maintained his concern with New York City life, its architecture and its moods. For the next thirty years he was one of the finest interpreters of people and crowds in movie and burlesque houses, night clubs and other places of entertainment—particularly Coney Island, where he portrayed skimpily dressed young ladies at the amusement park and even more scantily clad figures on the beach. The vitality and movement of the human figure as revealed in the activity of the metropolis were his principal subject and wedded to this was a sensual concern with the female body. To this end, some of his finest paintings and drawings were taken from burlesque houses, and, when these were banned in New York City, Marsh returned to New Jersey, drawing his subjects particularly from the Hudson Burlesque Theatre in Union City. In these works, in oil, tempera, and Chinese ink drawings, Marsh immortalized one now-past aspect of the entertainment world of New Jersey.

One of the most famous artists to live in Nutley, although for only a short while around 1915, was Guy Pène du Bois (1884-1958). Du Bois was born in Brooklyn and studied at the Chase School in New York City with William Merritt Chase, Robert Henri, and Kenneth Hayes Miller. In 1905 he went to France. On his return to America he was as active as an art critic on the *Evening Post* and the *New York Herald Tribune* as he was as a painter. For about seven years, part of which time he lived in Nutley, he was editor of *Arts & Decoration,* and one of his articles for that publication dealt with the collection of Arthur

Reginald Marsh, "Hudson Burlesk Chorus," 1950
Collection of The Newark Museum

Egner, the prominent Newark art patron, later president of the Newark Museum Association. Du Bois' paintings are fascinating representations of men and women interpreted almost as mannequins, with a quiet ironic incisiveness. They bear suggestions of the art of the earlier French painters, Honoré Daumier, Jean-Louis Forain, and Henri de Toulouse-Lautrec. Du Bois' home in Nutley was at the Enclosure, No. 16, occupied previously by Frank Fowler and Fred Dana Marsh, and afterwards by Michael Lenson. Even during his short residence there, however, he also maintained a studio in New York City.

Newark itself has had several local artists who devoted much of their talent to painting the life of the State's largest city. Particularly active was Russian-born Bernar Gussow (1881-1957), who was an instructor at the Fawcett School (later the Newark School of Fine and Industrial Arts) from 1910 to 1955. His paintings are somber visions of urban life, peopled by somewhat automaton-like figures. Another painter of city scenes of a more vital nature is John R. Grabach (1899-). Grabach was born in Greenfield, Massachusetts, and studied in New York at the Art Students League with, among others, H. August Schwabe of Newark. He lives in Irvington and was Director of the Irvington Art Museum Association; for many years he has taught at the Newark School of Fine and Industrial Arts.

Another area of the State that became prominent in its art life in the early years of the twentieth century was Fort Lee. It has already been pointed out that Van Dearing Perrine was active there. Another of the leading realist painters of the period to make his home there was George Overbury "Pop" Hart (1868-1933). Within a realistic, sometimes reportorial style, Hart was perhaps America's finest watercolorist, investigating life all over the world—Mexico, the West Indies, Hawaii, Tahiti, Samoa, Egypt, and Iceland, as well as different parts of the United States—in a dashing style combining brilliant draftsmanship with broad, freeflowing washes of color. He loved brilliant, sparkling sunlight and preferred the

George O. "Pop" Hart, "Cock Fight, Mexico," 1926

southern climes, but the New York area always remained his base of operations.

In 1907, Hart returned from several years spent in Europe and bought some land in Coytesville, just north of Fort Lee, where he built a shack which he used as his headquarters between travels. For the next five years he painted signs for amusement parks in New York and New Jersey and after that he was often employed painting stage sets for a movie studio at Fort Lee. This was during the summers; in the winters he went south, often to the West Indies. While most of his paintings, in oil and in watercolor, were done in exotic places, some depict the local area in and around Fort Lee, where the artist showed a particular preference for the Palisades.

Hart was a genial person and fond of people, but he would allow nothing to interfere with his painting and few visitors were invited to Coytesville. A close friend of Hart's in his early days at Coytesville, however, was an even better-known artist, Walt Kuhn (1877-1949), who lived in Fort Lee from about 1909 to 1919. Kuhn had been born and educated in Brooklyn, before going out west to San Francisco where he started drawing newspaper cartoons. In 1901 he went to Paris, and later to Munich, to study art, but he was back in New York in 1905, drawing cartoons for newspapers and magazines again. On February 6, 1909, he married Vera Spier, a designer of handmade jewelry, and for the next ten years they lived in New Jersey, summering in Nova Scotia and Maine.

Fort Lee was Kuhn's home, but his painting often related to his vacations, and his most important activity of this decade—organization of the world-famous Armory Show of 1913, which introduced modern art to America on a grand scale—took place, of course, in New York City. Meanwhile, Kuhn had to spend much of his time in occupations that had no relationship to painting in order to support his family. He had his first one-man show in the winter of 1910-1911 in New York, and after 1919 he lived in that city.

Walt Kuhn, "Harlequin," 1918
Collection of the Maynard Walker Gallery, New York

Nevertheless, Kuhn enjoyed an active life during his years in Fort Lee. He had a house on Hudson Terrace and built a studio there where he not only painted but did some little-known carvings. Many artists visited him, including Perrine and Hart, Gus Mager, and Jules Pascin; the last named did a portrait of Kuhn at his Fort Lee home. Many were the parties given there and at Fred Albig's restaurant. Much of the area where these artists lived and worked was swept away with the building of the George Washington Bridge.

A number of Kuhn's paintings done in Fort Lee are known, including his "Harlequin" and his "Master at Arms." His work of the early years of this period was a dashing, straightforward realism, sometimes tinged with Impressionistic qualities. With the Armory Show, however, many American artists felt the influence of the new movements which had originated in Europe, and Kuhn was no exception. His works immediately after it show the simplification and brilliant coloration of the Fauves, but it was not until the 1920's that Kuhn began painting figures in the blocky, monumental style with which he is particularly associated.

Just a little west of Fort Lee was another art colony in Ridgefield, an art colony that has lasted to the present. Early in the century, around 1910, a number of painters who were to become quite famous in the annals of American art built studio shacks there, Man Ray (1890-), Samuel Halpert (1884-1930), and Bernard Karfiol (1886-1952). Karfiol was born in Budapest, the son of American parents, and spent his boyhood on Long Island. He studied in New York City and in Paris and returned to this country in 1906, to New York and Ridgefield. It was during a visit at Ridgefield by the art patron, Hamilton Easter Field, in 1912 that Karfiol got his first real "break" and subsequently he was invited up to Ogunquit, Maine, where Field owned land and a house. From then on, Karfiol's reputation grew, and he became one of the country's leading figure painters, working with a simplified, classical approach to the naked form.

Samuel Halpert had been one of the first American painters to fall under European post-Impressionist theories, particularly the coloristic movements of the time, both Robert Delaunay's Orphism and the Fauvism of Henri Matisse and Albert Marquet, and he produced creditable work in the vein of both those movements. It was Samuel Halpert who brought Man Ray to the art colony in Ridgefield in 1913, where a Polish farmer and his wife rented summer cottages to artists. One house was still available for the summer, and Man Ray rented it; Halpert agreed to come out on occasional weekends and share the twelve-dollars-a-month rent. Living was very simple there; there were no shops and the nearest village was quite a distance away. Milk, bread, chickens, and eggs were available from the farmer, and water was gotten from a nearby well. Oil lamps were the source of illumination. For Man Ray, Ridgefield was a symbol of escape from the sordidness of the city and at the same time had the advantage of being close to it, and he likened his existence to that of Thoreau at Walden.

Man Ray decided, therefore, to make Ridgefield his permanent home. When Halpert came out for his first weekend he brought with him the poet Alfred Kreymborg, who joined them in the house. The poet Loupov also visited with his ex-wife, Donna, who remained with Man Ray. Loupov himself was interested in founding a liberal colony of cultural expression in Ridgefield and even went so far as to send out a printing press, but this was damaged in transit and the project eventually fell through. At the time both Max Eastman, editor of the *Masses,* and the poet, William Carlos Williams, were interested in the project and came out to Ridgefield.

Halpert's visits to Ridgefield gradually came to an end but Man Ray remained there. He moved with Donna from the larger building to a small house, and later they were married. He did paintings of Ridgefield as well as a stylized portrait of Donna asleep. The year of his move to Ridgefield was also the year of the Armory Show in New York City, and the experience of European modern-

Man Ray, "Woman Asleep," 1913
Collection of the Whitney Museum of American Art, New York

ism was a profound one for Man Ray as for so many American artists. During the winter of 1913-1914 he was at work on a large canvas influenced by Cubist painting but very colorful. In 1915 he was visited by Walter Arensberg, the collector, and Marcel Duchamp, the Dada painter, and it was from this visit that Man Ray's art took its mature course, under the influence of Duchamp. In 1915 he returned to New York City and became one of the leading American artists of the Dada movement. In 1921, Man Ray went to Paris and the greater part of his artistic activity has taken place there, but his Ridgefield experience was decisive in his development.

This Ridgefield group was succeeded in the 1920's by another group of writers and musicians, Manuel Komroff, Floyd Dell, and Anton Rovinsky, and painters, some of whom are still active in that town, Robert J. Martin (1888-   ) and William Tisch (1879-   ). Others who were there include Powers O'Malley (1870-   ), Walter Farndon (1876-   ), and Charles Duncan (1892-   ). They were young painters who had been students of Robert Henri and subsequently of Homer Boss, and were associated with the Society of Independent Artists. The artists' studios in Ridgefield were small and inexpensive; the area was still farms and beautiful wooded hillsides, but within easy commutation to New York City—thanks to the ferry from 130th Street to Fort Lee and the trolley from there south. Nevertheless, despite the cheap living, most of the painters held other jobs during the day to support themselves. Other painters came; the Belgian-French artist, Jules Pascin, who had a great deal of influence in America at the time, spent a summer there. Among other artists visiting the area was Emil Holzhauer, who spent weekends sketching in Ridgefield; he had sketched and painted in Newark earlier. Popular activities included skating, dancing, and walking trips during Sunday excursions out of New York. In this area, too, lived the painter that many consider the greatest of all New Jersey painters of the twentieth century, John Marin (1870-1953). Geographically speaking, Marin is often identified with the State of Maine and certainly many of his finest and most exciting watercolors and oils were painted there, but both his life and his art were intimately bound up with New Jersey also. Marin's mother, in fact, was Annie Louise Currey of Weehawken, who married John Cheri Marin in 1867, and the couple was living in Rutherford when their son John was born. Marin's mother died a few days after his birth, and the infant was left with his maternal grandparents in Weehawken to be raised.

As a boy, John Marin spent much time traveling between northern Jersey and a farm owned by his grandfather south of Milford, Delaware; these trips by sailboat and steamer were Marin's first acquaintance with the ocean which he was to paint and interpret so often in his maturity. Marin's boyhood was spent in New Jersey public schools and Hoboken Academy, and then at Stevens Institute in Hoboken, while during the summers he hunted, fished, and sketched along the Jersey coast. As a young man he practiced architecture, building a series of houses on Forty-Eighth Street in Union City, and when he could he roamed the countryside around the Palisades and along the Hackensack and Passaic rivers. There still survives a group of watercolors done in Weehawken in the last decade of the nineteenth century.

In 1898, Marin finally entered art school, the Pennsylvania Academy of the Fine Arts. In 1903-1904 he painted a series of oil paintings in Weehawken, which already show the expressive simplifications which were to become a hallmark of his style, this before he had any contact with European Fauvism. In 1905, his father agreed to send the young man to Europe to study, and here his style developed further, acquiring a Cézanne-like sense of structure although Marin claimed not to have been acquainted with Cézanne's work until his return to America. In any case, the distinction between the two artists is great: the Frenchman was a formalist, while Marin's approach was basically an expressionistic one,

John Marin, "Eastern Boulevard, Weehawken, New Jersey," 1925

The Metropolitan Museum of Art,
The Alfred Stieglitz Collection, 1949

devoted to a dynamic, explosive interpretation of nature, painted symbolically and often ideographically.

Marin returned to America in 1910 and began to do a series of paintings of Manhattan Island, including some famous interpretations of the Woolworth Building, in a style far different from that of the more realistic painters of "The Ashcan School." At this time he was staying in Union Hill, New Jersey, with his aunts. In 1914 he discovered Maine, the landscape and coast of which were to be a major source of inspiration to him all his life. Marin summered in Maine almost every year from then on, still living with his aunts in Weehawken. In 1920, John Marin and his wife moved to Cliffside Park, New Jersey, where they bought a house on Clark Terrace, down toward the Hudson River across from Grant's Tomb. There Marin was near open country suitable for his brush, and in the house he was able to knock out a partition in two upstairs rooms to form a studio. Although the majority of Marin's watercolors in the ensuing years were interpretations of Maine, the Palisades also figured in his subject matter.

More remote regions began later to figure in Marin's work, first New Mexico, where he spent two summers, 1929 and 1930, and Cape Split, Maine, where Marin purchased a house in 1934. The former was a new and exciting country which he investigated rather factually; in his Maine home he was able to proceed with more experimental elaboration of subjects which had become familiar to him. In this period, too, Marin returned to the oil medium along with his favored and better-known watercolors, working both in Maine and in Cliffside Park. When National Art Week was declared in November, 1940, Marin contributed a guest editorial to the *Palisadian,* a newspaper edited in Cliffside Park and published at Palisade. During the following year he wrote a piece, "Comments on the Pictures in this Exhibition," for a show of New Jersey art at Princeton University. These activities indicate Marin's continuing assocation with the state where he spent so much of his life; when his wife died in 1945, she was buried in a cemetery in Fairview, near Cliffside Park. The artist himself continued active both in New Jersey and in Maine until his death in 1953. Marin had no real follower or pupil in New Jersey, although Swedish-born Bror J. O. Nordfeldt (1878-1955), who lived in Lambertville at the end of his life, combined the ideographic symbolism of Marin with solid rocklike form of another Maine painter, Marsden Hartley, in his expressionistic interpretations of the New England coast.

If the realists of the early twentieth century were quite active in New Jersey, John Marin and Samuel Halpert were among the few major artists of the more avant-garde trends to be associated with New Jersey. Alexander Altenburg (1884-1940), little remembered today, was born in Greenville, New Jersey, and moved to Elizabeth, about 1910, where his family's Altenburg Piano House still flourishes today. Altenburg worked for much of his life in France, however, painting landscapes in a rich and exciting expressionist style recalling that of the great European modern, Chaim Soutine; his connections with his native state were limited. Joseph Stella (1880-1946), the famous American Futurist artist, had close contacts in Newark where his major work, the five panels of "New York Interpreted," is in the Newark Museum. One of Stella's finest oils depicts the industrialization of the Jersey meadows, his "Factories at Night—New Jersey," but Stella himself was never a resident. One other painter who had lifelong associations with New Jersey and who was influenced by some of the more advanced European art movements was Charles "Gus" Mager (1878-1955). Though never an innovator or a major influence in American art, Mager's career deserves to be noticed in a discussion of New Jersey art.

The career of Charles "Gus" Mager is little known today, though he was a figure of some significance in his own time. This is neither surprising nor by any means unique—and the one thing we can be sure of is that, as the history of the confusing and complex period of the early twentieth century is studied, figures like Mager and many others will re-emerge and their work will be re-examined.

The reason for Mager's anonymity is not difficult to find, for he remained a "hick," as he called himself, preferring to isolate himself in and around Newark which was his home and the home of his parents. Mager had been born there, and his early interest in art is evidenced by his membership in the Newark Sketch Club. For Mager, the most significant person in the Club was Paul Reininger. It is impossible to evaluate Reininger either in terms of his influence upon Mager or as an artist in his own right, since his paintings have completely disappeared from the public eye, but he, too, may well deserve investigation, for Mager acknowledged Reininger's profound influence upon him and called Reininger an "abnormal little genius." Mager likened Reininger's art to that of Vincent van Gogh, even to their similar deaths by suicide, and it is pretty certain that Reininger's work must have had an emotional, expressionist quality, since this is what was transmitted to Mager as they painted together and exchanged ideas. Another member of the Club whose influence Mager also acknowledged was Will Crawford, equally unknown today.

Mager's father, who was a diamond setter, had hoped that his son might become a jewelry designer, and Gus did go to work in a jewelry factory, but he sent drawings to New York newspapers in the hope of becoming a cartoonist, and he was soon hired by the *Journal,* and then by the *World.* Perhaps Mager, the artist, has suffered by his reputation as primarily a cartoonist, for he drew "Groucho the Monk," and a long line of "Monk" satirical drawings, and "Hawkshaw the Detective"—the last for twelve years in the *World.* These comic and illustrative commissions certainly provided a living for Mager, but they unavoidably helped to obscure his position as an artist.

Nevertheless, an artist he was, and well known among

many of the leading American painters of his time. He was a friend and companion of John Sloan, George Bellows, William Glackens, and Walt Kuhn in the early days, and the latter persuaded him to send two works to the famous Armory Show of 1913. He knew artists like Leon Kroll, Robert Henri, Ernest Lawson, and others, as well as Sloan and Bellows, through the McDowell Club Painters Group, with which he exhibited annually; he also had two shows in these well-known New York galleries: Brummer, Daniel, and the Artists' Gallery, as well as later exhibitions at the Rabin & Krueger Gallery in Newark. Other artists who have admired his work are Guy Pène du Bois, Robert Laurent, Chaim Gross, Nicolai Cikovsky, Joseph Stella, Bernard Karfiol, and Jules Pascin, some of whom came to visit him in his Jersey home. With Kuhn, "Pop" Hart, and others, he used to go to Albig's Pavilion on the Palisades in what is now Fort Lee, and the wild times they had there were mixed with talk about art.

Nor were Mager's interests and influences based only upon the more advanced aspects of American art; his early works particularly were strongly dependent upon the great post-Impressionist painters, Cézanne and Van Gogh. From the first he gained particularly a sense of largeness, solidity, and monumentality which marks many of his most impressive canvases. The greatest of all influences was probably that of Van Gogh, and the thick, rich impasto, the love of nature, and, above all, the expression of emotion through Nature relate Mager's art to Van Gogh's. At times, also, Mager, like Van Gogh, used an excited Impressionist-derived linear, broken brushwork, to express his reactions to the world about him.

If Mager responded to Van Gogh and if his work has some qualities of that great Dutch artist, it is also akin to the Frenchman, J. F. Millet, whose influence Van Gogh also acknowledged. Like Millet, and also like the Dutch artist Josef Israels, Mager was very close to the earth. There is a ruggedness to his art, and a feeling for nature which is devoid of grace and charm, but which has power. These artists were heavy-handed in their use of pigment, rich and heavy. In Mager's case, much of his devotion to the soil was centered about the New Jersey landscape, and about the people who inhabited it. At one time he owned a farm at Sand Brook near Flemington; his later years were spent in South Orange. It is Mager's unique contribution that he was able to combine some of the elements of Millet, Van Gogh, and Cézanne, and even of the Cubists, together with influences of his early teachers and colleagues, and fuse them into a distinct whole. The ruggedness of Mager's art negates the possibility of slickness or tricks, and his best pictures are vividly direct. What is more, they are very masculine paintings, and he was a very masculine painter. He was an active and intelligent naturalist, which brought forth elements present in his paintings. He was a sportsman, too, and among his best works are some which deal, vibrantly and vividly, with the art of wrestling, a subject which also intrigued his contemporary, George Luks.

In the period between the two World Wars, American art took on a relatively conservative character, despite the creative activity of such painters as Stuart Davis and John Marin. Some of the painters, like Halpert, who had experimented with Cubist, Orphist, and even abstract approaches, retreated into a more representational manner. It was a period of the development of regional schools of paintings, too, some of which were definitely insular in character, stressing subject matter drawn from different areas of the country, consciously avoiding European influences and emphasizing a sometimes militant nationalism. This was the period of growth of such groups as the painters of the Southwest, and of the Midwest, the latter numbering among its artists such well-known regionalists as Grant Wood, Thomas Hart Benton, and John Steuart Curry. One of this group, the artist

Charles "Gus" Mager, "Country Road," 1932
Collection of The Newark Museum

Joe Jones, is well known in the annals of New Jersey art, but his association with the State came after his concern with the representation of midwestern farm scenes.

The more conservative, sometime academic, painters who were popular at the time included a number who lived in New Jersey. Probably the best known figure and portrait painter of this group is James Chapin (1887-) of Annandale, Hunterdon County. He was born in West Orange and studied first in New York City and then in Antwerp. On his return he began to gain fame for his representations of New Jersey farmers, drawn from the Marvin farm near Middleville, west of Newton, where he rented a log cabin. A number of Chapin's portraits depict screen and theatre celebrities, including Katherine Hepburn and Aline MacMahon. In addition to his easel paintings, Chapin was commissioned by the Treasury Department in the 1930's to paint a mural for the Glen Ridge Post Office.

Among the best-known more conservative painters of landscape, a subject so popular in the history of New Jersey art, have been Gustave Cimiotti, Jr. (1875-) and Luigi Lucioni (1900-). The landscapes of the former often depict simplified, eloquent shapes and have a lyrical mood a little reminiscent of the work of Whistler, a painter whom Cimiotti admired in his youth. Lucioni's work is characterized by a precise, almost magic realism. Cimiotti was born in New York but grew up in Verona. While his home is, and was, in New York City, as Director of the Newark School of Fine and Industrial Art from 1935 to 1943, he had an important and influential place in the development of New Jersey painting. Lucioni, born in Italy, also lives in New York but was a resident of Union City for many years. Both artists have drawn upon New England for their subject matter, particularly Vermont, where the lack of industrialization, a wealth of picturesque scenery, and a contented, rural population remote from commercial progress have offered them the necessary inspiration.

In the period of the 1920's and 1930's, the most progressive aspect of American painting was probably the development of the painters known as the "Precisionists" or the "Immaculates." Both names are descriptive, for this group, led by Charles Sheeler, Niles Spencer, and Georgia O'Keeffe, created forms very precisely drawn, free from accident or impurity, and cleanly presented. In some cases, particularly in O'Keeffe's flower pictures, elements from nature were enlarged, and all extraneous material eliminated. The group has also been called "Cubist-Realist," for while their subjects were clearly representational, the forms were often interpreted with an emphasis upon geometric relationships deriving from Cubism. Their subject matter, except for O'Keeffe's paintings, often derives from the urban world, drawn from aspects of the city and the factory, and Precisionist paintings often glorify the industrial scene.

While the leaders of the precisionist movement were not New Jersey artists, one of the important members of this group and one of the most faithful to it, has long lived in the State. This is Louis Lozowick (1892-), who was born in Russia but studied in New York City. Lozowick explored industrial subject matter thoroughly, interpreting it with emphasis upon the geometry of its mechanical precisionism. Rather than the static forms of some of the work of his contemporaries, there is imaginativeness and a dynamism in Lozowick's art which likens it to some of Stella's Futurist interpretations. The inventive aspect of Lozowick's painting may be due to the early inclusion of his mechanistic paintings in the First International Exhibition held in Düsseldorf, in 1922, along with the works of such European abstract artists as Naum Gabo, László Moholy-Nagy, Theo van Doesburg, and El Lissitzky. Lozowick's reputation rests as much upon his lithographs as upon his paintings. He has been a resident of South Orange for many years.

The other major Precisionist in New Jersey was Charles Goeller (1901-1956), an artist not so well known as Lozowick. Goeller was born in Irvington and studied and painted in France. After an absence of seventeen years, he

Louis Lozowick, "Relic," 1949
Collection of The Newark Museum

returned to New Jersey and made his home in Elizabeth; he was an instructor at the Newark School of Fine and Industrial Arts. Goeller worked in a variety of styles, but his major approach to painting was in the Precisionist vein, in which style he interpreted the urban scene, factory buildings, still lifes, and figures; some of his subject matter, too, was drawn from his native state. Elsie Driggs (1898-   ), the wife of the artist Lee Gatch, has lived in Lambertville since 1936, but her best-known Precisionist work was done in the previous decade.

One of the major developments in American art of the 1930's stemmed from relief measures taken as a result of the Depression. The first of these was inaugurated under the Treasury Department in 1933 as the Public Works of Art Project. This was succeeded in August, 1935, by the Federal Art Project of the Works Progress Administration. Artists were thereby permitted to work in their own studios and upon their own subjects, and over five thousand unemployed artists received government patronage. While a great deal of mediocre work was produced, many of America's most famous artists were able to continue painting, and other younger painters received their first opportunity for professional work under the Project.

In addition to giving support to easel painting, the graphic arts, and sculpture, the Project supported fresco and mural projects for public buildings such as schools, hospitals, airports, housing projects, libraries, and post offices. Over thirteen hundred of these were created, including the post office murals by Westfield's Gerald Foster (1900-   ) at Freehold. Probably the most significant State artist connected with the Project was Michael Lenson (1903-   ). Lenson was Assistant New Jersey Supervisor in the mural and easel division of the Federal Arts Program. He executed major mural projects for the Treasury Department like those in the Mt. Hope, West Virginia, Post Office, as well as murals in the Verona sanatorium, in the Weequahic High School, and City Hall in Newark, and murals for the New Jersey Pavilion at the 1939 New York World's Fair. Lenson's service to New Jersey has not stopped with his mural work nor with his super-realistic, humanistic easel paintings. He was Director of the Newark School of Fine and Industrial Arts from 1944 to 1946, and he has been the State's most distinguished art critic, serving on the *Newark Sunday News* in that capacity for almost ten years. Lenson lives in Nutley in the house and studio previously used by Frank Fowler and Fred Dana Marsh.

The most important murals created in New Jersey during the Project were not the work of a local artist but were created by Armenian-born Arshile Gorky (1904-1948), destined to become in the 1940's one of the greatest and most influential of America's abstract painters of the period. Gorky joined the Project in 1935, and his first project was murals intended for Floyd Bennett Field and later executed for the Newark Airport. These murals, "Aviation: Evolution of Forms under Aerodynamic Limitations," were to consist of ten large panels covering 1530 square feet. Gorky made use of radically simplified geometric forms on bright fields of solid color, the whole conceived two-dimensionally. The airplane was dissected into component parts, these becoming symbols of the machine age. Gorky's models and one completed panel caused unfavorable comment in New Jersey newspapers, but critics rushed to their defense and, with Newark's approval, the murals, painted on canvas, were finally installed. Unhappily, these murals disappeared sometime during World War II and are known today only through studies, photographs, and the artist's own written description of them. A like fate has indeed befallen all of Gorky's mural projects. His World's Fair murals also disappeared, and those painted for Ben Marden's Riviera night club in Fort Lee were extensively repainted.

Fortunately, the beautiful aluminum sculpture, "Flight," created by José Ruíz de Rivera (1904-) in 1938 for the Newark Airport, also for the Federal Art Project, is extant today and, appropriately enough, in the collection of the Newark Museum. Like Gorky's

José Ruíz de Rivera, "Flight," 1938
Collection of The Newark Museum

murals, this work also is extremely simplified and semi-abstract, again lauding the machine age with suggestions of both bird and airplane forms. De Rivera is not a New Jersey artist, however, and actually, the major monuments created here in the early twentieth century were done by sculptors from other states. This was a period of great activity in the creation of public sculpture, and among the most important pieces to be seen in New Jersey are the Princeton Battle Monument by Frederick W. MacMonnies (1863-1937), and a number of works in Newark, the statue of George Washington in Washington Park by John Massey Rhind (1860-1936), and several works by Gutzon Borglum (1867-1941), "The Wars of America" in Military Park and the statue of Lincoln in front of the Essex County Court House. The Washington and the Lincoln monuments were provided for by a Newark patron, Amos H. Van Horn. The artists of all these works were well known American sculptors, and all achieved national fame for the creation of historical monuments.

Probably the best-known native sculptor of the period in New Jersey was Frederick G. R. von Roth (1872-1944). Von Roth was born in Brooklyn and spent his early years in Bremen, Germany. He studied in both Vienna and Berlin, in the Berlin Veterinary School as well as its Academy of Fine Arts. He spent much time analyzing the anatomy of animals and began to do small bronzes of such subjects as elephants and trainers, and equestrian portraits. On returning to this country he achieved a reputation as one of the finest sculptors of animals in the country and received a number of major public commissions. As chief sculptor for the Park Department of New York City under the Public Works Administration, he created many monuments in Central Park, the Baltic Monument, the fountains on the cafeteria porch of the Concessions Building, and the decorations of the animal houses in the Zoo, and the Sophie Irene Loeb memorial fountain on the Heckscher playground. Von Roth lived in Englewood; probably his best-known New Jersey work is the Washington Monument in Morristown.

More advanced tendencies in early twentieth-century sculpture did not follow either the style of vigorous realism or the tendencies toward abstraction which characterized avant-garde painting of the time. In sculpture, rather, a somewhat decorative and stylized approach appeared, particularly in the art of Paul Manship, dependent upon a svelte linearism and a suggestion of movement and flow. A later artist in New Jersey to be affected by this style was Waylande Gregory (1905-), who settled in the State in 1932 and lives in Bound Brook; he was born, grew up, and studied in Kansas. Much of his earlier sculpture was done in ceramic. During the Federal Art Project, Gregory was Director for Sculpture, and he designed in terra cotta the colossal fountain for Roosevelt Park, choosing as his theme "Light Destroying Darkness," appropriate for a sculpture so close to Edison's Menlo Park. Later works by Gregory include the four giant statues depicting the elements for the Fountain of the Atom at the 1939 New York World's Fair, the 90-foot-long ceramic wall of the Municipal Center in Washington, and a series of portraits of Hungarian Freedom Fighters.

IX

NEW JERSEY PAINTING AND SCULPTURE TODAY

THE CONCLUDING CHAPTER of this book by necessity must be a short one, amounting to a résumé of what seems at the moment to be the most significant work being done by New Jersey painters and sculptors. For one thing, the sheer productivity is on so great a scale, even in this relatively small state, that an attempt to analyze it completely and to cover the artists of national, regional, and local significance, would require a volume as large as the present one, just to set forth the details of the major work of the last thirty years. Secondly, a book such as this is concerned primarily with trying to unravel the confusion that is apparent at a given moment, and to create order out of seeming chaos, the better to present to the reader a comprehensible sequence of events. That could only be very imperfectly done at present, without the advantage of historical perspective, not only in evaluating the merits of the various artists at work in the State today, but also in relating New Jersey painters and sculptors to what will in the future emerge as the most significant esthetic trends of the present in American, and indeed international, art.

On one factor, however, all would agree now: the great blossoming of interest in the creative arts which has affected the country as a whole and the State of New Jersey no less than any other area. It has led to the emergence of thousands of artists in the State today, some on a sound professional basis, others on a semi-professional, amateur, and even beginning basis. It has led to the existence in the State of commercial galleries, some of which seem to promise longevity, others which have lasted only a few years. Another factor has been the creation of art centers in different regions throughout the State. In most of these, both the commercial galleries and the art centers, work by New Jersey artists appears to constitute the bulk of the material exhibited.

Another factor in the cultivation of art in the State has been the activities of the various educational institutions, where the interest in the fine arts has vastly increased in recent years. In many of these, important creative artists from outside the State have taught classes in painting and sculpture, exerting their influence upon students here and also becoming part of the esthetic growth of New Jersey for at least a short time. Among the leading American artists who have acted in this capacity are the sculptors, Richard Lippold (1915-) and Joseph Konzal (1905-), the former as head of the Art Department of Trenton Junior College from 1945 to 1952 and the latter at the Newark School of Fine and Industrial Art. That Newark institution has brought over numerous excellent contemporary painters who have provided further stimulus for the students of that institution, such as Angelo Ippolito 1922-). Princeton University, too, with its artist-in-residence series, has provided the services of such outstanding painters as Stephen Greene (1918-) and Hyde Solomon (1911-). In Madison, the art departments of Drew University under Elizabeth Korn, and Fairleigh Dickinson University under Tosun Bayrak (1926-), both of whom are themselves very talented artists, have stimulated art education greatly and Fairleigh Dickinson has also, through its summer "International Artists' Seminars," brought new talent from all over the world to the area.

The museums of the State, particularly those in Newark and Montclair, continue to do great service to the contemporary artists through their State exhibitions, and this has been emulated by such organizations as Bamberger's Department Store in Newark which holds an annual exhibition of work by New Jersey artists. From all of these, too, works of art are purchased. No major private collector seems yet to be specializing in work by artists of the State, but this may only be a matter of time.

As to contemporary art in New Jersey, the approaches which the leading artists of the State have taken are as diverse as the forms of art which exist throughout the Nation. In other words, more than ever before, New Jersey art can be said to mirror the state of art in the country as a whole, with special emphasis existing in certain areas which might be regarded as of more peculiarly New Jersey interest and contribution.

One movement in American art of particular force in the 1930's was social realism, a form of expressionism in which emphasis was placed upon the relationship of man to man, which revealed oppression, injustice, and strife, and which dealt with such themes as war, labor, and political corruption. It was an art form which bore some similarities to the realism of the very early 1900's, but which was stimulated by the Depression at home and political and social events abroad. The American artist who has been the most consistent investigator of this approach and concern in painting and who has brought to it the widest vision, is the dean of New Jersey artists, Ben Shahn (1898-   ) of Roosevelt. He has dealt with subject matter ranging from the ordeal of Sacco and Vanzetti to children playing among war ruins, always with a lyrical humanism. His first completed mural was a single-wall fresco in the community center of New Jersey Homesteads (Roosevelt) where Shahn lives. Mural work and easel painting as well as printmaking have all involved Shahn, and his artistic interest has been shared by his wife and children. There is actually a coterie of expressionist artists in Roosevelt, which in-

Ben Shahn, "Bartolomeo Vanzetti and Nicola Sacco," 1931-1932
Collection, The Museum of Modern Art, New York
Gift of Abby Aldrich Rockefeller

cludes Gregorio Prestopino (1907-) and Jacob Landau (1917-), whose work has savage, surreal overtones.

Other artistic styles are equally well represented in New Jersey. Henry T. Gulick (1871-1964) of Middletown is one of the most revered of New Jersey painters and is the State's leading self-taught or "primitive" painter, drawing his brightly painted scenes from in and around his country home and farm. Among the realist painters in New Jersey today there are many of great competence, as might be expected in a state which has, for quite a while, responded to an esthetic deriving inspiration directly from its natural beauty. Here, Maxwell Stuart Simpson (1896-), born in Elizabeth and living today in Scotch Plains, is highly proficient in figure, and perhaps even more, in landscape painting. A poet of the urban scene, particularly in a transcription of the older architecture of Newark, is Adolf Konrad (1915-), once a resident of that city and now enjoying rural life in Flanders. One of the strongest realist strains has emanated from the Newark School of Fine and Industrial Arts—from Charles Goeller, previously discussed, and at present from German-born Hans Weingartner (1896-) of Lyndhurst and Belleville and from his most talented young disciple, Leo Dee (1931-), both instructors at the School. Indeed, Weingartner and Dee have both created figure paintings and still lifes in a style of great technical virtuosity, a kind of magic realism which goes beyond the approach of the *trompe-l'oeil* painters of the late nineteenth century and the work of the Precisionists. Another extremely talented former student of the school, who paints in a hyper-realistic style, is Weehawken's Werner Groshans (1913-).

Nor has Surrealism lacked its exponents among contemporary New Jersey artists. Among the long-established painters to work in a style featuring an emphasis upon fantastic forms often drawn from the dream world and the unconscious is Leon Kelly (1901-) of Harvey Cedars. Edward John Stevens, Jr. (1923-) was born in Jersey City where he lives today, and has been the Director of the Newark School of Fine and Industrial Arts since 1959; he had been an instructor since 1947. Stevens' work, often painted in gouache, consists of highly fanciful, often amazingly decorative and exotic compositions with expressionist, primitive, and surreal overtones. Maynard Sandol (1930-) creates large imaginative compositions, both figural and landscape, which sometimes have topical connotations but which often draw for their inspiration upon past masters of fantasy—Goya, Turner, Ryder, and Redon. Finally, one of the newest and finest surreal artists to appear on the scene is Manuel Ayaso (1934-) of Newark, in whose paintings and drawings there is a savage fierceness combined with a haunting melancholy which has been likened to the work of Goya.

A number of leading New Jersey artists have worked in a style which can be considered semi- and near-abstract. This was true of the one-time Midwest regional

Adolf Konrad, "End of Day," 1952
Collection of The Newark Museum

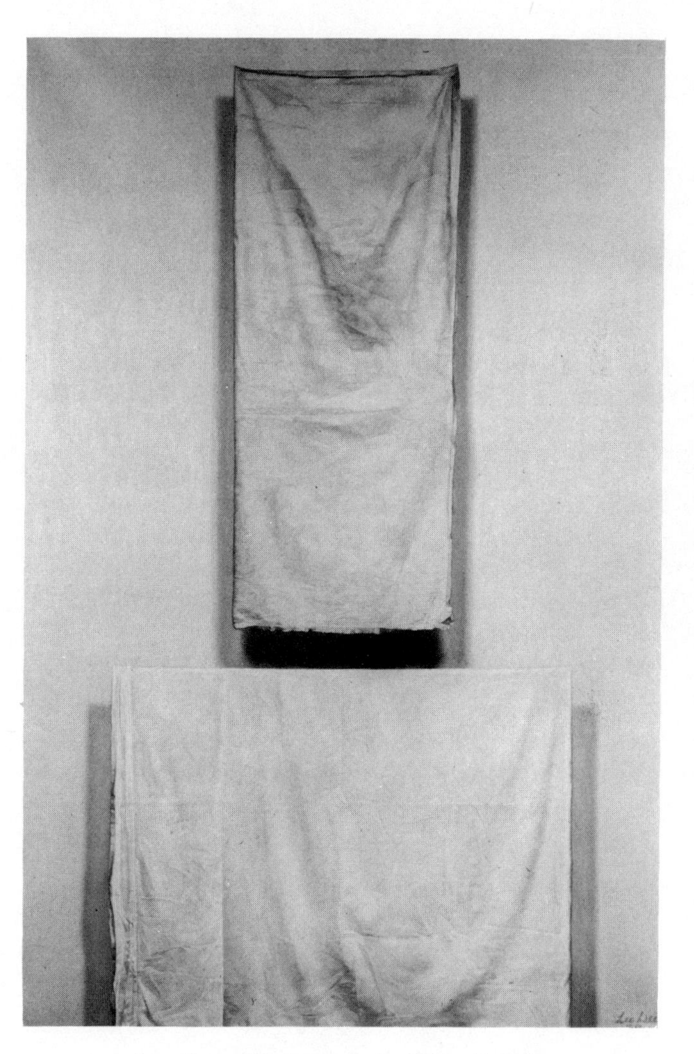

Leo Dee, "Reflections in White," 1959
Collection of The Newark Museum

Lee Gatch, "High Tension Tower," 1945
Collection of the Munson-Williams-Proctor Institute, Utica

artist, Joe Jones (1909-1963), who lived in Morris Township for his last twenty-two years From 1948 on, Jones favored subject matter drawn from the beaches and harbors of New Jersey and Bermuda, with forms and colors radically simplified, and large fields of subtly graded tones interrupted by sharp staccato-like linear accents of ships and other elements. Among other major commissions, Jones did murals of New York harbor scenes for the American Export Line's Mediterranean passenger vessels.

One of New Jersey's most noted artists is Lee Gatch (1902-), who has lived in "Coon Path," his Lambertville home, for many years. Gatch had studied in America with Leon Kroll and John Sloan, and in Paris with the Cubist, André Lhôte, but it was only on his return that the artist began to evolve the unique style which was to bring him fame. Very contemporary in its concern with and recognition of the two-dimensional surface of the canvas, and involving interesting juxtapositions of thinly-painted planes contrasted with rich strokes of the brush and, later, the palette knife, Gatch's work nevertheless does not conceal his love of nature, and subject matter is emphasized rather than suppressed in his work. There is a lightheartedness, a poetry, and a wit in his painting which makes it unique in American art, though it shows some similarity to the work of the very individual Swiss artist, Paul Klee. Gatch's use of ideographs as well as his tendency toward a created inner enframement in his paintings relate in some ways to the work of John Marin, but for Gatch the ideographs become symbols of somewhat visionary significance, and the shapes and forms in his paintings function also as carefully constructed abstract designs. In his recent work the artist has developed a unique form of collage, utilizing different stones cut extremely thin and interrelated with areas of canvas, in extremely subtle low-keyed tonalities. In all of his work, oil paintings and collages alike, the suggestions of derivations from nature abound, and much of his work constitutes a modern transcription of the rural setting of his home.

Burgoyne Diller, "Construction #16," 1938
Collection of The Newark Museum

A third figure of national and international reputation living in New Jersey is Burgoyne Diller (1906-   ) of Atlantic Highlands. Diller is one of the leading geometric abstractionists in the country and, beginning in 1934, was the first American artist to work in pure horizontal-vertical relationships in a mode ultimately begun by the great Dutch artist, Piet Mondrian. Diller has created exquisitely pure paintings, sculptures, and constructions. A different direction in the exploration of spatial, dynamic, and psychological meanings of interrelated abstract geometric forms was taken by the team of Marshall Simpson (1900-1958) of Middletown and his pupil, Roslynn Middleman of Plainfield (1929-   ), who worked together.

The major esthetic movement to evolve after World War II in America was "Action" painting, or "Abstract Expressionism," but strangely enough, New Jersey had few artists working in this vital, sometimes explosive vein of painting. One of the finest of the Abstract Expressionist artists to live in New Jersey for some time was Julius Hatofsky (1922-   ) of Hoboken. Grace Hartigan (1922-   ) is a major artist of the movement who was born in Newark, grew up in Millburn, and worked as a mechanical draftsman in Newark and Bloomfield before moving to New York City in 1947. What New Jersey did produce, however, in which it can take great pride, is a group of abstract and near-abstract painters who studied and worked together, emanating from the Newark School of Fine and Industrial Arts and Newark State Teachers' College, who evolved a very distinct abstract style. This group, Carmen Cicero (1926-   ), George Mueller (1929-   ), Frank Roth (1936-   ), Maynard Sandol (1930-   ), and Seymour Shapiro 1927-   ), created an abstract form of great subtlety, with a restrained surface appearance, muted tonalities, and soft floating forms. Their work differed among the different artists of the group, somewhat classical in the case of Mueller, more dynamic in the work of Shapiro and Roth, and suggesting aspects of representational form

Seymour Shapiro, "W. C. W.," 1960
Collection of The Newark Museum

in the painting of Cicero and Sandol. Some of the painters have moved away from abstraction now, toward equally imaginative and daring explorations of reality, but all made an important contribution to the story of New Jersey art and, indeed, to American art. All except Roth continue to live in New Jersey—Mueller and Sandol in Long Valley, Cicero in Englewood, and Shapiro in Rutherford. Another abstract painter of national reputation, again working along very individual lines, is the Canadian-born William Ronald (1926-), now living in Princeton.

These artists have all worked in oil for the most part, but New Jersey artists have contributed to the development of other media, too. One of America's finest artists in collage was Anne Ryan (1889-1954), who found inspiration for her delicate and refined abstractions in paper and textile in the work of the great European collage maker, Kurt Schwitters. New Jersey artists have shown a strong penchant for the watercolor medium, as a geographic analysis of the painters in that medium in such annual shows as those of the National Academy of Design would show. The New Jersey Watercolor Society has furthered this interest. Among the outstanding watercolorists in the State one might note particularly Henry Gasser (1909-), who was born in Newark, studied under John Grabach at the Newark School of Fine and Industrial Arts, and was director of that institution between 1946 and 1955. Gasser lives in South Orange.

While New Jersey has never been a sculptor's state, there are a number of distinguished artists working in wood, metal, stone, and plaster who live in New Jersey and have gained national acclaim. One of the best known is Dorothea Greenbaum (1893-) of Princeton, who has produced many poetic figures in both stone and metal, and is particularly renowned for her distinctive work in hammered lead. James Kearns (1924-) of Dover is a sculptor and painter who has produced profoundly moving images in an expressionist vein. Jason Seley (1919-), who has a summer studio in Long Valley, worked earlier in a radically simplified figurative style and has lately produced glistening abstract works fashioned from automobile bumpers and other mechanical parts. One of the best known of the younger sculptors or creators of "assemblages" in the State is Lucas Samaras (1936-) of West New York, who has created fascinating and complex objects within a new art form.

Dorothea Greenbaum, "Bathsheba"
Collection of The Newark Museum

James Kearns, "Seated Model"
Collection of The Newark Museum

At this writing the newest artist of importance to enter the range of New Jersey sculptors is Sahl Swarz (1912-), who has moved to Cliffside Park, where John Marin had spent so many years. Swarz has created impressive, somewhat totemic figures of bronze, sometimes in open linear mesh, sometimes with the addition of mosaic.

Abstract art is still today a foremost aspect of American painting and sculpture but in the past four or five years new movements have evolved which have engendered great excitement and enthusiasm among artists and collectors alike. One aspect of contemporary art has been a new concern with the figure, re-investigated in terms of the contributions of abstract art; this has been one interest of Henry Niese (1924-), who lived in Hackettstown for many years.

The newest of all the significant artistic movements at the time of this writing is "Pop" Art, the investigation and presentation of the more crass, commercial, and mediocre aspects of American culture, from comic strip to advertisement, which are used as the raw material for a new art form, totally distinct from abstraction, non-expressive technically, and totally recognizable. A number of artists, among the leaders of the "Pop" Art group are in New Jersey, thanks to the activity of Douglass College and Rutgers University in New Brunswick which have championed an advanced point of view in the teaching of the creative arts. Associated with Rutgers for a number of years was Allan Kaprow (1927-), best-known for his creation of "happenings," events of a theatrical nature involving exciting visual and aural manifestations with audience participation. On the Douglass faculty at present are Roy Lichtenstein (1923-), whose comic-strip enlargements constitute one of the best-known "Pop" Art forms, and Robert M. Watts (1923-), who has offered sleek, automobile dashboard constructions. Nearby, in Metuchen, is George Brecht (1926-), who creates boxes filled with fascinating assortments of oddly juxtaposed everyday objects. Per-

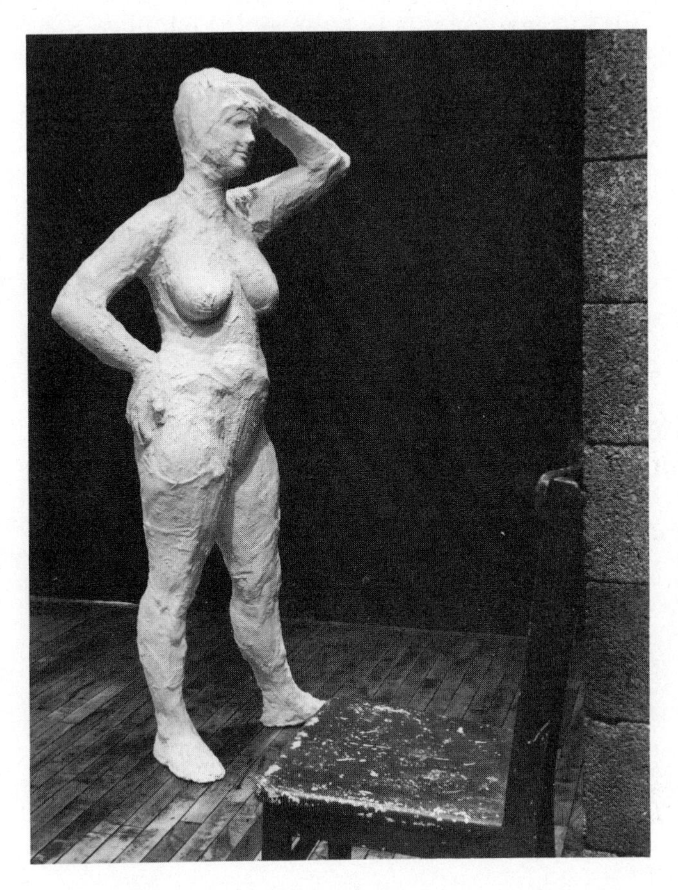

George Segal, "Model in the Studio," 1963
Collection of the Abrams Family, New York City

haps the best-known of all the artists in New Jersey allied with this movement is George Segal (1924-   ), whose plaster "Everyman" images suggest instant identification to a powerful and disturbing degree.

These, then, are some of the outstanding artists in the State. The State continues, too, to attract visitors to paint here, and one might mention Walter Stuempfig (1914-   ) and Hobson Pittman (1900-   ), to name just two artists from the Philadelphia area who continue the long-established practice of visiting the Jersey shore.

One might then suggest that New Jersey art life proceeds even more vigorously than ever before, yet following the traditions that have existed over many, many years. It presents a record perhaps too little known, one which should inspire pride among the residents of the State, and a record which testifies to a cultural heritage of significance and strength.

BIBLIOGRAPHICAL NOTE

As stated in the text, there is no general volume on the history of painting and sculpture in New Jersey. Most useful for even a brief survey of these developments would be the catalogues of a number of exhibitions which have attempted to cover the subject. These include *Early New Jersey Artists, 18th and 19th Centuries,* The Newark Museum, March 7th-May 19th, 1957; *Art in New Jersey from 1776 to 1876,* Montclair Art Museum, January 1-28, 1945; and *New Jersey Art in Retrospect,* The New Jersey State Museum, February 12-June 18, 1961. There is also material published in William H. Gerdts, "People and Places of New Jersey," *The Museum,* XV, Numbers 2 and 3—New Series, Spring-Summer, 1963. The Newark Museum maintains a file on early artists of the State in which information gleaned from individuals, from analysis of old newspapers, exhibition catalogues, city directories, and diverse other sources is recorded. Other depositories of material on New Jersey artists include The New Jersey Historical Society, the Newark Public Library, the Trenton Public Library and the libraries at Rutgers and Princeton Universities.

On developments in American painting and sculpture in general, see Louisa Dresser (ed.), *XVIIth Century Painting in New England . . .* (Worcester, Mass., 1935); Edgar P. Richardson, *Painting in America, the Story of 450 Years* (New York, 1956); and Virgil Barker, *American Painting, History and Interpretation* (New York, 1950).

In addition, there are the three standard pioneering works in the field: William Dunlap, *History of the Rise and Progress of the Arts of Design in the United States* (New York, 1834); Henry T. Tuckerman, *Book of the Artists* (New York, 1867); and Samuel Isham, *The History of American Painting* (New York, 1905), each especially valuable for the period immediately preceding publication. Invaluable, too, for artists active before 1860 is George C. Groce and David H. Wallace, *The New-York Historical Society's Dictionary of Artists in America 1564-1860* (New Haven, 1957). For later artists see volumes of the *American Art Annual,* especially the obituaries. On the career of John Watson, see Theodore Bolton, "John Watson of Perth Amboy, Artist," *Proceedings of The New Jersey Historical Society,* LXXII, 233-247. See also two articles by John Hill Morgan, "John Watson Painter, Merchant and Capitalist of New Jersey, 1685-1768" and "Further Notes on John Watson," both in the *Proceedings of the American Antiquarian Society,* October, 1940, and April, 1942, respectively.

On Patience Wright, see Everett Parker Lesley, "Patience Lovell Wright, America's First Sculptor," *Art in America,* XXIV, 148-154, 157; and Ethel Stanwood Bolton, *American Wax Portraits* (Boston, 1929). Mr. John C. Long of Princeton is presently working on the life and art of Patience Wright.

On Francis Hopkinson, see the article concerning him in the *Dictionary of American Biography.* Numerous works by New Jersey artists are listed in the following cumulative exhibition records: Mary Bartlett Cowdrey, *American Academy of Fine Arts and American Art-Union*

(New York, 1953); Mary Barlett Cowdrey, *National Academy of Design Exhibition Record, 1826-1860* (New York, 1943); and Anna Wells Rutledge, *Cumulative Record of Exhibition Catalogues, The Pennsylvania Academy of the Fine Arts, 1807-1870, the Society of Artists, 1800-1814, the Artists' Fund Society, 1835-1845,* in *American Philosophical Society Memoirs,* XXXVIII (1955).

PORTRAITURE: THREE GENERATIONS

For early portraiture, in addition to the general works mentioned above, see Alan Burroughs, *Limners and Likenesses; Three Centuries of American Painting* (Cambridge, 1936); and Charles Coleman Sellers, *Charles Willson Peale* (Philadelphia, 1947). For material on Joseph Wright and his mother, Patience Wright, see Sidney Fiske Kimball, "Joseph Wright and His Portraits of Washington," *Antiques,* XV, 376-382; XVII, 35-39. Edward Savage's career is discussed in Louisa Dresser, "Edward Savage 1761-1817," *Art In America,* XL, 157-212. The best discussion of Gilbert Stuart's career can be found in William T. Whitley, *Gilbert Stuart* (Cambridge, 1932); in Lawrence Park, *Gilbert Stuart, an Illustrated Descriptive List of His Works . . .* (New York, 1926); and particularly in Charles M. Mount, *Gilbert Stuart, A Biography* (New York, 1964).

For the Empire Period see the exhibition catalogue, *Classical America, 1845-1845,* The Newark Museum, 1963. On the life and art of William Dunlap, see the two works by this artist-writer, *Diary of William Dunlap (1766-1839) . . . ,* edited by Dorothy C. Barck (New York, 1930), and his *History of the Rise and Progress of the Arts of Design in the United States* (New York, 1834), as well as Oral Sumner Coad's *William Dunlap, a Study of his Life and Works and of his Place in Contemporary Culture* (New York, 1917), and his forthcoming article on Dunlap in the *Proceedings of The New Jersey Historical Society.* On Henry Inman, see Theodore Bolton, "Henry

Inman" and "A Catalogue of the Paintings of Henry Inman," *The Art Quarterly,* III, 353-375, and 401-418. Inman in New Jersey is treated by William H. Gerdts, "Henry Inman in New Jersey," *Proceedings of The New Jersey Historical Society,* LXXVIII, 178-187. For the Rankin family portraits and for Oliver Tarbell Eddy in general, see Edith Bishop, "New Portraits by Rembrandt Peale and Oliver Tarbell Eddy," *The Museum,* I, No. 4, new series, and the same author's catalogue, *Oliver Tarbell Eddy 1799-1868,* The Newark Museum, 1950. Information concerning Jefferson Gauntt came from the artist's descendant, Edwin A. Gauntt of Jobstown. George Durrie is discussed by Mary Bartlett Cowdrey in the exhibition catalogue, *George Henry Durrie, 1820-1863, Connecticut Painter of American Life,* Hartford, Wadsworth Atheneum, 1947. For Micah Williams, see the articles by Irwin F. Cortelou: "A Mysterious Pastellist Identified," *Antiques,* LXVI, 122-124; "Henry Conover: Sitter, Not Artist," *Antiques,* LXVI, 481; "Notes on Micah Williams, Native of New Jersey," *Antiques,* LXXIV, 540-541.

Charles Loring Elliott is discussed by Thomas Bangs Thorpe, "Reminiscences of Charles L. Elliott, Artist," *N. Y. Evening Post,* September 30, October 1, 1868; and by Theodore Bolton, "Charles Loring Elliott: An Account of his Life and Work," *Art Quarterly,* V, 59-96. George Gates Ross' activities are mentioned in numerous issues of the *Newark Daily Advertiser.* The information on Joseph Beitl is in the files of The Newark Museum, given at the time of the artist's presentation of one of his works. Douglas Volk and Frank Fowler are mentioned in S. C. G. Watkins, *Reminiscences of Montclair* (New York, 1929), and Elizabeth Stow Brown, *The History of Nutley, Essex County, New Jersey* (Nutley, 1907).

LANDSCAPE PAINTING BEFORE THE CIVIL WAR

For landscape painting in general, see Frederick A. Sweet, *The Hudson River School and the Early American Landscape Tradition,* catalogue of an exhibition at the Art Institute of Chicago and Whitney Museum of American Art, New York, 1945. On early paintings of Passaic Falls, see Harold J. Dahl and George Connor, "The Falls of the Passaic," *Antiques,* LXXIV, 326-328. For Thomas Whitley and his relationship to the Art-Unions, see E. Maurice Bloch, "The American Art-Union's Downfall," *New-York Historical Society Quarterly,* XXXVII, 331-359. For Joshua Shaw, see the *Bordentown Register,* November 29, 1956. The standard work on Asher B. Durand is still John Durand, *The Life and Times of A. B. Durand* (New York, 1894). Information on Elias Durand came from his granddaughter, Mrs. Walter Gray of Irvington, New Jersey. Jacob Caleb Ward is discussed by Joseph F. Folsom, "Jacob C. Ward, One of the Old-Time Landscape Painters," *Proceedings of The New Jersey Historical Society,* III, new series, 89-93. Information on the activity of William Mason Brown in Newark came from the *Newark Daily Advertiser* for August 16, 17, and 18, 1852. Rutgers University Library has information on John Jesse Barker. For Edward Kranich, see William H. Gerdts, "Edward Kranich, 1826-1891," in *Proceedings of The New Jersey Historical Society,* LXXIX, 16-20. Information on Jasper Cropsey was made available by William Steinschneider, Hastings-on-Hudson. The standard work on Martin Johnson Heade is Robert G. McIntyre, *Martin Johnson Heade 1819-1904* (New York, 1948).

NEWARK AT MID-CENTURY

Information on artistic activities in Newark in the 1840's and 1850's can be found in the daily editions of the *Newark Daily Advertiser,* which made frequent mention of art exhibitions, the showing of panoramas, and ran occasional notes on local artists and art activities. In this newspaper there was also frequent discussion of the proposals, plans, and operations of the New Jersey Art-Union. On the Art-Unions in general, see Mary Bartlett Cowdrey, *American Academy of Fine Arts and American Art-Union* (New York, 1953). On Rembrandt Lockwood, see William H. Gerdts, "Rembrandt Lockwood, an Artist of Newark," *Proceedings of The New Jersey Historical Society*, LXXVI, 265-279.

OTHER THEMES IN THE NINETEENTH CENTURY

For still-life painting in general, see Wolfgang Born, *Still-Life Painting in America* (New York, 1947), and William H. Gerdts, *Nature's Bounty and Man's Delight, American 19th Century Still Life Painting,* exhibition catalogue of the Newark Museum, 1958. Information on Susan Waters was supplied by Mrs. Florence Magee of the *Bordentown Register.* On late nineteenth-century still-life painting in general, and on John Frederick Peto, see Alfred Frankenstein, *After the Hunt* (Berkeley and Los Angeles, 1953), and the catalogue of the John Frederick Peto Exhibition, Smith College Art Gallery, 1950.

On the various painters of birds and animals, Alexander Wilson is mentioned in Joseph F. Folsom, *Bloomfield, Old and New* (Bloomfield, 1912), and the work of John James Audubon in New Jersey can be found in Maria Rebecca Audubon, *Audubon and His Journals . . .* (New York, 1897). Information on William D. Travis was found in N. R. Ewan's "William D. T. Travis, Burlington's Forgotten Artist," *The Burlington Press,* October, 1945.

William Ranney's life and art are discussed in Francis S. Grubar, *William Ranney, Painter of the Early West* (Washington, D. C., 1962). For Lilly Martin Spencer, see Ann Byrd Schumer, "Aspects of Lilly Martin Spencer's Career in Newark, New Jersey," *Proceedings of The New*

Jersey Historical Society, LXXVII, 244-255. On E. L. Henry, there is Elizabeth McCausland's *The Life and Work of Edward Lamson Henry . . .* (Albany, 1945). Robert Weir and his New Jersey stay are discussed by Irene Weir, *Robert W. Weir, Artist* (New York, 1947). The definitive book on William Page is Joshua C. Taylor, *William Page, The American Titian* (Chicago, 1957). For Frank Paul Sauerwein, see Van Deren Coke, *Taos and Santa Fé* (Albuquerque, 1963) and an unpublished thesis on the artist by Elaine Maher Harrison (West Texas State College, 1958). Information on Thomas Buchanan Read was provided the author by Orson Brown of Bordentown.

LANDSCAPE AND SEASCAPE PAINTERS

The most useful works on George Inness' career are the following: George Inness, Jr., *Life, Art, and Letters of George Inness* (New York, 1917); Elizabeth McCausland, *George Inness, An American Landscape Painter, 1825-1894* (New York, 1946); and the catalogue of the show, *George Inness of Montclair,* The Montclair Art Museum, 1964. Information on Elisha W. Hall was supplied by his descendant, Woodruff English of Summit. Many of the lesser but capable landscapists of the period are mentioned in Helen L. Earle (comp.), *Biographical Sketches of American Artists* (Lansing, 1924). George Inness, Jr., Harry Fenn, and other artists of Montclair are mentioned in S. C. G. Watkins, *Reminiscences of Montclair* (New York, 1929). Information on Joseph Tubby was supplied by his daughter, Miss Gertrude Tubby of Montclair. For Andrew Melrose, see Walter T. Eickmann, *History of West New York, New Jersey* (West New York, 1948). Thomas Moran is discussed in William H. Gerdts, *Thomas Moran, 1837-1926,* catalogue of an exhibition at The Picture Gallery, University of California, Riverside, 1963. For (Thomas) Worthington Whittredge, see John I. H. Baur (ed.),

"The Autobiography of Worthington Whittredge, 1820-1910," *Brooklyn Museum Journal,* I, 5-68. Information on the Hartwick family can be found in Edythe Helen Browne, "A Master of Rival Accomplishments," *Art and Archaeology,* XXX, No. 6, 211-220. Ralph Blakelock's career in New Jersey is discussed in William H. Gerdts, "Ralph Albert Blakelock in New Jersey," *Proceedings of The New Jersey Historical Society,* LXXXII, 121-127. Louis Eilshemius is the subject of William Shack's *And He Sat Among the Ashes* (New York, 1939). Information on George Alfred Williams was generously given by Mrs. Donald Liddell. For Thomas Buttersworth, see Helen Comstock, "Marine Paintings by Two Buttersworths," *Antiques,* LXXXV, No. 1, 99-103. For Antonio Jacobsen, see "A. Jacobsen, 705 Palisade Ave. West Hoboken, N. J.," *The Bulletin Old Dartmouth Historical Society and Whaling Museum,* Winter, 1958, 3.

NINETEENTH-CENTURY SCULPTORS

For nineteenth-century sculpture in general, see Lorado Taft, *The History of American Sculpture* (New York, 1925), and William H. Gerdts, *A Survey of American Sculpture: Late 18th Century to 1962,* an exhibition at the Newark Museum, 1962. For John Frazee, see his autobiography at The New Jersey Historical Society, and excerpts from it in *American Collector,* XV, 15-16, and 12-13. A thesis on Frazee by Henry Bryan Caldwell is on file at New York University. For William John Coffee, there are two articles, George C. Groce, "William John Coffee, Long-lost Sculptor," *American Collector,* XV, 14-15, 19-20; and Anna Wells Rutledge, "William John Coffee as a Portrait Sculptor," *Gazette des Beaux-Arts,* XXVIII, 297-312. James Thom is mentioned in the *Bulletin* of the American Art-Union, May, 1850, 28. Thomas Dow Jones in Newark is mentioned in the *Newark Daily Advertiser,* October 2, 1850. The sculptors of Montclair are mentioned in S. C. G. Watkins, *Reminiscences of Montclair* (New York, 1929). The standard work on Thomas Ball is his autobiography, *My Threescore Years and Ten* (Boston, 1891), but this was written before the artist had settled in Montclair. Charles Schreyvogel is discussed in "Monograph Number Three" of *The Mentor Reading Course* (Springfield, Ohio, 1915). For Karl Bitter, see Ferdinand Schevill, *Karl Bitter* (Chicago, 1917).

THE EARLY TWENTIETH CENTURY

For the history of painting and sculpture in America of this period, the most useful books are Milton W. Brown, *American Painting from the Armory Show to the Depression* (Princeton, 1955); and John I. H. Baur, *Revolution and Tradition in Modern American Art* (Cambridge, Mass., 1951). Concerning art in New Jersey of the period, see Lolita L. W. Flockhart, *Art and Artists in New Jersey* (Somerville, 1938). On the Newark Museum, see *A Survey: 50 Years of The Newark Museum* (Newark, 1959); on the Montclair Art Museum, see *Forty Years of Collecting,* an exhibition at the Montclair Art Museum, 1953.

For Theodore Robinson, see John I. H. Baur, *Theodore Robinson 1852-1896* (Brooklyn, 1946). Stuart Davis' comments on Gar Sparks are recorded in the catalogue of the exhibition of the work of Gar Sparks, Julien Levy Galleries, New York City, 1946. For Davis himself, see Stuart Davis, *American Artists Group,* New York City, 1945, and James Johnson Sweeney, *Stuart Davis* (New York, 1945). On Reginald Marsh, see Lloyd Goodrich, *Regional Marsh,* Whitney Museum of American Art, New York City, 1955.

For George Overbury "Pop" Hart, see *"Pop" Hart 1868-1933,* an exhibition at the Newark Museum, 1935. Information on Walt Kuhn came from the artist's daughter, Miss Brenda Kuhn, as well as the catalogue, *Walt Kuhn 1877-1949,* Cincinnati Art Museum, Cincinnati, 1960. For the early artists at Ridgefield, see Man Ray, *Self Portrait* (Boston and Toronto, 1963). Robert Martin of Ridgefield and Mrs. Mildred Baker of the Newark Museum supplied the information about the various later artists who lived in Ridgefield. The literature on John Marin is quite extensive; the most useful publications, particularly for his life in New Jersey, are MacKinley Helm, *John Marin* (Boston, 1948); *John Marin, Watercolors, Oil Paintings, Etchings,* an exhibition at The Museum of Modern Art, New York City, 1936; and Charles E. Buckley, *John Marin in Retrospect. An Exhibition of His Oils and Watercolors,* at The Corcoran Gallery of Art, Washington, D. C., 1962, and The Currier Gallery of Art, Manchester, New Hampshire, 1962. Bernard Rabin and the late Nathan Krueger supplied the information on Charles "Gus" Mager.

For the "Immaculates" or "Precisionists," and Louis Lozowick in particular, see Martin L. Friedman, *The Precisionist View in American Art,* an exhibition at the Walker Art Center, Minneapolis, 1960. On Arshile Gorky, see Ethel Schwabacher, *Arshile Gorky,* an exhibition at the Whitney Museum of American Art, New York, 1951.

NEW JERSEY PAINTING AND SCULPTURE TODAY

On contemporary New Jersey painters and sculptors, see the catalogues of the triennial exhibitions, *Work by New Jersey Artists,* held at the Newark Museum, beginning in 1952, and those of the *Annual New Jersey State Exhibition* series at the Montclair Art Museum, beginning in 1931. For two of the leading contemporary New Jersey artists, see James Thrall Soby, *Ben Shahn* (West Drayton, Middlesex, England, 1947), and Perry T. Rathbone, *Lee Gatch,* The American Federation of Arts (New York, 1960). Other material relating to present-day New Jersey painters and sculptors can be found in the catalogues of their exhibitions published by the commercial art galleries in which they exhibit, and in the reviews of their exhibitions in such magazines as *Arts* and *Art News.*

INDEX

Titles of works of art are in italics.

Titles of books are in quotation marks.

Adams, John, 10
Adams, Woodhull, 196
Albig, Fred, restaurant, 215, 224
Alexander, Cosmo, 12
Alexander, John W., 162
Alexis, Grand Duke of Russia, 136
Allston, Washington, 131, 139
Altenburg, Alexander, 222
Altman, Benjamin, 151
Amati, Nicolo, 177
American Art-Union, 53-55, 84, 86, 91
Ames, Ezra, 20
Annandale, 227
Arensberg, Walter, 218
Art Institute of Chicago, 172
Art-Union, 53-55, 84-92, 120
Asbury Park, 172
Asssmann, Franz, 167
Atlantic City, 172, 173, 179
Atlantic Highlands, 154, 245
Audubon, John James, 117-118
Ayaso, Manuel, 239

Babbage, family, 168
Baithe, Cora Rebecca, 167
Baldwin, Isaac, 61
Baldwin, Ward, 181
Ball, Caroline Peddle, 191
Ball, Thomas, 190-191
Emancipation Group, 190; *George Washington,* 190; *Daniel Webster,* 190
Bamberger, Louis, 198
Barker, John Jesse, 67-69, 88, 89, 144
Chetwood family portraits, 69; *De Hart family* portraits, 69; *East Entrance to Rahway, New Jersey,* 69 illus. 68; *Woodruff family* portraits, 69
Barlow, Joel, 10
Barnwell, G. (artist), 88
Basking Ridge, 67
Bay Head, 119
Bayrak, Tosun, 236
Beale, G. D., 82
Panorama of California, 82; *Panorama and Diorama of the Creation and the Deluge,* 82
Beard, James, 117, 125
Beard, William, 117
Beckwith, J. Carroll, 165
Beers, Julie Hart, 71
Beitl, Joseph G., 48
Bell, Clarke, 150
Belleville, 66, 239
Bellows, George, 205, 224
Belly, Léon, 150
Bennett, Ernest H., 168
Bennett, William James, 61
Weehawken, 61
Benton, Thomas Hart, 225
Berchem, Nicholas, 57, 59
Bergen County, 56
Bergen Hill, 36
Beverly, 57

Beyer, Edward, 75, 80
Skating on the Passaic, 75
Bierstadt, Albert, 123, 153, 157, 166
Bingham, George Caleb, 123
Birch, Thomas, 56-57
Birch, William, 36
Bitter, Karl, 194-195
John Fairfield Dryden, 195; Prehn mausoleum, 194, 195; Jacob H. Schiff fountain, 194; *Carl Schurz Memorial,* 194
Blashfield, Edwin, 198
Blakelock, George, 167
Blakelock, Ralph, 166, 168
Blakelock, Ralph Albert, 165-170, 198
Alfred George and Ernest F. Bennett, 168: *The Artist's Garden, East Orange, New Jersey,* 168; *Grace E. Washburn in Her Garden,* 168; *illus.* 169; *Moon Rise, Androscoggin River,* 167; *South Orange,* 168
Bloomfield, 61, 66, 117, 156, 245
Bloomsdale, 36
Blythe, Benjamin, 12
Blythe, David, 123
Bodmer, Karl, 56
Boggs, R. (artist), 89
Bonaparte, Charlotte Julie, 55-56
Cora Monges, 56; *Passaic Falls,* 55-56
Bonaparte, Joseph, 56
Bonfield, George R., 57
Bonnat, Léon, 154
Bordentown, 8-9, 12, 14-15, 17-18, 20, 47, 56, 57-59, 67, 109, 111, 131, 139, 175, 180
Borglum, Gutzon, 233
Abraham Lincoln, 233; *The Wars of America,* 233
Boss, Homer, 218
Boston Athenaeum, 184
Bosworth, Sala, 125
Boucher, François, 59
Bound Brook, 234
Boutelle, De Witt Clinton, 67
The Voyage of Life (with Thomas Cole), 67; *Winter on the Passaic,* 67
Boyle, Ferdinand Thomas Lee, 29
Ford family portraits, 29
Brecht, George, 250
Brevoort, James Renwick, 166
Brielle, 199
Bristol, John Bunyan, 73-75
Brown, John George, 136, 138
Brown, Mary Ann, 67
Brown, William G., 67
Brown, William Mason, 44, 66-67, 80, 83, 90, 105, 107
English Coast Scene, 67
Browne, Mathilda, 111
Brundage, Frances, 102
Bryant, William Cullen, 53, 61, 65
Bull, Ole, 177
Burlington, 12, 14, 17, 20, 25, 26-27, 36, 57, 59, 118
Burns, Robert, 187
Buttersworth, James E., 175-178
New York Harbor Scene, illus. 178
Buttersworth, Thomas, 175

Caldwell, 204-205
Califano, John, 115
Camden, 115, 118
Canova, Antonio, 185
Carmiencke, Johann Hermann, 150
Carter, Dennis Malone, 90
Casilear, John William, 63
Catlin, George, 123, 129
Cézanne, Paul, 219, 224
Chagaray, Eloise, 29
Chalfant, Jefferson David, 113
Chapin, James, 227
Glen Ridge Post Office murals, 227; *Katherine Hepburn,* 227; *Aline MacMahon,* 227
Chapman, Cyrus Durand, 137
Chappel, Alonzo, 90
Chase, Harry, 177
Chase, William Merritt, 137, 163, 199, 200, 209
Chatham, 172
Chicago Art-Union, 85
Childs, Cophas, 23-24, 26
Childs & Inman, 23
Church, Frederic, 153, 166
Cicero, Carmen, 245-246

Cikovsky, Nicholai, 224
Cimiotti, Gustave, Jr., 227
Clarke, Thomas B., 151
Cliffside Park, 221-222, 250
Coffee, William John, 185-187
Jefferson family portraits, 185; *Bust of a Man,* 186-187; illus. 186
Cole, Thomas, 50, 65, 66, 67, 73, 89, 144, 150
Coleman, Glenn O., 205-208
Coles, Abraham, 87, 90, 92
Coles, J. Ackerman, 198
Collins family (Morristown), 69
Colman, Samuel, 150
Colton, G. Q., 81
Conarroe, George, 20
Anne L. Hubbell, 20
"Conover, Henry," 40
Constable, John, 145
Constant, Benjamin, 137
Convent Station, 29, 109
Cook, Edith, 71
Cooley, J. P., 72
Cooper, James Fenimore, 19
Copley, John Singleton, 12, 13, 14, 94, 104
Cornelius, Peter von, 94, 99
Corot, Jean Baptiste Camille, 77, 145, 151
Cosmopolitan Art Association, 85, 125
Couper, William, 191
John A. Roebling, 191
Coypel, Noël-Nicolas, 56
Coytesville, 212
Craig, Thomas Bigelow, 155
Cranch, Christopher Pearse, 42, 63
Crane, Bruce, 154, 156-157, 197
Crawford, Will, 223
Crawley, John, 16
Cropsey, Jasper, 71-74, 75, 88, 89, 90, 91, 122
Autumn on the Hudson River, 73; *The Good Shepherd,* 72; *Greenwood Lake,* 72; illus. 74; *Janetta Falls, Passaic Co.,* 72; *Lake WaWayanda,* 72; *Passaic River,* 72
Culverhouse, Johannes, 90, 91
Cummings, Thomas Augustus, 86
Cummings, Thomas Seir, 84
Currey, Annie Louise, 219
Currier & Ives, 175
Curry, John Steuart, 225
Curtis, George William, 42
Curtis, William J., 162

Dana, John Cotton, 196-197
Danckaerts, Jasper, 51
Passaic Falls, 51
Da Salo, Gasparo, 177
Dassel, H. (artist), 89
Daubigny, Charles François, 145
Daumier, Honoré, 211
Davies, Arthur B., 170, 171
Davis, Stuart, 205-208, 225
Hoboken, illus. 207
Deane, George Hobart, 27, 137
Deane, George Washington, 26-27, 59
Deane, William Croswell, 27
Dee, Leo, 239-241
Reflections in White, illus. 241
Delaunay, Robert, 216
Dell, Floyd, 218
De Loutherbourg, Philippe-Jacques, 57, 59
Dennis, Martin R., 87
Depew, Chauncey, 150
De Rivera, José Ruíz, 231-233
Flight, 231-233; illus. 232
Dickens, Charles, 171
Dickeson, Montroville, 83
Dielman, Frederick, 162
Diller, Burgoyne, 244-245
Construction #16, illus. 244
Dolph, John Henry, 117
Doughty, Thomas, 50
Douglass College, 250
Dove, Arthur, 200
Dover, 247
Drake (artist), 90
Drew University, 236
Driggs, Elsie, 230
Du Bois, Guy Pène, 209-211, 224
Duchamp, Marcel, 218
Duffey, Mrs. E. B., 108-110
Lillies, illus. 110; *October,* 109
Dummer, George, 36
Duncan, Charles, 218
Dunlap, William, 2-3, 20-22, 38, 57, 146
The Dunlap Family, 21; *Self-*

Portrait, 22; *George Washington,* 22; *"History . . . of the Arts of Design"* (book). 2, 20
Durand, Asher B., 27, 60-66, 67, 73, 89, 90, 91, 95, 120, 122, 144, 162
Ariadne (engraving), 61; *The Capture of Major André,* 61-63; *Declaration of Independence* (engraving), 60-61; *The Evening of Life,* 65; *Landscape,* illus. 64; *The Morning of Life,* 65; *Aaron Ogden,* 61; *Old Pat* (engraving), 60; *Primaeval Forest,* 63; *Portrait of Mrs. Durand and her Sister,* 63; illus. 62; *The Wrath of Peter Stuyvesant,* 63
Durand, Cyrus, 61
Durand, Elias Wade, 66
Durand, John, 60
Durrie, George Henry, 38-40
Conover family portraits, 40
Duveneck, Frank, 48, 199

Eagleswood, 134-136, 146-150, 153
Eakins, Thomas, 175, 198
Earl, Ralph, 14, 50
Earle, Lawrence C., 138
East Orange, 167-168, 206
Eastman, Max, 216
Eastman, Seth, 123
Eaton, Charles Warren, 156
Eddy, Ansel Doane, 35
Eddy, Oliver Tarbell, 32-35, 36, 38, 44
Alling Family portraits, 35; *Matthias Day,* 35; *Mrs. Matthias Day,* 35; *Reverend Ansel Doane Eddy,* 35; *David Hayes,* 35; *The Four Youngest Children of William Rankin and Abigail Ogden Rankin,* 33; illus. 34; *Phebe Ann Rankin,* 34-35; *William Rankin,* 32-33
Egan, John J., 82-83
Panorama of Ireland, 82; *Panorama of the Mississippi,* 83
Egner, Arthur, 198, 209-210
Eichholtz, Jacob, 20
Eilshemius, Louis, 170-171
Elizabeth, 32-33, 48, 69, 126, 157, 222, 230, 238
Elliott, Charles Loring, 42-44, 46, 53, 121, 122, 133
Mrs. Thomas Goulding, 44; illus. 43
Englewood, 233, 246
Enzing-Müller, Johannes Michael, 92-93, 100
Essex County, 66
Essex County Institute Fair, 83
Essig, George, 179
Evans, William T., 190, 197-198

Fagleswood, see Eagleswood
Fairleigh Dickinson University, Madison, 236
Fairview, 222
Falconer, John M., 65
Farndon, Walter, 218
Fawcett School; *see* Newark School of Fine and Industrial Arts
Fay, Gaston, 63
Federal Art Project, 230-233, 234
Feke, Robert, 13
Fenn, Harry, 154
Field, Hamilton Easter, 215
Fisher, Alvan, 50
Flanders, 238-239
Forain, Jean-Louis, 211
Forbes, Edwin, 138
Fort Lee, 200, 206, 211-215, 218, 224, 231
Foster, Gerald, 230
Foulke, Doctor, 104
Fowler, Frank, 48, 165, 208, 211, 231
Luxembourg Palace Frescoes, Paris, 48; Waldorf-Astoria ballroom Frescoes, 48; *William Dean Howells,* 48; *Helena Modjeska,* 48
Francis, John F., 105
Frankenstein, Godfrey, 83
Panorama of Niagara Falls, 83
Frankenstein, John, 128
Franklin, Benjamin, 9, 15
Franklin, William, Governor, 12
Frazee, John, 180-185
The Artist's Son, 182; *Basket of Grapes and Peaches,* 182;

Nathaniel Bowditch, 184; *John Jay,* 184; *Lafayette,* 182; *John Lowell,* 184; *John Marshall,* 184; *Thomas S. Perkins,* 184; *William Prescott,* 184; *Joseph Story,* 184; illus. 183; *Daniel Webster,* 184
Freehold, 38, 40, 230
French, Daniel Chester, 191, 195
Frerichs, William C. A., 177
Fuller, George, 165, 198

Gabo, Naum, 228
Gainsborough, Thomas, 19, 57
Gasser, Henry, 247
Gatch, Lee, 230, 242-243
High Tension Tower, illus. 242
Gaul, William Gilbert, 141
Gauntt, Jefferson, 38-39
Portrait of Uz Gauntt, 38-39
Gauntt, Uz, 38-39
Gérôme, Jean Louis, 165
Gifford, Sanford, 75
Gignoux, Regis, 88, 89, 90, 91, 144
Glackens, William, 224
Glen Ridge, 170, 227
Gleyre, Charles Gabriel, 129
Glintencamp, Henry, 205-206
Lackawanna Ferry Terminal, 206
Goddard, Ralph Bartlett, 191
Goeller, Charles, 228-230, 239
Goodell, Ira, 40
Gorky, Arshile, 231
Aviation: Evolution of Forms under Aerodynamic Limitations (mural, Newark Airport), 231; Murals, Ben Marden's Riviera night club, 231; Murals, New York World's Fair, 231
Goya y Lucientes, Francisco José de, 239
Grabach, John R., 211, 247
Grant, Ulysses S., General, 136
Gray, Henry P., 88, 89
Greacen, Edmund, 200
Greacen, Nan, 200
Greenbaum, Dorothea, 247-248
Bathsheba, illus. 248
Greene, Stephen, 236
Greenville, 222
Greenwood Lake, 72, 74
Gregory, Waylande, 234
Hungarian Freedom Fighters, 234; *Light Destroying Darkness,* 234
Griffith, Ella, 111, 113
Groshans, Werner, 239
Gross, Chaim, 224
Gulick, Henry T., 238
Gussow, Bernar, 211
Guttenberg, 157

Hackettstown, 250
Haggerty, Ogden, 145
Hagny, John, 48
Hall, Basil, 56
Hall, Elisha W., 147-149
Hall, George Henry, 105
Hall, John G., 87
Hall, William, 149
Halpert, Samuel, 215-216, 222, 225
Hamilton, Alexander, Dr., 3
Hamilton, James, 172-173, 179
Hardenbergh, Gerard Rutgers, 119
Harding, Chester, 20
Harnett, William Michael, 105, 111, 113-115
Harper, Fletcher, 150
Hart, George Overbury "Pop," 200, 211-213, 215, 224
Cock Fight, Mexico, illus. 212
Hart, James, 71
Hart, William, 71
Hartigan, Grace, 245
Harting, Marinus, 88
Hartley, Jonathan Scott, 188-190
Ralph Waldo Emerson, 190; *John Ericsson,* 188; *William T. Evans,* 190; *Nathaniel Hawthorne,* 190; *George Inness,* 190; illus. 189; *Washington Irving,* 190; *The Whirlwind,* 188
Hartley, Marsden, 200, 222
Hartwick, Christian, 163
Hartwick, George Ginter, 163
Hartwick, Herman, 163, 199
Harvey Cedars, 239
Harvey, George, 86
Hatofsky, Julius, 245
Hawkes, E. Z., Dr., 172

Hayes, David A., 87
Hays, William Jacob, 117
Haywood, George, 27
Heade, Martin Johnson, 75-79, 155
Jersey Meadows, 79; illus. 78
Heed, Sarah Johnson, 77
Heights, Island, 114
Heinrich, F. (artist), 89
Henri, Robert, 201, 205, 206, 207, 209, 218, 224
Henry, Edward Lamson, 129-131
Departure for the Seat of War from Jersey City, 131; *"Planet,"* 131; *Station on Camden and Amboy Railroad,* 131; *Station on Morris and Essex Railroad,* 131; illus. 130
Hesselius, Gustavus, 2, 8
Heyde, Charles L., 89, 90, 91
Hicks, Thomas, 63
Hill, John, 57
Hinckley, Thomas, 115
Hoboken, 42, 52-53, 71, 75, 79, 89, 105, 106, 122, 132-133, 138, 165, 170, 193, 204, 205-206, 219, 245
Hoeber, Arthur, 165
Hogarth, William, 60, 131
Hohokus, 155
Holbein, Hans, the Younger, 1
Holzhauer, Emil, 218
Homer, Winslow, 75, 138, 173-176, 198
Long Branch, New Jersey, 173; illus. 176
Hopkinson, Francis, 12
James Hopkinson, 12
Hoppner, John, 9
Hornblower, Joseph C., 97
Hughes, Robert Ball, 10
Hunt, Richard Morris, 194
Hunterdon County, 29, 56, 72
Huntington, Daniel, 95, 99
Huntington, Reverend, 95

Ibbetson, Julius Caesar, 59
Inman, Henry, 20, 22-29, 33, 38, 40, 42, 44, 72, 119, 137
George Washington Doane, 26; *Children of Bishop Doane,* 27; illus. 28; *James McMurtrie,* 24-25; *Paterson,* 23; *Self-Portrait in a Top Hat,* 25; *Bishop White,* 27
Inness, George, 69, 122, 134, 142-154, 155, 156, 159, 161, 163, 165, 175, 188-190, 191, 198, 199
The Delectable City, 150; *On the Delaware River,* illus, 148; *Peace and Plenty,* 146; *The Valley of the Shadow of Death,* 150; *View at the Foot of Newark Cemetery,* 144; *View Near Newark,* 144; *View on the Passaic,* 144; *Winter Morning, Montclair,* illus. 152
Inness, George Jr., 147, 151, 153-154, 188, 196
Inness, Helen, 188
Insley, Albert B., 155
Ippolito, Angelo, 236
Irving, Washington, 19, 190
Irvington, 137, 211
Irvington Art Association, 211
Isidor, Joseph, 198
Israels, Josef, 224

Jacobsen, Antonio Nicolo Gasparo, 175-177
Janetta Falls, Passaic County, 72
Jarvis, Charles Wesley, 27-29
Henry Clay, 29
Jarvis, John Wesley, 20, 22, 27-28
Jefferson, Joseph, 155
Jefferson, Thomas, 9, 10, 12, 185
Jefferson Village (Maplewood), 60
Jersey City, 36, 75, 102, 129, 131, 141, 155, 157, 163, 165, 170, 239
Jersey City Museum 165
Jewett, William, 35-36
Jobstown, 38
Jocelyn, Nathaniel, 38
Johnson, David, 73, 75
Old Mill, West Millford, New Jersey, 73
Johnson, Eastman, 63, 138
Johnston, Henrietta, 2, 8
Johnson, James Arthur, 166-168
Jones, Joe, 227, 243
Jones, Thomas Dow, 88, 89

Henry Clay, 188; *General Harrison,* 188; *Abraham Lincoln,* 188; *General Scott,* 188; *Zachary Taylor,* 188

Kaprow, Allan, 20
Karfield, Bernard, 215, 224
Keane, William, 115
Kearns, James, 247-249
Seated Model, illus. 249
Kearny, 171
Keefe, Edward, 205
Keith, William, 154
Kellner, Augustus, 55
Passaic Falls, 55
Kelly, Leon, 239
Kempson, Julie Hart Beers, 71
Kempson, Peter T., 71
Kensett, John F., 63, 75, 162
Kirk & Kirkpatrick, 87
Kirschbach, Frank, 193
Klee, Paul, 243
Kneller, Sir Godfrey, 7
Komroff, Manuel, 218
Konrad, Adolf, 238-240
End of Day, illus. 240
Konzal, Joseph, 236
Korn, Elizabeth, 236
Kranich, Edward, 69-71
The Old Homestead, illus. 70
Kreymborg, Alfred, 216
Krimmel, John Lewis, 119
Kroll, Leon, 224, 243
Kruger (artist), 88
Kühn, Justus Englehardt, 2, 8
Kuhn, Walt, 213-215, 224
Harlequin, 214-215; illus. 214; *Master at Arms,* 215

Lacroix, Paul, 105-108, 121
Still Life with Grapes and Watermelon, illus. 107; *View of New York City from Hoboken,* 106
LaFarge, John, 99, 200
Lake Wawayanda, 72
Lakewood, 205
Lambdin, George Cochran, 105
Lambertville, 222, 230, 243
Lancret, Nicolas, 170
Landau, Jacob, 238
Lanman, Charles, 88
Launitz, Robert, 184
Laurent, Robert, 224
Lawrence, Charles B., 56
Lawrence, James S., 40
Lawrence, William, 181
Lawson, Ernest, 197, 204, 224
Le Gallienne, Richard, 171
Lely, Sir Peter, 1
Lenson, Michael, 211, 230-231
Lever, Hayley, 204-205
Leyers, Charles, 48
Lhôte, André, 243
Library Hall (Newark), 44, 67, 83, 87, 92
Lichtenstein, Roy, 250
Lincoln, Abraham, 48, 188, 233
Linen, George, 36
Lippold, Richard, 236
Lissitzky, El, 228
Little Falls, 187
Livingston, 46, 48
Llewelyn Park, 75
Lockwood, Rembrandt, 86, 88, 89, 90, 91, 93-103, 125
Genevieve (sculpture), 94 *Interior,* 94; *Last Judgement,* 94-101; illus. 96; *Lily of the Valley,* 94; *Sheepfold,* 94; *A View on the Passaic River,* 94
Long Branch, 72, 173, 179
Longfellow, Henry Wadsworth, 139
Longpré, Paul de, 115
Long Valley, 246, 247
Longworth, Nicholas, 95, 125, 126
Lorrain, Claude, 150
Loupov, Donna, 216
Loupov (poet), 216
Lozowick, Louis, 228-229
Relic, illus. 229
Lucioni, Luigi, 227
Luks, George, 201, 225
Lungren, Ferdinand, 129, 165
Lyndhurst, 239

Mabie, Hamilton W., 162
McCord, George Herbert, 156
Whippany River, 156
McDougall, John Alexander, 46-47, 80, 86, 196
Portrait of a Lady, illus. 47
McEntee, Jervis, 63
McEwan, William, 147-149
MacMonnies, Frederick, 195, 233

Princeton Battle Monument, 233
McMurtrie, James, 24-25, 27
Madison, 236
Mager, Charles A. (Gus), 196, 215, 222-226
Country Road, illus. 226
Manship, Paul, 234
Manley, Thomas R., 156, 188
Maplewood, 60, 63-65, 200
Marchant, Edward, 172
Marin, John, 218-222, 225, 243, 250
Eastern Boulevard, Weehawken, New Jersey, illus. 220
Marin, John Cheri, 219
Marquet, Albert, 216
Marr, Carl, 193
Marsh, Frederick Dana, 208, 211, 231
Marsh, Reginald, 208-210
Hudson Burlesk Chorus, illus. 210
Marshall, P. B., 31
Martin, Homer D., 198
Martin, John, 99
Martin, Robert J., 218
Matisse, Henri, 201, 216
Maurer, Alfred, 200
Maverick, Peter, 60-62
Mayer, Alfred M., 63
Meeker, Joseph Rusling, 67, 75
Melrose, Andrew, 157-158
Valley of the Hackensack from the Estate of J. Becker, Esq., Union City, New Jersey, illus. 158
Menlo Park, 234
Metuchen, 71, 250
Meyer, Rachel Post, 60
Michaelangelo, 94, 98, 99
Middleman, Roslynn, 245
Middlesex County, 38
Middletown, 238, 245
Middleville, 227
Millburn, 164, 245
Miller, Alfred Jacob, 129
Miller, Delia, 144
Miller, James, 88
Miller, Kenneth Hayes, 205, 209
Miller, William Rickarby, 75-76
Weehawken Bluff on the Hudson, illus. 76
Millet, Jean François, 224-225
Millmore, Martin, 190
Moeller, Louis Charles, 48-49
Moholy-Nagy, László, 228
Mondrian, Piet, 245
Monet, Claude, 77, 199, 200
Monmouth County, 38, 179
Montclair, 48, 138, 151-154, 156, 165, 175, 188-191, 205, 236-237
Montclair Art Museum, 196-198, 236-237
Monticelli, Adolphe, 170
Moran, Edward, 159, 173, 179
Moran, Mary Nimmo, 159-161
Newark from the Meadows, 161
Moran, Peter, 159
Moran, Thomas, 157-161, 173
Lower Manhattan from Communipaw, 159; illus. 160; *Mountain of the Holy Cross,* 159
Moreland, George, 59
Morris Township, 243
Morristown, 69, 156, 234
Morse, Samuel F. B., 20, 36, 94, 131
Mount Holly, 23-27, 38
Mount, William Sidney, 120, 123, 124
Mueller, George, 245-246
Murphy, J. Francis, 154
Museum of Fine Arts, Boston, 173

Natt, Thomas J., 30-31
Landscape of Belleville, 31; *Portrait of a Newark Gentleman,* 31; illus. 30
Neagle, John, 20
Newark, 16, 29, 31-35, 36, 38, 44-48, 55, 60, 66, 67, 68, 75, 79, 81-103, 111, 117, 125-128, 137, 143-144, 155, 159-161, 165, 167, 170, 171, 177, 181, 185-187, 188, 195, 196-197, 206, 211, 218, 223, 230, 231, 233, 236-237, 238, 239, 245, 247
Newark Academy, The, 33
Newark Art League, 137
Newark Drawing School; *see* Newark School of Fine and Industrial Arts

Newark Library Association, The, 33, 87, 92 (see also Library Hall)
Newark Museum, The, 16, 48, 137, 196, 197, 211, 222, 231, 236-237
Newark School of Fine and Industrial Arts (also Newark Drawing School and Fawcett School); 171, 196, 211, 227, 230, 231, 236, 239, 247
Newark Sketch Club, 137, 196, 223
Newman, Robert Loftin, 165
Newsam, Albert, 23
Newton, 227
New Brunswick, 40, 67-69, 89, 119, 131, 181-182, 250
New England Art-Union, 85
New Jersey Art-Union, 53, 86-92, 117, 188
New Jersey Historical Society, The, 48, 52, 129
New Jersey State Agriculture Fair, 126
New Jersey Watercolor Society, 247
New Providence, 172
Niese, Henry, 250
Nordfeldt, Bror J. O., 222
Northfield, 69
North Caldwell, 155
Nott, William, 120
Nutley, 48, 165, 177, 191, 208, 209, 231

Oak Ridge, 151, 200
Oddie, Walter M., 75, 88
Chimney Rock, 75
Oertel, Johannes, 86, 88, 89, 90, 93
O'Keeffe, Georgia, 228
Old Bridge, 48, 154
O'Malley, Powers, 218
O'Neill, Eugene, 205
Orange, 48, 111, 131, 155, 163
Orcagna, 99

Page, William, 63, 133-136, 146-147, 151
Admiral Farragut in the Shrouds of the Hartford at Mobile Bay, 136; *Winfield Scott,* 136; *Robert Gould Shaw,* 136; *Venus Guiding Aeneas and the Trojans to the Latin Shore,* 134; illus. 135; *Venus of Urbino,* 134
Palisade, 221
Palmer, Erastus Dow, 65, 188
Panoramas, 80-83
Paradise, John, 29, 30
Joseph Rue, 30; *Mrs. Joseph Rue,* 30
Paradise, John Wesley, 29, 30
Parker, Matthew, 25
Pascin, Jules, 215, 218, 224
Passaic Falls, 16, 23, 51-52, 55-56
Passaic River, 72, 75, 94, 128, 144, 219
Pater, Jean Baptiste Joseph, 170
Paterson, 23, 51, 52, 155, 187, 194
Peale, Anna Claypoole, 105
Peale, Charles Willson, 14, 17, 19, 31, 104
Captain Boyd, 14; *George Washington,* 14
Peale, James, 104, 105
Peale, Margaretta Angelica, 105
Peale, Maria, 105
Peale, Mary Jane, 105
Peale, Raphaelle, 104, 105
Peale, Rembrandt, 14, 31-32, 56, 80-81
Portrait of William Rankin, 32; illus. 32; *Portrait of Mrs. William Rankin,* 32; *Court of Death,* 80-81
Peale, Rubens, 105
Peale, Sarah Miriam, 105
Penington, Isaac, and family, 18
Pennington, 29
Pennington, William, Governor, 88
Perrine, Van Dearing, 200, 211, 215
Perth Amboy, 2-4, 21-22, 134-136, 146-150, 153
Peto, John Frederick, 113-116
Still Life, illus. 116
Philadelphia Art-Union, 85
Pierce, Amelia M., 109
Pine, James, 29
Pine, Theodore, 29, 86
Picasso, Pablo, 201
Pittman, Hobson, 252

Plainfield, 139, 245
Point Breeze (Bordentown), 56
Pomarede, Leon, 82
Panorama of the Mississippi River and Indian Life, 82
Poore, Henry Rankin, 155
Powell, William Henry, 83
Discovery of the Mississippi River by De Soto, 83
Powers, Hiram, 85, 147
Pownall, Thomas, 51
Passaic Falls, 51
Prestopino, Gregorio, 238
Princeton, 199, 233, 247
Princeton University, 48, 221, 236
Public Works of Art Project, 230, 233

Quinby, J. S., 91

Rabin & Krueger Gallery, Newark, 224
Rahway, 69, 181-182, 184
Rankin, William, and family, 32-35
Ranney, William Tylee, 120-124
Hackensack Meadows, 122; *The Match Boy,* 123; *The Old Oaken Bucket,* 123; *The Pipe of Friendship,* illus. 124
Raphael, 98
Rauschner, John Christian, 10
Ray, Man, 215-218
Woman Asleep, illus. 217
Read, Thomas Buchanan, 47, 139-141
Sheridan's Ride, 141; *Ward family* portraits, 139
Redon, Odilon, 239
Red Rank, 129
Reed, Luman, 61, 63
Reininger, Paul, 223
Remington, Frederick, 129, 193
Reuterdahl, Henry, 177
Reynolds, Sir Joshua, 19
Rhind, John Massey, 233
George Washington, 233
Richards, F. A. (artist), 89
Richards, T. H. (artist), 89
Richards, William Trost, 173-4
Twilight on the New Jersey Coast, illus. 174
Ridgefield, 215-218
Rix, Julian Walbridge, 155
Robertson, Archibald, 51
Passaic Falls, 51
Robinson, Theodore, 199
Rockwell, Horace, 31
Roesen, Severin, 108
Romney, George, 13
Ronald, William, 247
Roosevelt, 237-238
Roosevelt Park, 234
Roosevelt, Theodore, 200
Ross, George Gates, 44-46, 67, 80, 86, 97
James Ward, illus. 45
Rossiter, Thomas P., 63
Roth, Frank, 245-246
Rousseau, Theodore, 145
Rovinsky, Anton, 218
Runyon, Theodore, 91
Russell, Charles, 193
Rutgers University, 48, 132, 182, 250
Rutherford, 155, 219, 247
Ryan, Anne, 247
Ryder, Albert Pinkham, 165, 173, 239
Ryle, William, 155

Saint-Gaudens, Augustus, 191
Saint-Memin, Julien Fevret de, 16-17
Captain James Lawrence, 17
Salem, 20
Samaras, Lucas, 247
Sanderson, Henry, 131-132
The Drunkard's Progress, 131; *Washington Crossing the Delaware,* 132
Sandford, John, 181
Sandol, Maynard, 239, 245-246
Sargent, John Singer, 49
Sartain, John
"Reminiscences of a Very Old Man" (book), 25
Sauerwein, Charles D., 129
Sauerwein, Frank Paul, 129
Savage, Edward, 15-16, 17
James Ewing, 16; *Passaic Falls,* 16; *The Washington Family,* 16
Schiff, Jacob H., 194
Schlegel, Fridolin, 83, 86, 88, 89, 90, 91, 92
Schooleys Mountains, 56

Schreyvogel, Charles, 192-193, 194
The Last Drop, illus. 192; *My Bunkie,* 193
Schwabe, H. August, 137, 193, 196, 211
Schwitters, Kurt, 247
Scotch Plains, 238
Scott, Julian, 138-140
Battle of Cedar Creek, 139; *Blue and the Grey,* 139; *Capture of André,* 139; *In the Cornfield at Antietam,* 139; *Molly Pitchur,* 139; *Prussian Soldiers at the Time of Frederick the Great,* 139; *Rear Guard at White Oak Swamp,* 139; *Scene of the Civil War,* illus. 140
Scott, Sir Walter, 187
Seabright, 194
Sea Girt, 173
Segal, George, 251-252
Model in the Studio, illus. 251
Seley, Jason, 247
Shahn, Ben, 237-238
Bartolomeo Vanzetti and Nicola Sacco, 237; illus. 238; Murals, New Jersey Homesteads, 237
Shapiro, Seymour, 245-247
W. C. W., illus. 246
Shaw, Joshua, 57-60
The Deluge, 57; *English Landscape with Two Figures,* illus. 58; *The Progress of Vice,* 59; *Sea Piece—Morning during a Heavy Storm,* 58; *Storm and Shipwreck,* 58
Sheeler, Charles, 228
Sheridan, Philip, General, 141
Shinn, Everett, 201-204, 208
Trenton City Hall Murals, 204; illus. 202 and 203
Short Hills, 115
Silva, Francis A., 179
Simpson, Marshall, 245
Simpson, Maxwell Stuart, 238
Sloan, John, 201, 224, 243
Slocum, Lewis Bloomington, 168
Smibert, John, 3, 8
Smith, Christine Pearl, 114
Smith, DeWitt, 181
Smith, Enos, 60
Smith, F. Hopkinson, 162
Solomon, Hyde, 236
Somerset county, 75
Sommer, Otto, 66, 80
The Voyage of Life, 66; *Westward Ho!,* 66
Sonntag, William Louis, 166
South Orange, 131, 168, 225, 228, 247
South River (formerly Washington), 184
Soutine, Chaim, 222
Sparks, Gar, 206
Sparta, 131, 151
Spencer, Benjamin Rush, 125, 128
Spencer, George M., 87
Spencer, Lilly Martin, 47, 101, 123-129, 136
William Cullen Bryant, 128; *The Children of Governor Marcus L. Ward,* 126, illus. frontispiece; *Day Dreams,* 128; *General Grant,* 128; *Grandpa's Prodigies,* 128; *Mrs. Benjamin Harrison,* 128; *Washington Irving,* 128; *Jolly Washerwoman,* 128; *One of Life's Happy Hours,* 125; *The Picnic on the Fourth of July—A Day to be Remembered,* 128; *Truth Unveiling Falsehood,* 128; *The War Spirit at Home—Celebrating the Victory at Vicksburg,* 126; illus. 127; *Nicholas Longworth Ward,* 126
Spencer, Niles, 228
Spier, Vera, 213
Sprague, William, Senator, 128
Spring, Marcus, 146
Springfield, 29, 44
Stella, Joseph, 200, 222, 224, 228
Stephens, Thomas H., 92
Stevens, Edward John, Jr., 239
Stevens Institute, 219
Story, Emma Louise, 205
Stradivarius, Antonio, 177
Stuart, Gilbert, 12, 17-19, 20, 37, 56
Anne Penington, 18, 19; illus. 18; *Edward Stow,* 17; *Mrs. Edward Stow,* 17, 19
Stuempfig, Walter, 252

Sullivan, Charles, 125
Sully, Thomas, 20, 22, 33, 40, 55, 69
Passaic Falls, 55
Summit, 157, 161-162, 172
Swarz, Sahl, 250
Swedenborg, Emanuel, 133, 147, 150

Tait, Arthur Fitzwilliam, 90, 91, 117, 138
Talbot, Jesse, 52
Passaic Falls, 52
Thom, James, 154, 187
Thom, James Crawford, 154-187
Robert Burns, 187; *Old Mortality and His Pony,* 187; *Tam O'Shanter,* 187; *George Washington,* 187
Thompson, Launt, 65
Thorwaldsen, Bertel, 185
Tiffany, Louis Comfort, 149-150, 153
Palisades, 150
Tipson, William Arthur, 55
Passaic Falls, 55
Tisch, William, 218
Titian, 133, 134, 150, 151
Toms River, 114
Toulouse-Lautrec, Henri de, 211
Towne, John, 25-26
Travis, William, D. T., 118-119
Aftermath of War, 118; *The March of Mortality,* 118
Trenton, 16, 71, 77, 109, 115, 191, 202-204
Trenton Junior College, 236
Trott, Benjamin, 37-38
Mrs. Alexander N. McComb, 38; illus. 37
Trotter, Newbold, 172
Trumbull, John, 20, 60, 61, 94, 131, 138
Tryon, Dwight, 154
Tubby, Joseph, 156, 165, 188
Tuckerman, Henry T.
"Book of the Artists" (book), 24
Tuckerton, 56
Turnbull, Thomas, 3
Turner, Joseph Mallord William, 57, 145, 157, 239

Union City, 121-123, 157, 175, 209, 219, 227; *see also* West Hoboken
Union Hill, 221

Vanderbilt, George W., 194
Vanderlyn, John, 61, 81
Van Dyck, Sir Anthony, 1
Van Doesburg, Theo, 228
Van Gogh, Vincent, 223-225
Van Horn, Amos H., 233
Ventnor, 179
Vermeer, 115
Verona, 227
Vernet, Joseph, 177
Volk, Douglas, 48
Volk, Leonard, 48
Von Roth, Frederick G. R., 233-234
Central Park, New York, sculpture, 233; *Washington Monument, Morristown,* 234

Wagner, Richard, 171
Waldo & Jewett, 35-36
Portrait of George Dummer, 36; *Portrait of Mrs. George Dummer,* 36
Waldo, Samuel, 20, 35-36, 60, 182
Wall, William Guy, 55
Passaic Falls, 55
Wallace, Lew, General, 139
Walpole, Horace, 9
Wanamaker, John, 128
Ward, Caleb, 66
Ward, Charles V., 66
Ward, Jacob C., 66, 90
Hamilton-Burr Duel, 66
Ward, John Quincy Adams, 65
Ward, Marcus L., Governor, 83, 87, 88, 91, 94, 95, 101-102, 126, 139, 141
Washburn, Grace E., 168, 169
Washington (now South River), 184
Washington, George, 9, 14, 15, 16, 22, 98, 132, 187, 190, 233, 234
Waters, Susan, 109-112
Still Life with Squirrels, illus. 112
Waters, William C., 109

Watson, Alexander, 4
Watson, John, 2-8, 10-11, 12, 13, 21, 146
Bacchus, 4; *Governor William Burnet,* 4, 7; illus. 5; *Lady Burnet,* 4; *Gaius Caesar Caligula,* 5, 7; *Hercules,* 7; *Governor Lewis Morris,* 4, 7; illus. 6
Watson, Sophia, 4
Watteau, Antoine, 170
Watts, Robert M., 250
Waugh, Frederick Judd, 175
Waugh, Samuel, 47, 83, 175
Italia (panorama), 83
Weber, Max, 200
Weehawken, 48, 53, 61, 66, 75, 121, 165, 177, 194, 206, 219-221, 239
Weingartner, Hans, 239
Weir, John Ferguson, 133
Weir, Julian Alden, 133
Weir, Robert Walter, 132-133
The Belle of the Carnival, 132; *Columbus Before the Council of Salamanca,* 132; *The Embarkation of the Pilgrims,* 132; *Out in the Garden,* 132; *Portia at the Palace of Octavia,* 132; *Titian in his Studio,* 132; *Virgil and Dante Crossing the Styx,* 132
Wells, Rachel Lovell, 9, 10, 12
Wertmüller, Adolph, 87
Western Art-Union, 53, 85, 125
Westfield, 191, 230
West, Benjamin, 12, 57, 80
West Hoboken, 121-123, 157; *see also* Union City
West Millford, 73
West New York, 157, 247
West Orange, 227
Whistler, James McNeill, 200, 227
White, E. (artist), 88
Whitley, Thomas W., 42, 52-55, 88, 89, 90, 91, 121
Country Seat of Charles L. Elliott in Hudson Co., N. J., 42; *Passaic Falls,* 52; illus. 54
Whittredge, Euphemia, 162
Whittredge, Worthington, 65, 161-164
Millburn, New Jersey, illus. 164
Wiggins, Carlton, 149-150, 153
Will, John M. August, 163-165
Williams, Frederick Ballard, 170-171
Williams, George Arthur, 171-172
The Drama of Life, 172; *The Drama of Nature,* 172, *The Drama of the Spirit,* 172; *The Marginal Way,* 172; *Tristan and Isolde,* 171
Williams, John Insco, 81-82
Panorama of the Bible, 81-82
Williams, Micah, 40-41
Sarah Hasbrouck, illus. 41
Williams, William Carlos, 216
Wilson, Alexander, 117-118
Wilson, John R., 91
Witkowski, Karl, 137
Wood, Mrs. Earl LeRoy, 167
Wood, Grant, 225
Woodbury, 108
Woodman, George, 63
Woodruff, Samuel, 90
Woodstown, 201
Woodville, Richard Caton, 123
Works Progress Administration, 230-233
Wright, Elizabeth, 9, 10
Wright, Joseph (elder), 9
Wright, Joseph (younger), 9, 10, 12, 15, 17, 22
Mrs. Wright Modelling a Head in Wax, 15; *George Washington,* 10, 15
Wright of Darby, Joseph, 13
Wright, Patience Lovell, 8-12, 15, 21, 56, 180
Charles Fox, 10; *Admiral Richard Howe,* 10, illus. 11; *James Johnson, Bishop of Worcester,* 10; *Lord Lyttleton,* 9; *Thomas Penn,* 9; *William Pitt the Elder,* 9, 10; *George Washington,* 9-10
Wright, Phoebe, 9
Wyant, Alexander, 157

Zion, 205

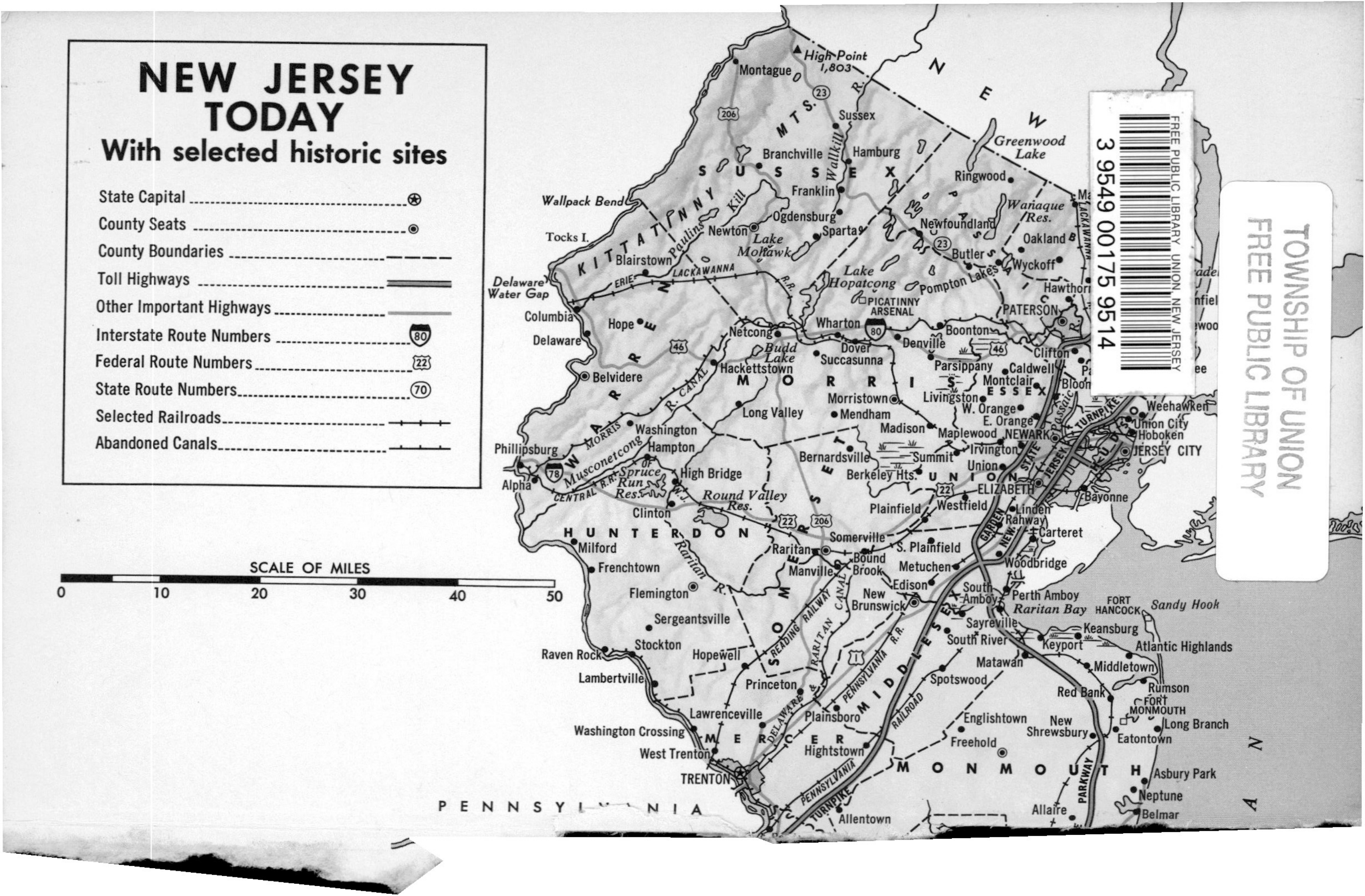
NEW JERSEY
TODAY
With selected historic sites
State Capital
County Seats
County Boundaries
Toll Highways
Other Important Highways
Interstate Route Numbers
Federal Route Numbers
State Route Numbers
Selected Railroads
Abandoned Canals
SCALE OF MILES
0
10
20
30
40
50
SUSSEX
WARREN
MORRIS
PASSAIC
ESSEX
HUDSON
UNION
SOMERSET
HUNTERDON
MIDDLESEX
MERCER
MONMOUTH
PENNSYLVANIA
NEW
High Point 1,803
Montague
Sussex
Hamburg
Branchville
Franklin
Ogdensburg
Newton
Sparta
Lake Mohawk
Blairstown
Tocks I.
Wallpack Bend
KITTATINNY MTS.
Delaware Water Gap
Columbia
Delaware
Hope
Belvidere
Phillipsburg
Alpha
Washington
Hampton
Musconetcong
Spruce Run Res.
High Bridge
Round Valley Res.
Clinton
Milford
Frenchtown
Flemington
Sergeantsville
Stockton
Raven Rock
Lambertville
Hopewell
Princeton
Lawrenceville
Washington Crossing
West Trenton
TRENTON
Greenwood Lake
Ringwood
Wanaque Res.
Newfoundland
Oakland
Butler
Wyckoff
Pompton Lakes
Lake Hopatcong
PICATINNY ARSENAL
PATERSON
Hawthorne
Wharton
Netcong
Budd Lake
Dover
Succasunna
Hackettstown
Boonton
Denville
Parsippany
Caldwell
Clifton
Montclair
Livingston
Morristown
Mendham
Long Valley
W. Orange
E. Orange
Madison
Maplewood
NEWARK
Irvington
Bernardsville
Summit
Berkeley Hts.
Union
ELIZABETH
Plainfield
Westfield
Linden
Rahway
Carteret
Somerville
S. Plainfield
Raritan
Bound Brook
Manville
Metuchen
Woodbridge
Edison
New Brunswick
South Amboy
Perth Amboy
Raritan Bay
Sayreville
South River
Keyport
Keansburg
FORT HANCOCK
Sandy Hook
Atlantic Highlands
Middletown
Matawan
Spotswood
Red Bank
Rumson
FORT MONMOUTH
Long Branch
Eatontown
New Shrewsbury
Englishtown
Freehold
Plainsboro
Hightstown
Allentown
Allaire
Asbury Park
Neptune
Belmar
Weehawken
Union City
Hoboken
JERSEY CITY
Bayonne
LACKAWANNA
ERIE
MORRIS CANAL
CENTRAL R.R. OF N.J.
READING RAILWAY
DELAWARE & RARITAN CANAL
PENNSYLVANIA R.R.
PENNSYLVANIA TURNPIKE
NEW JERSEY TURNPIKE
GARDEN STATE PARKWAY
Passaic
Raritan R.
Paulins Kill
Wallkill R.